THE SECRET ATLAS OF NORTH COAST FOOD

Published by The Heavy Table
3515 31st Ave. South
Minneapolis, MN 55406

ISBN 978-0-9897982-0-4

For information about bulk or bookstore purchases, email editor@heavytable.com.

Proudly printed in Minnesota

www.heavytable.com

second printing

(Heavy) TABLE OF CONTENTS

::THE SECRET ATLAS OF NORTH COAST FOOD::

A Book Dedicated to the Farmers, Chefs, and other Foodmakers of the Upper Midwest made possible by the generous financial, moral, and emotional support of our Kickstarter backers, who demonstrated that even in chaotic times, creation is possible

EDITOR James Norton
DESIGNER Tod Foley
LEAD CARTOGRAPHER Matt Dooley

with
Robb Burnham (also known as WACSO) *ILLUSTRATOR*
Nat Case *CARTOGRAPHER*
Lindsay Christians *WRITER*
Andy DuCett *ILLUSTRATOR*
John Garland *WRITER*
Tim Gihring *WRITER*
Peter Hajinian *WRITER*
Soleil Ho *WRITER*
Jerry Ingeman *ILLUSTRATOR*
Maja Ingeman *WRITER*
John Kovalic *WRITER & ILLUSTRATOR*
Allegra Lockstadt *ILLUSTRATOR*
Maria Manion *WRITER*
Jeff Nelson *ILLUSTRATOR*
Susan Pagani *WRITER*
Joshua Page *WRITER*
Sarah Barga Pollasch *ILLUSTRATOR*
Brandon Raygo *ILLUSTRATOR*
Emily Schnobrich *WRITER*
Andy Sturdevant *WRITER & ILLUSTRATOR*
Chuck Terhark *WRITER*
Emma Trithart *ILLUSTRATOR (INCIDENTAL ILLUSTRATIONS)*
Adam Turman *ILLUSTRATOR*
Anne Ulku *ILLUSTRATOR*
Alyssa Vance *WRITER*
Jason Walker *WRITER*
Sean Weitner *WRITER & ILLUSTRATOR*
David Witt *WRITER & ILLUSTRATOR*

OF MAPS AND MEAT SHOPS: AN INTRODUCTION TO THE BOOK

BY JAMES NORTON

"We mix our own mythologies, we push them out through PA systems."
— "Chicago Seemed Tired Last Night," The Hold Steady

This is not a book about "local food." It was not created by or for "foodies." And, God help me, it is not a guide to great eating filled with handy recipes and capsule summaries of the same 20 restaurants you've read about 20 times before.

This is a book about the food that is eaten where we live, and the people who create it. It is written by writers; it is illustrated by cartographers and illustrators. If I'm backing into this introduction in a defensive crouch, it's because of what has happened to food writing over the past decade or two: it has been largely transformed from being a sedate and learned niche into a vulgar goldmine of crass stupidity. It has been exploited, bastardized, buried in keywords, wrapped in bacon, and optimized for search engines.

The Secret Atlas is optimized for people who are curious about where they live and have the sneaking suspicion that something great is going on right around the corner.

Something great is, in fact, going on right around the corner. And three blocks over. And in that small town you've never visited that's just a mile off I-94. And on farms, and in orchards, and in bars, and home kitchens, and in the creameries, and on the butcher blocks and in curing rooms.

It's happening in cocktails, in fact, if you go to the right bars.

This book is an attempt to take back some of the conversation about food in the Upper Midwest, to get past the cronuts, the ill-considered sushi bars, and the fuzzy longing for Paris. Here, we tell our own stories.

To write this book we ate ox tongue and tripe with chili sauce on Park Street in Madison. We drove the interstates and back roads sketching some of the world's best cheesemakers.

We fished trout streams with a black Labrador retriever named Cricket, traced the steps of Dylan, Fitzgerald, and Liberace, and sank our teeth into porketta roasts, funeral hotdish brats, and braunschweiger up and down the Mississippi River. We followed a single order of huevos rancheros through the mind-boggling labyrinth that is Hell's Kitchen during brunch.

And we also drank some bad Upper Midwestern wine.

A FEW WORDS ABOUT THE NORTH COAST

The term "North Coast" confuses people. North, sure, but we're not a coast, are we? Well, no. But, wait — yes.

Geographically, economically, and culturally speaking, the importance of a coast is that water is a great way to travel and transport goods. If you live in a port town, you can leave and see the world; meanwhile, you can stay where you are, and the world will also come to you. You are connected.

Minneapolis and St. Paul are situated on the Mississippi River, one of the great American arteries of commerce and culture. Wisconsin and Minnesota both front on the hard-working and scenic Great Lakes, gateways to the East Coast and the world beyond.

If you bring a global perspective and eat at Heartland in St. Paul, or Corner Table in Minneapolis, or The Old Fashioned in Madison, you'll recognize that we don't live in flyover country — we live in a part of the world that is, in every meaningful sense of the word, connected, and increasingly in touch with its own profound strengths.

HOW THIS BOOK CAME TO BE

You are reading this book because 439 people believed enough in the project to support it with money. If it falls short of your expectations, blame me, as editor — if it delights you, credit the community that rallied to make its production and distribution possible.

One of this book's many highlights - perhaps its central one — is the chapter that our high-rolling Kickstarter backers wrote for us by contributing their favorite "hidden gem" restaurants throughout the region. (Thanks, Kickstarter backers!) Touring the region through your eyes was a kick.

Without the support of our backers, you would not be holding this book - we couldn't afford to do it on our own, and a publisher would not, if history is any guide, have handled such esoteric and eclectic material with the delicacy required to keep the package intact. We are blazing new trails through the jungle: editorial process, sales, marketing, distribution, and more. Whether those trails will lead to quicksand pits or the lost city, we don't know, but they look a hell of a lot more appealing than the beaten path at this moment.

We are honored that you've joined us on this journey. Now... to the food!

Guten appetit,

James Norton
Minneapolis, Minnesota
2013

CHAPTER 1
DINNER WITH DYLAN

WRITER: TIM GIHRING :: **CARTOGRAPHER:** MATT DOOLEY

I've never broken bread with Bob Dylan. Or Bobby Zimmerman for that matter. It's not even clear to me that the man eats anymore; he may subsist on applause, memories of a young Joan Baez, and the whiff of an old guitar case. But he was a famished teenager once, and I know where he ate then, what he ate, and who paid (hint: it wasn't him).

I know what starving artists eat, too, when they get around to it, like Scott Seekins, the ubiquitous Minneapolis painter who makes wry portraits of himself fly-fishing in a white suit (which he's done) and marrying Britney Spears (which he hasn't). I once spent an afternoon in his spare, splintery studio above the late Nate's Clothing store downtown, the sink out in the hall, the closet containing nothing but a row of well-worn black suits and a row of white. He now lives upstairs from Cafe Maude in Loring Park and holds court in its bar every Thursday night, as reliable as a painting on the wall.

These are a few of the places haunted by Upper Midwestern artists, where they revive, reconnect, and occasionally perform, solitary creatures returning to the fold. In the act of eating a hamburger, they have never painted, never played a note, never written an interesting phrase—they are not artists. They are simply and sublimely hungry.

Hibbing, MN

1st Ave

Sportsmen's Café
and Taverna

L&B Café

Zimmy's

E Howard St

Androy Hotel

Hibbing

Ely

Virginia

Sunrise Bakery

Bob Dylan

0   ½ Mile

International Falls

Atikokan

Nipigon

Thunder Bay

Hancock

0   50 Mile

Duluth

Superior

Ironwood

Esca

Brainerd

Milwaukee, WI

Rhinelander

Mader's

Usinger's
Sausage

Plankinton
Arcade

Green B

Ma

St. Cloud

Fisher's Club
Garrison Keillor

Willmar

Minneapolis   St. Paul

Eau Claire

The Joynt
Justin Vernon

Lakeville

Faribault

Mankato

Rochester

Winona

Little Nick's

0   1 Mile

A&J Polish Deli

Sheboy

Brookings

Sioux Falls

Albert Lea

La Crosse

Liberace

Minneapolis/St. Paul

Madison

Waukesha

Milwauk

Janesville

Racine

St Anthony

Roseville

Little
Canada

Dubuque

Waukegan

Rockford

Elgin   Evan

John Berryman

Minneapolis

Brass Rail Lounge

Augie's Bourbon
Street Cabaret

First Avenue
Prince

John Berryman

The Kenwood
Louise Erdrich

Rudolph's
Barbecue

F. S. Fitzgerald

Saint Paul

Aurora

Chi

St Louis Park

CC Club
Alt-rockers

Prince

W.A. Frost

Mickey's Dining Car
Garrison Keillor

Davenport

Joliet

Minneapolis

Vintage Restaurant
and Wine Bar
Garrison Keillor

Commodore Hotel
University Club
F. Scott Fitzgerald

Edina

West
Saint Paul

Kankakee

Richfield

0   5   Miles

Galesburg

Peoria

Bloomington

BOB DYLAN

L&B CAFÉ | *417 East Howard St., Hibbing (defunct)*

Echo Helstrom was a minx from the wrong side of the mine, an Iron Range Brigitte Bardot, when she became Bobby Zimmerman's high school steady. After class, they would shock the squares at this homey café on the main drag, smoking cigs and devouring his favorite dish: cherry pie a la mode. He never had any money, or didn't cough it up, so Helstrom—the real-life "Girl from the North Country"—would pay. "Please don't let on that you knew me when," he would later sing, "I was hungry and it was your world." Today, the space is occupied by Red Rock Capital Advisors, an investment firm.

ZIMMY'S | *531 East Howard St., Hibbing*

This cavernous, newish place hosts the annual Dylan Days festival, pegged to his birthday, when amateur musicians perform his songs, the walls are covered with unintentionally Cubist paintings of him, and the menu features "North Country porketta" (the Iron Range staple) and sometimes his beloved cherry pie a la mode. "Don't think twice, we're open," the sign outside admonishes, displaying Dylan's youthful mug on one side and his former girlfriend Echo's on the other, weirdly preserving a genius's seminal crush.

SUNRISE BAKERY | *2135 First Avenue, Hibbing*

In the former Lybba Theater, where Zimmerman and Helstrom would hold hands and pretend to watch cowboy serials, hand-scrawled signs now advertise sarma dinner (minced meat wrapped in cabbage, $6.95), cheese-filled potica bread, and other great staples of the Iron Range, peddled with about as much fanfare as grandma pulling cookies from the oven. Winters can be brutal here — Dylan claimed to have worn three or four jackets just to keep from freezing—but this place supplies all the caloric armor you'd need.

SPORTSMEN'S CAFE AND TAVERNA | *509 East Howard Street, Hibbing*

Craving pizza burgers (patties with pizza sauce and mozzarella cheese, no longer on the menu), Zimmerman and Helstrom would slide atop the chrome stools at this Main Street café, shined by a century's worth of overworked asses. In Dylan's day, when the mines were slowing, the workingman's routine must have terrified him. Taking a request at an early New York concert, he joked, "So long as I don't have to work for a living."

ANDROY HOTEL | *502 East Howard Street, Hibbing*

The open-pit mine at the edge of town, the world's largest, threatened to swallow Hibbingites alive by 1919, surrounding them on three sides, and there was still plenty of ore beneath their homes. So the mining honchos moved the town. In return, they built a new City Hall, a high school with marble floors and chandeliers, and this hotel — host to Bobby Zimmerman's bar mitzvah bash. Later dubbed the "Androy Motor Inn, Hibbing's finest supper club," as the faded advertising on the brick exterior still declares, it has since been converted to senior housing.

OLD HIBBING

The mining companies moved 180 homes and 20 businesses, but not everything. The streets, foundations, and quaint old lampposts remain amid the creeping woods. One can imagine Zimmerman smoking and necking on the steps of the old school at the corner of Lincoln and Second avenues, an imaginary saloon in a ghost town now used as a campground and disc golf course.

F. SCOTT FITZGERALD

UNIVERSITY CLUB | *420 Summit Avenue, St. Paul*

Even after 80 years, it seems possible that the drink stains and cigarette burns inflicted by F. Scott, Zelda, and their Summit Avenue set remain in this cozy enclave of fireplaces, bookshelves, dining nooks, and surprisingly affordable membership. In the small bar downstairs, Fitzgerald reportedly carved his name, though the closest anyone has found is the mysterious moniker "John F. Scott." What has survived is an *Onion*-esque newspaper from 1922, the *St. Paul Dirge*, written by Fitz and circulated at the Bad Luck Ball that he and Zelda held in a club room hung with black crepe. The party had already been immortalized in a headline: "Frightful Orgy at University Club."

W.A. FROST & COMPANY | *374 Selby Avenue, St. Paul*

When Fitz was growing up on Cathedral Hill, this upscale restaurant was a drugstore and soda fountain. And in the summer of 1919, while slaving over his first novel, he would drop by for Cokes and procrastination.

COMMODORE HOTEL | *79 Western Avenue, St. Paul*

Sinclair Lewis, the Fitzgeralds, and outlaws like John Dillinger crashed if not burned in this former residential hotel (now condos). In an obscure 1934 essay, F. Scott reminisced about his and Zelda's autumnal idyll here in 1921: "We got to the Commodore in St. Paul, and while the leaves blew up the street we waited for our child to be born." And drank, conveniently at the small, glass-and-mirror Art Deco bar on the first floor. The owner of the University Club and W.A. Frost now wants a Fitz trifecta: he's been expanding the moth-balled lounge for years now with plans to reopen as a jazz club fit for a flapper.

GARRISON KEILLOR

MICKEY'S DINING CAR | *36 West Seventh Street, St. Paul*

A refugee from an Edward Hopper painting, this Art Deco diner is around the corner from the Fitzgerald Theater, where Garrison Keillor hosts his radio show. Open 24 hours, it's just the kind of place where Keillor — or Guy Noir — would tuck into eggs in the dead of night, as he did with Lindsay Lohan, Meryl Streep, Lily Tomlin, and others in Robert Altman's *A Prairie Home Companion.*

THE VINTAGE RESTAURANT AND WINE BAR | *579 Selby Avenue, St. Paul (defunct)*

Keillor would wander over from his home to this four-story red-brick pile, a Victorian out of a Scooby Doo ghost story, to drink on the patio. It's now a casual cafe named as though you need a golden ticket to enter: Dr. Chocolate's Chocolate Chateau.

FISHER'S CLUB | *425 Stratford Street West, Avon*

Avon is Lake Wobegon country. And for a few weirdly meta years, Keillor was part-owner of this lakeside supper club. He'd show up for a beer and a bump, entertaining the guests, until early 2013, when the place was put up for sale, as surreal a thing as if Our Lady of Perpetual Responsibility was converted to condos.

ALT-ROCKERS

CC CLUB | *2600 Lyndale Avenue South, Minneapolis*

"Here comes a regular," Paul Westerberg sang in the Replacements' ballad about this notorious tavern, open like any respectable business at 8 a.m. Though before the city smoking ban, it was hard to see anyone coming through the haze. Soul Asylum, Axl Rose, Poison, Uncle Tupelo, and other rockers sat enshrouded in dark booths as though setting fire to the healthy lifestyle epitomized by the French Meadow Bakery across the street. Now the smoke has cleared, the musicians have moved on, and the French Meadow has bought the bar.

PRINCE

FIRST AVENUE | *Seventh Street and First Avenue, Minneapolis*

Who knows what Prince ate here, much less Joe Cocker, who inaugurated the nightclub in 1970. (Before then, it was the city's Greyhound station and a cafe occupied what is now the 7th Street Entry side stage.) But in the club's 1990s heyday, you could get pizza on paper plates from a hole in the wall near the stage. Now it has a full-service restaurant next door, the Depot Tavern, open to the fresh air and hosting as many tourists in jean shorts as pale night owls.

RUDOLPH'S BARBECUE | *Franklin and Lyndale Avenues, Minneapolis*

As hard as it is to imagine Prince spilling barbecue sauce on his lacy sleeves, remember this: the progenitors of the Minneapolis funk sound were breaking barriers of all kinds and there weren't many places in Minneapolis—in the 1980s or today—where black and white folks mixed in equal numbers. Rudolph's has long been one of them. And after singing about sex in butt-less chaps for three hours, you too might crave the carnivorous if not carnal pleasures of tearing into saucy flesh.

LOUISE ERDRICH

THE KENWOOD | *2115 West 21st Street, Minneapolis*

When Louise Erdrich was plotting the stage debut of her novel, *The Master Butchers Singing Club*, she would meet the director here, over lemonade. It was a simple coffee shop then, and there was a passageway to Birchbark Books next door, her labor of love. Now, it's a superb neighborhood restaurant with an ironic preppie vibe straight out of an Andover headmaster's home—plaid wallpaper, paintings of dogs and deer—and a cheeky humor: "If your name is Rob Binelli," the menu announces, "you drink for free." Good to know. Still, sandwiched between Birchbark (now sealed off), the Bockley Gallery, and an art studio for kids, there will always be artists here, spending the fruit of their labors on the walnut crepes.

JOHN BERRYMAN

THE BRASS RAIL LOUNGE | *422 Hennepin Avenue, Minneapolis*

John Berryman left Iowa City for Minneapolis in the 1950s, having shat on the doorstep of a fellow university instructor. He left the world altogether in 1972, having won the Pulitzer Prize and the National Book Award for his confessional poetry. He'd been drinking for two days, probably here at his favorite haunt, a windowless, low-ceilinged holdover from skid row. It hasn't changed much, except to add a few perfunctory TVs—oh, and some "famous male dancers." Berryman might have liked that. But on a freezing morning, he took a bus to the University of Minnesota, where he taught, walked out on the Washington Avenue Bridge, waved to passersby, and hurled himself into the Mississippi River.

AUGIE'S THEATER LOUNGE & BAR | *424 Hennepin Avenue, Minneapolis*

Next door to the Brass Rail, this place was once the unlikely crossroads of Jewish gangsters like Icepick Willie (who wasn't exactly in the ice-delivery business) and performers like Groucho Marx, Lenny Bruce, and Gypsy Rose Lee, who wandered over from the theater district. One minute you'd be laughing at a zinger from Henny Youngman, the next the joke was on you.

[WISCONSIN]

LIBERACE

PLANKINTON ARCADE | *161 West Wisconsin Avenue, Milwaukee (defunct)*

Something happened to Wladziu Valentino Liberace when he sat at the piano in the Red Room, the basement lounge of this glass-roofed entertainment palace, for the first time in 1938. Soon, the shy teenager would be wearing white suits to these gigs, going by "Walter Busterkeys," and winking at waiters carrying broiled African lobster tail ($1.60) to fans who hadn't known they wanted Liberace until he manifested himself on stage.

MADER'S | *1041 North Old World Third Street, Milwaukee*

Liberace, in his salad days, reportedly threw all-night parties in this temple to medieval mischief, a vaulted beer-hall lined with steins as big as half-barrels and statuary of drunken monks. At noon, families drink beside suits of armor in the Knights Bar while young women in dirndls and heels heave sauerbraten and apple strudel onto big round tables. Cary Grant ate here, as did Audrey Hepburn, Frank Sinatra, several presidents, and, more recently, Justin Bieber. It's easy to imagine Liberace using the nine-foot spear hanging in the dining room to extend a knockwurst to someone he fancied two tables over. It'd make about as much sense as when Wilco shot the cover for their 2009 release, *Wilco (The Album)*, just outside the parking lot — with a camel wearing a birthday hat.

USINGER'S SAUSAGE | *1030 North Old World Third Street, Milwaukee*

The *wurstmachers* here still grind meat into goodness — blood sausage, beer brats, braunschweiger—as they have in this building since 1880. Liberace and anyone else entering Mader's across the street has never needed to guess at Milwaukee's heritage.

LITTLE NICK'S | *Corner of Muskegon and Mitchell streets, Milwaukee (defunct)*

Once a beer hall where a teenage Liberace played, this corner building still sports an onion dome, marking the old Polish neighborhood on Milwaukee's south side. Now it's primarily Hispanic and there's a *panaderia* across the street.

A&J POLISH DELI | *1215 Lincoln Avenue, Milwaukee*

One block from Kosciuszki Park, near St. Cyril and St. Methodius churches, this place remains the sausage-clogged heart of an old Polish neighborhood. Liberace, who got his start in the area, would have recognized the offerings — kielbasa, hunter sausage, herring, and Old World cheeses—from the grocery his parents ran out of the front of their home.

JUSTIN VERNON (BON IVER)

THE JOYNT | *322 Water Street, Eau Claire*

It's easy to see why Justin Vernon drank here before he was famous. One in a long line of bars near the University of Wisconsin-Eau Claire, stumbling distance from the Chippewa River, it's a narrow, cozy cave with 50-cent happy hour beers. It's even easier to understand why he returns — sometimes after hunting — now that he's Bon Iver. His apartment and studio are nearby. And from the "no light beer" sign to the pitchers of local Berghoff, thick as the surrounding woods, this place is as real as celebrity is not.

CHAPTER 2
WISCONSIN OLD FASHIONEDS

WRITER: LINDSAY CHRISTIANS :: **ARTIST:** BRANDON RAYGO

It takes Jennifer DeBolt's bartenders about 29 seconds to make Wisconsin's signature cocktail.

"We want to make the best Old Fashioned anyone has ever had," said DeBolt, who has managed the **Old Fashioned** restaurant on Madison's Capitol Square since it opened in 2005.

"I would rather have people know what a true Old Fashioned tastes like than go with a mix that's not quite the same."

"Old Fashioned" means something different in the Dairy State than it does in other parts of the country. What was once an austere combination of sugar, whiskey and bitters has become a sweet brownish-red cocktail served in a lowball glass, made with a healthy slug of brandy, lemon lime soda and a colorful maraschino cherry/orange garnish.

The Old Fashioned restaurant sells hundreds of its namesake cocktail in a single weekend, as many as 500 if there's a Badger game on. On "customer appreciation day" every September, bartenders muddle hundreds of $1 Old Fashioneds in a two hour span.

"For the regulars, it's tradition," DeBolt said. "I think everything goes in cycles; my numbers can attest to that. But the Old Fashioned has such staying power.

"I hope it stays forever as a popular drink. If it's done correctly, I think it will."

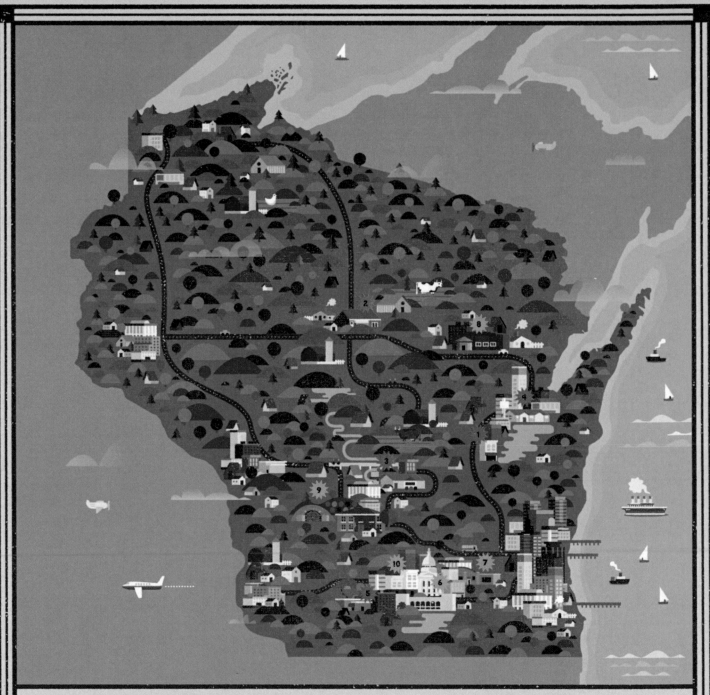

THE 'NEW' OLD FASHIONED

6	**THE OLD FASHIONED** 23 N Pinckney St. #1, Madison, WI 53703	PHONE	(608) 310-4545
7	**OLD SUGAR DISTILLERY** 931 E Main St., Madison, WI 53703	PHONE	(608) 260-0812
8	**ARTY'S (THE NEW OLD FASHIONED)** 18 6th St., Clintonville, WI 54929	PHONE	
9	**WOLLERSHIEM WINERY** 7876 Wisconsin 188, Prairie du Sac, WI 53578	PHONE	(608) 643-6515
10	**THE TORNADO STEAKHOUSE** 116 S Hamilton St., Madison, WI 53703	PHONE	(608) 256-3570

THE 'OLD' OLD FASHIONED

1	**BROOKLYN GRILL** 607 South Main St., Oshkosh, WI 54902	PHONE	(920) 230-4477
2	**PINEWOOD SUPPER CLUB** 1208 Halfmoon Lake Dr., Mosinee, WI 54455	PHONE	(715) 693-3180
3	**TRAIL'S LOUNGE RESTAURANT** 125 Wauona Tr., Portage, WI 53901	PHONE	(608) 742-2325
4	**THE RED OX** 2318 Oneida St., Appleton, WI 54915	PHONE	(920) 830-4121
5	**SMOKY'S CLUB** 3005 University Ave., Madison, WI 53705	PHONE	(608) 233-2120

LOST IN TRANSLATION

With the exception of a splash of cherry liqueur or a fruity garnish, the Old Fashioned hipsters sip in next generation Manhattan speakeasies bears little resemblance to the drink that Wisconsin long ago adopted as its own.

The Old Fashioned is a drink of many translations, some sneered at by the cocktail establishment but nonetheless beloved. In an effusive, rambling exploration of the drink on *Slate*, Troy Patterson called it "the seminal cocktail of a pluralistic nation."

Cocktail historians agree that the Old Fashioned originated as a simple "whiskey cocktail," made with a sugar cube, a few dashes of bitters and a double shot of bourbon or rye. In his book *Imbibe*, David Wondrich notes early references to the drink in the Chicago Tribune in the 1880s.

By 1895, Wondrich writes, the Old Fashioned represented "a drinker's plea for a saner, quieter, slower life, one in which a gent could take a drink or two without fear that it would impair his ability to dodge a speeding streetcar or operate a rotary press."

Rye remains the go-to spirit in most older recipes. The classic Old Fashioned in *The World's Best Bartenders' Guide* calls for Angostura bitters, a sugar cube, water, rye and a twist of lemon peel, with orange and cherry relegated to garnish. Wondrich adds a mixer — club soda — but pares the remainder to sugar, bitters and rye.

There is no exact origin for when fruit became part of the drink. Some blame Prohibition.

"When America's love affair with the cocktail was forced underground, the quality of the spirits consumed degraded basically to the point of poison," wrote Minneapolis bartender Nick Kosevich on the *Heavy Table* in 2009. "Cutting these spirits with fruit juices and sugar was one way the speakeasy barkeeps could get their guests to stomach the quality of product that they had to sell."

> "I do the works — orange, cherry, sugar muddle. I don't think you want to destroy the integrity of an awesome drink invented in the 1800s just for speed."

Recipes with muddled fruit have been common for decades, though traditionalists still protest. On an instructive website called oldfashioned101.com, cocktail writer Martin Doudoroff pleads with his readers to agree that "there is no slice of orange in an Old Fashioned. There is no cherry in an Old Fashioned."

He goes further, quoting *Crosby Gaige's Cocktail Guide and Ladies' Companion* from 1945:

"You do not mash up fruit of any kind in an Old Fashioned. To do so implies a perverted nastiness of mind."

Wisconsinites beg to differ.

"I do the works — orange, cherry, sugar muddle," said Sarah Marcin, who tends bar at the **Brooklyn Grill in Oshkosh.** "I don't think you want to destroy the integrity of an awesome drink invented in the 1800s just for speed."

"We love Old Fashioneds in Wisconsin," Marcin added, calling the Wisconsin version "modern." "If you go out of state they have no idea what that is. The Old Fashioned is super popular here."

BRANDY IN THE BADGER STATE

It's only a slight stretch to say that every bar in Wisconsin has its own take on the Old Fashioned. It's a drink that adapts to both the bar and the drinker, with dozens of possible combinations.

The sugar at the bottom of the rocks glass may be a cube — The Old Fashioned restaurant uses brown sugar — a teaspoon of granules or simple syrup. Angostura is the usual choice for bitters, between three and seven dashes for those who like more spice.

Sometimes this muddle of sugar and bitters includes a wedge of orange and a maraschino cherry; sometimes it doesn't. Bartenders feel strongly about it both ways.

While an Old Fashioned may be made with nearly any spirit from bourbon to gin, to drink like a Wisconsinite, order brandy first — preferably Korbel from California.

Why brandy? One theory goes that excited German ex-pats returning from the Chicago world's fair in 1893 fell in love with the spirit. Wisconsin has been a brandy state ever since. The state's appetite accounts for nearly half of Korbel's annual shipments.

"Go out of state, and any time you order anything brandy, they say, 'What part of Wisconsin are you from?'" said Steve Allen, who co-owns the **Pinewood Supper Club in Mosinee** with his wife, Joan.

"Especially if you order a brandy Old Fashioned sweet."

Sweet is by far the most popular way to get an Old Fashioned, and it means lemon lime soda — Sprite, 7-Up or Sierra Mist. Ordering an "Old Fashioned soda" will bring a less sweet drink made with seltzer; "press," short for Presbyterian, means a mix of Sprite and seltzer. "Sour" calls out the sour mix or Squirt.

"I've had people drink it with ginger ale," said Jerry Ewig, owner of **The Red Ox in Appleton.** "Everybody adds their own little thing to it."

The garnish is equally malleable. Beyond a lipstick-red maraschino cherry and slice of orange on a tiny plastic sword, people who take their drink sour might go for a Bloody Mary-style skewer of pickled onions and mushrooms. At the Red Ox, the Old Fashioned muddle starts with lemon instead of orange, and a favorite garnish is olives.

All of this muddling and stirring takes longer than the average cocktail prep, which has led supper clubs across the state to seek shortcuts.

At **Trails Lounge in Portage,** the bartenders don't muddle because "it will take too long," according to owner Manoucher Madani. In Mosinee, staff at the Pinewood use a premade mix of simple syrup and bitters.

"We used to muddle bitters with the sugar cube, but when you're trying to make a heavy amount of them, it's really tough to do that," Allen said. "We sell a lot of Old Fashioneds."

Bob Perry, bar manager at **Smoky's Club in Madison,** has been tending bar for nearly 50 years. He learned to make an Old Fashioned at Cathay House, a Madison Chinese restaurant, in the 1960s.

"Some places are still muddling orange and cherry — I don't do that here," Perry said. "To me, muddling gets a little too sweet. I like it smoother."

Perry does muddle the sugar and bitters, but allows that it takes time and training to get the balance right. Using a mix could be more consistent.

"Some places now are trying to cut back," Perry said, "make it a little simpler, where it doesn't take them much time to make a drink.

"I like doing it from scratch because there's an art to it. If you make it right, it's going to be a great drink. The mixes get too bitter."

As a cocktail, the Wisconsin Old Fashioned has a mixed reputation. It's too sweet and gooey, some protest; the maraschino is full of high fructose corn syrup and dye; it's a "boozy smoothie," practically a dessert drink.

Badger state bartenders are used to it. They make no excuses.

"Everywhere in America talks dry and drinks sweet," said Bob Hemauer, general manager of the **Tornado Steakhouse,** a Madison supper club. "To paraphrase H. L. Mencken, nobody has ever lost money underestimating the sugar consumption of the American public. Everyone likes sweet stuff."

Hemauer called the evolution of the Old Fashioned "a boozy game of telephone."

"I look at it like dialects, like language," he said. "People from the Midwest have the same accent.

"It's unique in that (the Old Fashioned) is identifiably Wisconsin, like fried cheese curds. But I don't think the phenomenon itself is that unique... like scrapple in Pennsylvania, poutine in Canada."

THE LOCAVORE'S COCKTAIL

Beyond the default accompaniment for Friday night fish fry, some in Wisconsin view their neighbors' bottomless appetite for muddled fruit and brandy as a business opportunity.

Philippe and Julie Coquard, owners of **Wollersheim Winery** in Prairie du Sac, said some 3,000 folks lined up for a bottle when Wollersheim released its first brandy in April 2013.

The Coquards already produce of the state's most popular wine, Prairie Fume, made from seyval blanc grapes grown in New York. For the new brandy, "we decided to go all Wisconsin, everything from the grape variety to the oak we use for the barrels," said Julie Coquard.

With an eye toward expansion, Wollersheim is already adding local growers of LaCrosse and St. Pepin grapes, cold-hardy varietals developed in Wisconsin. In its second year, the company plans to double the 360 gallons it aged for the first batch and eventually build a dedicated distilling facility.

As for the taste, Coquard Brandy takes after Wollersheim's wines — it's fruity, easy to drink.

"Our brandy is well-balanced, approachable," Julie Coquard said. "It has a floral side (that) makes it interesting."

But despite its roots, a Wisconsin-made brandy may not be a good fit for the state's favorite cocktail.

At **Old Sugar Distillery,** founder Nathan Greenawalt can — and does — make a locavore-friendly Old Fashioned with Brandy Station, made since 2010 with grapes grown in McFarland. But he'd rather use Old Sugar's Cane & Abe rum.

"Our rum is very oaky and unsweetened," said Greenawalt. "Old Fashioneds were traditionally made with whiskey. The rum fits because the oak is so dominant."

Greenawalt isn't surprised that the Wisconsin-style brandy Old Fashioned ("a glorified punch") is a big seller at the distillery on Madison's east side. His bartenders put a twist on it by cutting out the sugar and doubling the bitters.

"They're super popular and really tasty," he said. "But in a way, the subtleties of brandy are covered up by the rest of the cocktail."

Further north in Clintonville, the founders of **Arty's** hope the new frontier in Old Fashioned consumption is of the bottled variety. Arty's, sold in six packs around Wisconsin, proudly bears the tagline "the New Old Fashioned" and offers three premixed twists on the cocktail — brandy sweet, whiskey sweet and whiskey sour.

"When I was a child, my parents owned a supper club," said Timothy Pappin, who founded the company in July 2012 with his nephew, Ryan Mijal. He still remembers "washing dishes behind the bar and people ordering Old Fashioneds."

When the pair noticed a growing interest in old school craft cocktails and "microdistilleries popping up" around the state, they had the idea to make the statewide cocktail obsession easier to pair with fishing and football.

Pappin wouldn't share the ingredients, but said it took six months of tinkering with flavorings and concentrates to come up with Arty's recipe.

"We made some pretty miserable recipes in the process," Pappin said. "All of our neighbors were guinea pigs... some things we passed out were embarrassing."

At 6.9 percent alcohol by volume in a seven ounce bottle, Arty's is more alcoholic than a Coors or a Spotted Cow, but packs a lighter punch than the cocktail version.

"A muddled Old Fashioned is a much heavier drink," Pappin said.

Arty's "sweet, light and refreshing" flavor could court a new generation of Old Fashioned drinkers.

It shouldn't be a hard sell. Bob Hemauer already sees college students sitting next to middle aged businessmen at the Tornado Steakhouse bar, all drinking variations on the same thing.

"The Wisconsin style Old Fashioned gets ordered at the Tornado by people from 21 to as old as they come in, in their 80s or sometimes 90s," said Bob Hemeauer. "Elevated cocktails are not going anywhere anytime soon, and I don't think the Wisconsin-style supper club Old Fashioned is either.

"We serve hundreds and thousands of them. There's plenty of room for creativity."

CHAPTER 3
LADIES BOOKS AND TACKLE SOCIETY

WRITERS: SUSAN PAGANI AND MARIA MANION :: **ILLUSTRATOR:** DAVID WITT

The Ladies Books & Tackle Society was founded in the mid-1800s in the Yorkshire Dales by a small band of adventuring women who spent their summers angling the freestone rivers and their winters reading the works of the Brontë sisters, Thomas Hardy, George Eliot, Jane Austen, and Anthony Trollope. The club migrated to the United States after World War II, and a chapter was started in Minneapolis by the convivial Maeve Burpee, who maintained the traditions of angling and English literature and added a new emphasis on food, reflecting her own particular fondness for a hearty repast and a strong cocktail.

Although rather quiet about membership and club outings, the Ladies Books & Tackle spends most weekends fishing the local streams. They may be recognized by their club patches and extraordinary dedication to snacking, which will be evident in some great encumbrance, such as a chest of china, set streamside and awaiting the next meal.

The Ladies Books & Tackle bylaws clearly state that the angler must have her rod, vest, boots, waders and fly boxes organized and stowed in a fishing duffle the evening before an expedition. This ensures not only a quick departure in the small hours of the morning but also, and perhaps more importantly, that the sleepy and muddled angler will not inadvertently leave a piece of important equipment behind.

However, it is a fact that an early departure and all the preparation in the world will not ensure success. The important thing is not to return home defeated, but to make the best of whatever the day may bring. For us, this generally means a good meal or two.

A DAY OF POOR FISHING IS A DAY OF FINE EATING
IN WHICH WE TRAVEL WIDELY IN SEARCH OF SNACKS

One morning in early summer, we awoke to a storm, the rain flying sideways at our windows and the wind whipping the tops of the trees. Unsure how long or how hard it had been or would be raining, we determined to set off and try our luck on the Lower Kinnickinnic. Sure enough, as we crossed the St. Croix River, the clouds blew away, and we were rewarded with a gloriously sunny day. Yet things at the river were not so brilliant. The banks were all sludge and a downed tree forced us off the path, where our boots muddled the damp, wild plants, so that the air around us was redolent with mint and flowers. But the water was high and it resembled fast-moving chocolate milk. Nothing was hatching, and though we tried our brightest flies — a soft-hackled partridge and orange — the trout could not see them to be tempted.

There would be no fishing this water, so we let Cricket, our black Labrador retriever, take a dip, and tossed him sticks while we considered the day. It would be hot, but if the breeze held, it would be a good day for a picnic at the rainbow trout pond in Plum City. And so we set off, stopping here and there to pick up the things we like to eat in the area. With its striped awning, the **Dish and the Spoon Café** presents an unimposing but friendly face among the old buildings that line Main Street in River Falls. It's a pleasant spot, and we often see a pair of old fellows sitting out front with their coffees. On this particular morning, they smiled and wore sandals and seemed relaxed enough, but our eavesdropping ears found them engaged in a combative review of the world's news. We slipped past with a "Good morning," and headed to the counter, where we built our sandwiches by circling and checking bread, protein, dairy, condiments and various veggies on a clipboard. The choices were not startling — turkey, tuna, roast beef, etc. — but we knew from past experience that everything in the sandwich would be fresh and crisp. Of course, it was still much too early for lunch, so the nice people delivered our sandwiches and a few Sprecher ginger ales in a brown bag and we put them away for later.

The trick to making what is solid and wholesome streamside fare into something quite lovely is to doctor it up with cheese from Cady Cheese Factory. However, the factory's retail shop does not open until mid-morning. Our stomachs were growling for breakfast, so we overshot the factory by a few miles and headed to the **Spring Valley Bakery.** This little bakery has been turning out pastries, cookies, and doughnuts for more than 60 years. From the outside, it resembled a pub — with a crimson façade and black trim — but inside it was warm and smelled of sweet dough and melting chocolate. We took away a bag of raised doughnuts. Among them, a plump and rather racy thing called the Honeymooner, glazed and topped with a heavy crown of dark sour cherries.

We inhaled the doughnuts under a tree on Wonderland Road. There, in the middle of a wheat farm, is a bit of the Rush River we like to fish. The water was just as murky, but the grass had been recently mowed and smelled of clover, the air was cool beneath the tree, and the doughnuts were tender and delicious. The wind ruffled the wheat. We heard the dull roar of a tractor at work somewhere, not far off. Cricket rolled in the grass delighted, and we were tempted to take a nap.

As a dairy, the **Cady Cheese Factory** belongs among the fields and farms, but it is still strange to turn into a parking lot and see the well-appointed retail shop, which looks like it should live between knicknackeries on the boulevard of some resort town. From its crowded cases, we tasted a 14-year-old sharp white cheddar. It broke off the block in shards and had a texture that was both creamy and granular. The flavor was wonderful too — salty, tangy, and bright. We bought a hunk of the cheese and stowed it in the brown bags with our sandwiches.

Plum City always seems ready for a parade. The street lamps are hung with American flags and baskets of pink peonies, and yet the city always feels empty and therefore a little eerie. On the day we visited, it was dead quiet but for the steady hum of a handful of motorcycles following us down Main Street. When we parked, their leather-clad and be-fringed riders cruised by with impassive faces, and then swung around and parked. Dismounted, the hellions turned out to be friendly retirees, who grinned and waved when a gaggle of towheaded boys and girls, pale even in summer, pattered by in bare feet, carrying bags of puppy chow. In Plum City, all roads lead not to plums but to a spring-fed pond at the center of town. If you don't have a bag of kibble, you can purchase a small amount for 25 cents at a vending machine. As we watched, the little plumlings tossed handfuls of the stuff into the pond, then backed away as the roiling water exploded with trout. These were not the wee speckled brownies of the local streams, but three-foot-long rainbow trout with massive sucking lips and commodious bellies that could easily tuck away a whole bag of puppy chow, a small child, or a sweet black Labrador. It was fascinating and upsetting all at once, especially in the dead calm of the little city. Crossing to the far side of the pond, we claimed a picnic table and spread out our fare. Cricket sat next to the pool, staring pensively into its deep green and blue depths. He was so attentive to the fish that he did not notice as we passed the Cady cheddar, cutting slabs of the musky cheese into our sandwiches.

After lunch, the Labrador enjoyed a biscuit, and we finished up our sodas — sugary and pleasing after the salty cheese — debated the ending of **Middlemarch,** which was either terribly romantic or a terrible waste of a smart woman, and revisited the merits of the cheese until the sun was too high and hot, and we realized the town bakery would be closing.

The **Bittersweet Bakery & More,** housed in what used to be Plum City's bank, specializes in bars, cookies, and doughnuts, but also has antique kitchenware, hand-knit scarves and hats, and aprons for sale. There was an air of nostalgia about the place. The windows were hung with vintage aprons — flouncy with rickrack and ribbons — that once belonged to the town's grandmothers. And a long hallway displayed black-and-white photographs of Plum City in its heyday. Our favorite featured the old Plum City Rod & Gun Club, which used to sit alongside the trout pond. It had nice windows and seemed the sort of place where the Ladies Books & Tackle might have held its annual meeting, voting in new bylaws with a lady-like roar. We recognized the spirit of the town in a photo of a man with a serious mien and a great, broomy mustache. He was receiving a shave on a horse cart decked out in stars and stripes for a Fourth of July parade. We tied the pretty aprons around our waists and, although it was by then a million degrees outside, looped the heavy, knitted cowls around our heads, and then bought a bag of molasses cookies to take home with us, dessert for the long drive home.

This was not the only treat. Many of the ladies are partial to ice cream, and we could not resist a soft-serve ice cream cone from the **Ellsworth Cooperative Creamery.** Once inside, cool and surrounded by cases of cheese, our appetite returned. We pondered a bag of dill curds, which are so very compatible with beer, but moderation dictated that we leave with only a swirl of the rich vanilla ice cream.

The light was still good, so we made a final stop on the Upper Kinnickinnic to look at the water. We call the spot Swinging Gate. It was rehabilitated not long ago, and now there are wildflowers, tidy gravel paths and rustic limestone steps down to the river. The water was brown and cloudy, but the flowers were in fine fettle — blooming and fragrant and fairly buzzing in the hot sun. Following Cricket, we wandered down to the bottommost step and hung our feet in the cold, cold water, reflecting on what a fine day it had been.

— Susan Pagani

IN WHICH WE PICNIC STREAMSIDE

An appreciation for picnics is not in the Ladies Books & Tackle Society bylaws — our members already have this in their makeup — but, in future, should a prospective lady seem indifferent, the executive council is prepared to take the trouble and add it to our constitution.

It's that important. In the height of summer, when the sun is high and fish are wary, a civilized picnic is a chance to celebrate the season and our own humility in the struggle to catch fish. Trout fishing and good eating are not for the dispirited.

The Ladies Books & Tackle trout outing picnic has varied in destination, but we've settled on Pine Creek the last few years. Pine Creek winds from the base of a Mississippi River limestone bluff to Lake Pepin, and the scenic drive from Minneapolis to this restored creek in Pierce County, Wisconsin, allows just enough time for members to chat over a Thermos of oolong and a hardboiled egg. We ponder the clarity of the creek's water; we recount the previous year's catches; we question which of our freshly tied flies may be likely to entice the jewel-tone brook trout; we wonder which of the native plantings along the creek-side will be in bloom and whether we have medication enough to combat them; we list the contents of our picnic hamper; and we retell the struggles of finding a decent plum for our summer chutney.

We ladies are always tentative upon arriving. Our car is air-conditioned; the creek valley is hot and bright, even by mid-morning. A ribbon of tall grasses and plantings along the creek-side falls in s-curves through the valley. The meadow on either side is mowed, cut grass crunchy and browning in the sun. We know the already skittish fish are disinclined to leave their rock ledge shadows, but we also know we'll feel better after trying to tempt them — for, if we don't catch fish, we better understand the joys of when we do. And we know we'll have a tipple at the end of it.

Trout outings require a fair amount of equipment — rods, reels, fly boxes, waders, wading boots, sunglasses, nets — and, after donning our gear, we wander to the creek, each of us disappearing inside the curtain of flowering plants to find our own private spot in the stream. Crouched, quiet, and stealthy, we wait and watch for a fish to rise.

It's here, in our personal, secret stretches of creek that our picnic really begins. For even if the trout are reluctant to rise to our tufts of feathers tied to a hook, the rest of the stream seems eager to play. Frogs plop from rock ledges into the water. Grasshoppers — green-bellied, brown-bellied and yellow-bellied — attempt creek-side jumps, sometimes landing in the current to kick their way downstream. An angler squeals, faintly, at plum-size, black and lemon-yellow spiders weaving sturdy webs. Cedar waxwings with their Zorro-mask marking and yellow-rimmed tail feathers chip and whistle and flit from here to there, catching insects in midair. Blades of grass that touch the water's surface leave wakes in the stream behind them, and every sort of blooming plant seems to have brought out its best china. The club's members enjoy the conviviality of each other's company, but these hours alone in our respective, in-stream retreats are fine. Quite fine.

While judicious with fly-fishing equipment, we find we are less so with the picnic provisions. It seems only right that after such splendor at the stream, we should dine in the stream's meadows, equally grand. Unfortunately this means a heavy hamper is hauled, at turns by teams of two, from here to there and here again, to gauge whether or not that particular spot suits our requirements. Although we each have personal preferences, we generally agree that we should picnic under a tree for shade, on an incline for the best prospect to the river, in an open area for cross-ventilation by which mosquitoes are kept at bay, and at some distance from the stream, should other anglers like to fish on the water near us. Once determined, we unload the hamper (now a vintage aluminum cooler, an upgrade from our plastic red eyesore of previous years), unfurl the picnic cloth (ideally coordinated with the china pattern for best effect), set the tableware (china, glassware, silver, linens), spread the picnic fixings, and decant the picnic tipple. One of us takes photographs for the club annual, while another hides all unsightly containers and paraphernalia in the cooler. We then sit down to dine.

Over the years, the appetites of our club members have aligned themselves. We have each come to enjoy sharp cheddar cheeses, pickles of the tangy variety, and chutneys featuring seasonal fruits. And in an effort to reduce the weight of our hamper this year, we tried to focus on these items, bringing only bits of roast chicken and hearty, baguette-like bread (small so that we ladies can each eat more than one without self-recrimination) as their vehicle. A little cheese, pickle and condiment go a long way. (Note: The hamper was not lighter as a result of this strategy. Our enthusiasm for each inclines us to bring more.)

The cheese and pickle needed no vehicle. Door County cherries were lovely this year, so we pickled a few handfuls with cider vinegar, sugar, and pepper flakes, packed in a jar with fresh parsley. Someone shoved a chunk of Cady Creek 14-year cheddar into a pickled cherry; a frenzy ensued. The cherries at the uppermost level of the jar were mild while those on the bottom were more assertive; they had a spicy bite that paired well with the toothsome cheddar. The crunchy, crystalline bits within the cheese were a delightful contrast against the firm, smooth cherries. When the cherries were gone, one lady declared that a drop of the ruby pickle juice on a bit of white cheddar was also quite pleasing.

Our chutney this year was fresh plum and dried apricot, and it was pink. We've had some society debate about whether all pink foods and drink are unnaturally sweet, but we endeavored to enjoy it without bias since we should not be judging our fellow ladies' contributions. Stewed slowly with red onion, jalapenos, garlic, black pepper and vinegar, the chutney was, in fact, only slightly sweet. In concert with the mayonnaise, it felt like custard on the tongue. We all thought it would also be stunning on duck. Perhaps another year.

Nibbling at the remainders and pondering this year's efforts is the cue for our ritual cocktail: spicy ginger ale cut with a bit of Kentucky bourbon and garnished with a slice of cucumber. The fragrant, cool-ish drink (we have yet to efficiently tote ice) puts us in a reflective mood. We toast trout — caught, lost, or elusive — nature's finery, good friends, and good food.

For dessert, after having packed up our hamper and fishing gear, we drive a farther bit south to pick up a triple berry pie at the **Stockholm Pie Company**. The wooden screen door and benches in the shade beneath the building's overhang remind us of a farmhouse porch and we're inclined to stay, feasting on our pie and watching other folks charge in to get theirs. Our darling Labrador would rather be rolling in grass, however, so we grab the pie and go.

Although intending to stop at a scenic rest area along the Great River Road and serve it on the china plates we lugged especially, the Ladies Books & Tackle members can't help but to grab their silver forks (pocketed from the hamper) and dig into the pie. The berries are sweet and tart and perfect with the faintly salty, very flaky crust. The best of summer is in that pie. Who cares if the beautiful crust is dashed to bits by a bunch of ladies who couldn't wait to taste it.

— Maria Manion

Dish and the Spoon Café
208 N Main Street
River Falls, Wisconsin 54022
Mon - Fri 6:30am - 8pm
Sat - Sun 7:30am - 3pm

Spring Valley Bakery
S232 McKay Avenue
Spring Valley, Wisconsin 54767
Mon-Fri 6:30am - 3:30pm
Sat 6:30am - noon
Sun Closed

Cady Cheese Factory Inc
126 Wisconsin 128
Wilson, Wisconsin 54027
Mon - Fri 8:30am - 5:30pm
Sat - Sun 9am - 5pm

Bittersweet Bakery & More
404 Main Street
Plum City, Wisconsin 54761
Tues - Fri: 7am - 3pm
Sat 7am - Noon
Sun & Mon Closed

Ellsworth Co-Op Creamery
232 N Wallace Street
Ellsworth, Wisconsin 54011
Mon - Fri 8am - 5:30pm
Sat- Sun 9am - 5pm

Stockholm Pie Company
N2030 Spring St #1
Stockholm, Wisconsin 54769
10am - 5pm (closed Wed)

CHAPTER 4

ALL-STAR CHEESEMAKERS OF THE UPPER MIDWEST

WRITER: JAMES NORTON :: **ILLUSTRATOR:** WACSO

We refer to cheese as a food, but that word is insufficient. Real cheese is alive, a product of microfauna, human attention, milk, and time. Harold McGee, writing in "On Food and Cooking," does it justice: "Cheese is one of the great achievements of humankind. Not any cheese in particular, but cheese in its astonishing multiplicity, created anew every day in the dairies of the world."

I'm eating a piece of Willi Lehner's cave-aged bandage-wrapped cheddar as I type these words, breaking off little pieces of cheese with my thumb and forefinger, and warming the cheese in my mouth a bit before I chew. I could toss out adjectives and descriptions: caramel-sweet, nutty, salty, earthy, bright without being sharp, increasingly powerful as you work toward the rind — but to gain anything like a meaningful picture of what's going on, you ultimately need to taste the cheese yourself.

Cheese is a product of geography multiplied by time, born in an animal and guided by human intelligence and innumerable microscopic helpers. It's not just delicious — it's deeply mystifying, and the eternal, ultimately hopeless quest to entirely resolve that sense of mystery sets cheesemakers apart from ordinary people. They are driven, sometimes to the brink of distraction, to decipher God's lactic mysteries.

And we should all be grateful to them for that sense of compulsion.

Willi Lehner - Bleu Mont Dairy

Bob Wills - Cedar Grove Cheese

Gianni Toffolon - BelGioioso Cheese

Jeff Jirik - Caves of Faribault

Katie Hedrich - LaClare Farms

Jeff Jirik

Keith Adams

Keith Adams - Alemar Cheese

Sid Cook - Carr Valley Cheese

Tony Hook - Hook's Cheese

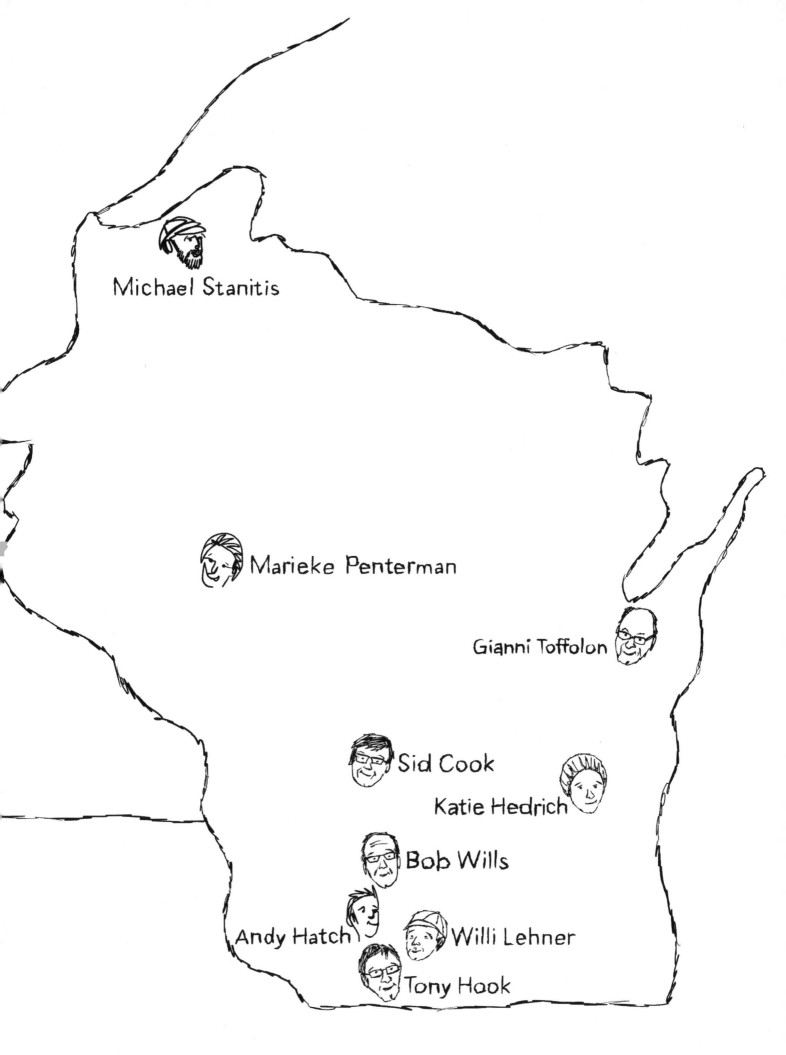

Michael Stanitis

Marieke Penterman

Gianni Toffolon

Sid Cook

Katie Hedrich

Bob Wills

Andy Hatch

Willi Lehner

Tony Hook

The Upper Midwest is one of the world's great cheese regions. Wisconsin in particular routinely wins more world awards for its cheese than entire countries (and we're talking about respectable cheesemaking countries, like Italy and France). That's thanks to the seriousness with which the art is approached, to the substantial state infrastructure that supports and encourages the cheesemaker, and to the state's heritage of cheesemaking. The tradition dates back into the early 19th Century and has produced a number of still-living, still-working 4th- and even 5th-generation cheesemakers.

The new vogue for local food has boosted the cheese industry (among others) and Wisconsin has pivoted from a cheese-as-commodity state to an artisan cheese state without missing a beat. The knowledge had always been there; with the permission of the market, it was tapped into, and a thousand cheeses bloomed and ripened.

Minnesota is beginning to catch up. Lacking the state and university support of its Eastern neighbor, it has a long way to go, but is also home to some masterful cheese makers and a blossoming freshman class of new makers.

This chapter of the Atlas isn't intended to be a definitive summary of all the great cheesemakers in Minnesota and Wisconsin; that demands a book of its own. Think of it as a sampler, an introduction to some of the dairy industry's best and brightest, individuals with stories as rich as their cheese, all of whom have made, are making and/or will make a serious contribution to our food culture.

In the course of writing these brief capsule biographies, we've nicknamed our subjects — not to define them completely, but to dramatize various points of view brought to cheese by its talented creators.

As artist Robb Burnham has sketched these cheesemakers with lines and color, so go these brief descriptions: impressionistic, iconic, abridged, and hopefully enough to get you started on your own voyage into cheese country.

Calling Minnesota's Jeff Jirik **"THE CAVEMAN"** isn't meant to imply a primitive approach to cheesemaking — he's a painter with flavor and cheese is his canvas. Jirik ages cheeses in the 29,000-square-foot Caves of Faribault, natural sandstone hollows that have been expanded and shored up to be used as a massive cheese-aging (or "affinage") chamber.

Faribault cheeses like AmaBlu Cave-Aged Blue show up on restaurant menus throughout the state and region, and Jirik scored a recent win at the Fancy Food Show. There his Jeffs' Select Aged Gouda received a Specialty Food Association sofi award for Outstanding Cheese or Dairy Product. The cheese is a collaboration between Jirik and Monroe, Wisconsin cheesemaker Jeff Wideman of Maple Leaf Cheese.

"It was truly a collaboration between friends," says Jirik. "We become friends after meeting at the American Cheese Society show in 2002. He makes a great Gouda, so we decided to age some in the caves. The caves really got it excited. When we turned the cheese loose in the caves naked, it loved the humidity and temperature, and we were able to pull a caramel note out of it which is unusual for a Gouda — in fact, I almost hate to call it a Gouda because after 12 months in that cave, it's almost a completely different cheese."

Jeffs' Select was intended for private distribution to friends and family, but after some fell into the hands of a distributor, "the rest, they say, is history."

"THE ARTISAN" is fellow Minnesotan Keith Adams of Alemar, who came to cheesemaking after a long, turbulent, initially successful foray into the bagel business that left him a bit wiser after its demise.

He ventured into cheese inspired by friends of his who made wine in California, and approached his goal cautiously: "I had an older-guy-who-had-his-ass-kicked idea of how to start a business: find really good milk, find really good mentors and once you've started, don't settle for pretty good, push through it and try to be great," Adams says. "I wanted to really try to do this the right way."

With help from Sue Conley of California's legendary Cowgirl Creamery and "The Cheesemaker's Manual" author Margaret Morris, Adams started making cheese in April of 2009. Adams insisted on good milk, and he got it: he works with grass-fed milk from Cedar Summit Farms. "If you're making wine," says Adams, "you'd want to start with super grapes, and for cheese, it's really great milk."

Adams's Bent River Camembert-style cheese and newly released Good Thunder washed-rind cheese are both mainstays in the Twin Cities area and beginning to spread thanks to West and East Coast distributors willing to give an upstart Midwestern cheesemaker — and his excellently regarded cheese — a chance.

Tony Hook of Hook's Cheese Company in Mineral Point, Wisconsin doesn't run the biggest or most diversified cheese business in the region, but we're calling him **"THE INVESTOR"** all the same. His aged cheddar sets a national standard not just for its longevity (the release of Hook's 15-year cheddar is an annual gourmet event celebrated from coast to coast) but also its excellence. Like a skilled banker, Hook and his wife Julie (who have been making cheese together for more than 35 years) are able to guide good milk into young cheese, and steer young cheese into old cheese without missing a beat.

"It keeps crystallizing as it gets older," says Hook of his aged cheddar. "It isn't a sharper flavor like the three- to five-year-old cheddar, but after you get to six, seven, eight years it smooths out like a fine wine and gains more flavor. I haven't found the peak in ours, but I'm sure there is one, somewhere. About 70 percent of what we produce would probably age out to 12-15 years, but most of that sells at three- to five-years-old."

The key to a cheese that ages out gracefully, says Hook, is "milk quality. If you start with poor milk, it'll start showing off flavors. I attribute 90 percent of the quality of our cheeses to good milk from our farmers, who all have small family farms. If you don't have the quality milk, you won't make the quality cheese."

Michael Stanitis of Sassy Nanny Farmstead Cheese is **"THE WANDERER,"** but he doesn't walk alone — his nightly walks with his goats through the woods near Cornucopia Wisconsin, make him a throwback to the days when goatherds and shepherds walked the hills and forests in search of food for their flocks. (It should be added that classical shepherds didn't typically make their rounds with a gin and tonic in hand, as is the norm for Stanitis.)

Stanitis started his business in his 40s, and says the transition has had its rough moments: "I used to make fun of rich people who started restaurants and had never worked in a restaurant a day in their lives," he says. "Well, I'm not rich, but I can tell you that the fantasy of having a herd of goats, milking them, making cheese, and marketing the cheese is nonstop, constant work... it's a hard way to make a living, but it's a great life to make."

"I do really enjoy 90 percent of it," he adds. "[But] I can't stand sitting at farmers markets. It makes me want to put an ice pick through my eye."

"I built my business plan on reconnecting people with their food," says Stanitis. "If people are going to take an extra four or five dollars out of their pocket and spend it on my cheese, they're doing it because they know me and they drive by my farm and see the goats outside in their manger, or they see them out walking with me, and they say 'hey, let's give our money to Michael.'"

"I love that I can raise the animals and I don't take their kids away from them or lock them up in a barn. They're out all day, their kids are out there with them. Every night I make a big stiff cocktail and head out down the road and into the woods with them, and that's the way it used to be done. There's a reason that people were shepherds and herders — the most natural way to feed your animals is to let them eat what they want to eat.

You can tell a true cheesemaker because he or she approaches cheese both as an artist and as a scholar. We're calling Sid Cook **"THE MAD SCIENTIST"** because he takes the cheesemaker's passion for guided dabbling to dizzying heights, creating dozens upon dozens of "Wisconsin Originals" cheeses in his time — new cheeses the world hasn't tasted before. His company, Carr Valley Cheese, operates four different small cheese plants, the better to handle the making of the company's more than 80 cheeses, available at four different retail outlets throughout the state.

"It's my mess," says Cook. "It's pretty expensive to build one big factory, and it really takes a lot of cheesemaking systems to make a lot of different cheeses. A big factory works real good if you want to make cheddar... or Swiss... or something like that, but we need a lot of flexibility, and a different scale."

Andy Hatch of Uplands Cheese is young, but he competes as a peer with the grizzled graybeards of his profession, making some of the world's most coveted cheese near Dodgeville, Wisconsin.

The alpine-style Pleasant Ridge Reserve (which according to the most recent Zingerman's catalog may be "the best American cheese being made today") commands so much respect that even coastal-based flyover country-bashers will sniffily admit that it's edible.

If Hatch is **"THE JOURNEYMAN,"** it's only because he learned from acknowledged master Mike Gingrich and is just now taking ownership of Uplands in order to lead it forward into the heart of the 21st Century.

"Luckily, we're at that size where I have to do everything — that's making cheese, marketing, bookkeeping... " says Hatch, who views his hands-on involvement as a blessing, not a curse. It's a positive attitude that is particularly helpful when it comes to dealing with Rush Creek Reserve, an aged raw milk soft cheese that now sparks an annual autumnal buying panic when the scarce wheels are released onto the market.

"Ripening a cheese is essentially controlling rot," says Hatch. "And when a cheese is wet [like Rush Creek Reserve], it ripens faster. So it's like driving a car at 80 miles an hour instead of, like Pleasant Ridge, going 25. It's a lot harder to keep it under control and in balance. It's also a small piece of cheese, so the amount handling is incredible — if you turn and wash a wheel of Pleasant Ridge [Reserve] every day, which we do when it's young, you've handled ten pounds of cheese. If you turn and wash a Rush Creek wheel every day, you've handled three quarters of a pound of cheese."

Cheesemakers all have a scientist's instinct: control for variables and learn more about what you're doing. Few, however, take it the level of Bob **"THE PROFESSOR"** Wills from Cedar Grove Cheese and Clock Shadow Creamery. Wills holds a doctorate in economics and a law degree, and his Living Machine (a series of plant- and aquatic-life stocked tanks that clean the waste water of his Plain, Wisconsin-based cheese plant) surely ranks among the Seven Wonders of Wisconsin Cheese.

"This is probably the most exciting time in the dairy industry in Wisconsin that there's ever been," said Wills in an interview with me for the 2009 book "The Master Cheesemakers of Wisconsin." "It's kind of like there's a renaissance. During history there have been these little periods when there'll be groups of writers in Paris or New York, or when Shelley and Keats and Byron and all those guys hung out together and all challenged each other, and in the music scene there's the same kind of stuff... and it just feels like that's what's happening in Wisconsin. Partly through necessity because you can't make a living here making normal cheese. And partly just because once it got rolling and there was a support system behind it, consumers got interested in what we were doing, and now people are just clamoring to see what we'll do next.

If twenty-something Katie Hedrich is **"THE ROOKIE"** of this group, it's not a knock on either her abilities or her results — in 2011, her farmstead goats' milk Evalon cheese won overall champion at the United States Championship Cheese Contest, among the most coveted awards in cheesedom.

Hedrich and her family broke ground on a new 35,000 sq. feet facility in Dec. of 2012 that marks a major expansion for LaClare Farms. "We're now milking in a Double 24 parlor, and the goats have a much larger area to roam and be free, and we're milking about 430 goats right now — by the end of this year, we hope to be up to 600 goats," she says.

The new facility in Chilton, Wisconsin has a retail store (which will feature some cows' milk cheeses made by Hedrich exclusively for this location), and a cafe (open 10am-7pm daily).

"I think cheesemaking in Wisconsin has made a really good change by focusing on quality rather than quantity," says Hedrich. "I think California's move into quantity pushed Wisconsin into quality, and I think we're now seeing a lot of really high quality product coming from Wisconsin. I think there's a lot of room for growth, but I think people need to be conscious of what they're doing. I see this in the goat cheese world: OK cheese isn't good enough anymore."

All the way from Cremona, Italy to Green Bay comes Gianni Toffolon of BelGioioso Cheese, one of Wisconsin's biggest and most distinguished makers of Italian- and Italian-inspired cheeses. Toffolon has made cheese in Wisconsin since 1979, and is a certified Wisconsin master cheesemaker. For him, it's not just about the cheese — it's about passing on the love and knowledge of cheese to the next generation, for which we christen him **"THE MENTOR."**

"I'm building up the factories, working with the young cheesemakers, and training up the next generation — I'm very pleased with life right now," says Toffolon. "I'm passing on everything I can of my past cheesemaking experience — things I found out the hard way, sometimes. And also to look into the 'why' of cheese, and to keep asking questions."

There's a common perception that the American work ethic is dead or dying, but Toffolon doesn't see it that way. "The thing that I find is that most young people want to learn, but that sometimes they're not given the time and the attention," he says. "Too often we patronize them, or label them: 'Oh, he doesn't have the patience, oh he doesn't care, all he wants to do is go out and drink.' It's not their fault — it's the teacher's."

Toffolon grew up in old, largely non-mechanized way of making cheese: "Your hands are in the product 24/7. It's the hard way, but you learn." Now, he says of younger cheesemakers, "when they start, the cheesemaker is basically a machine operator, but if you get him to start asking questions — all of a sudden, they get more and more curious about the cheesemaking. They get to the point when they start asking questions, and they want to know more and more."

We're calling Marieke Penterman **"THE GOUDA QUEEN"** in acknowledgement of what she has accomplished as cheesemaker for Holland's Family Cheese i n Thorp, Wisconsin: by combining Dutch experience with Wisconsin cows, Penterman has created some of the state's most popular and well-regarded cheese, an effort that culminated this year with the awarding of the 2013 U.S. Championship Cheese Contest Grand Champion award to her Marieke Gouda Mature, aged 6-9 months.

Penterman grew up on 60-cow dairy farm in Holland, and her husband's dream of larger-scale dairy farming led the family to Wisconsin.

"For us, America truly is a land of opportunity," she says. "What we're doing here we could have never done in our home country, in Europe. In Holland, farming is very expensive. In Canada and Europe, there's a quota system which means you have to buy the right to milk a cow before you can buy the cow. And land is very expensive in Holland."

One night while trying to figure out a way to create a bit of economic stability for her family, she put together her love of cheese ("I always asked family and friends to bring along cheese [from Holland]; In Holland, we're called 'Cheeseheads,' just like the people in Wisconsin) and the abundance of her family farm's milk.

"I woke up my husband and I said, 'I think I know what we can do — we should look into making the milk into cheese.'" She trained up, and the rest is recent dairy history.

"We make the cheese within five hours of the milk leaving the cows' udders, so that freshness is something you can taste in our cheese," she says. "It's a raw milk product — I truly believe in raw milk, I think it's better for your body, and it has a full flavor."

Willi Lehner of Blue Mounds, Wisconsin has picked up a reputation as fiercely independent — although his little company makes some of the best cheese in the country, he largely goes it alone on his farm in southwestern Wisconsin, where he relies on wind and solar power and yodels away the days while aging cheese in a cave that he built himself. Calling him **"THE RENEGADE"** isn't a knock on his stability or quality control — it's an acknowledgment of the fact that his Bleu Mont Dairy cheese truly stands alone, and that the methods he uses to produce it are truly his own.

"I only make cheese when cows are eating what they evolved to eat — grass," he says. "There are two windows of time when I make cheese — spring into early summer, and then again September into October. Pasture milk to me is the best milk you can get."

"Then it goes into what are the cows eating — not only the grass, but the breed of cow," he says. "The best milk I work with is this farm [Uplands], they make Pleasant Ridge Reserve. Their milk is spectacular, and great milk makes great cheese. As a whole I'm really fortunate with the milk I'm able to use. Every cow imparts certain enzymes to the milk."

"It wasn't until I spent a big chunk of my time in Switzerland in my 20s that I really got turned on to world class, fabulous cheese, you know? One of my experiences there was making cheese on an Alp," he says. "I was there with my brother — he milked the cows and I made the cheese in a copper kettle over a wood fire like it has been done for hundreds of years. It's there that I made the connection between what the cows eat and the final product."

Lehner's cave-aged bandaged cheddar is one of his best-known cheeses. "It's made in the traditional way most cheddars are made. It goes through the whole cheddaring process... the curds are poured into a form that's lined with a muslin cloth, and that cloth gets pressed onto the cheese the day it's made. The cheeses are cured in an underground vault that simulates a cave. Because of the temperature and humidity in a cave — 55 degrees temperature, and humidity of about 90 percent — the cheeses get completely covered in mold, and those molds give the cheese a lot of flavor."

"In addition to those molds giving the cheese flavor, the cheeses also lose 10 to 15 percent of their weight during the curing process, so the flavors get more and more concentrated," he says. "There are probably hundreds of strains of molds in my cave, and people say they can pick out my cheese during a blind tasting because of the terroir of my cheese cave."

As for flavor: "It has a milky component — it has some caramely flavors going all the way to butterscotch as it gets old — it's quite dense, denser than most cheddars you buy in a store because of the fact it has lost moisture. When the cheese is eaten, we encourage people to cut it so that you're getting a bit of what was under rind through to the center, because there's a flavor gradient to the cheese — the part under the rind is the most intensely flavored, and the center isn't quite like that — they mature differently."

The Wisconsin cheesemaker portraits that illustrate this chapter were made possible with the support of the Wisconsin Milk Marketing Board.

CHAPTER 5

LOUIE THE LOON in: THE CHEESEBURGERS OF WEST 7th St.

BY DWITT

I'M JUST GOING TO SAY IT... ST. PAUL IS A BURGER TOWN

THEY ARE EVERYWHERE. IT'S PRACTICALLY RAINING BURGERS ON WEST 7TH STREET THERE ARE 2 DOZEN DIFFERENT RESTAURANTS WITH CHEESEBURGERS ON THEIR MENU. SO I THOUGHT, LET'S TRY THEM ALL!

I WANTED TO KNOW WHO CAN TAKE BREAD, BEEF, & CHEESE, & MAKE SOMETHING AMAZING.

I ORDERED & ATE EVERY BASIC CHEESEBURGER THAT WEST 7TH HAD TO OFFER TO SEE & TASTE FOR MYSELF WHO HAS GOT THEIR FUNDAMENTALS DOWN.

I'M NOT INTERESTED IN WHAT YOU CAN STACK ONTO & STUFF INTO A BURGER. ALL OF THAT EXTRA BUSINESS OFTEN HIDES POOR BURGER CRAFTSMANSHIP.

I ATE EACH ONE AS IT CAME TO ME. I ADDED NOTHING TO ANY OF THE CHEESEBURGERS UNLESS IT CAME ON THE SAME PLATE.

LEGAL.

ILLEGAL.

ON EACH PAGE THERE IS A ROUGH MAP OF WEST 7TH SHOWING WHERE EACH RESTAURANT IS IN RELATION TO EACH OTHER.

I ALSO RATED EACH BURGER ON A SCALE OF 1 (BAD) TO 10 (AWESOME) & THAT RATING IS FOUND IN THE CIRCLE IN THE BOTTOM RIGHT OF EACH PANEL.

IN HERE

FOR CONSISTENCY'S SAKE, IF I WAS GIVEN A CHOICE OF CHEESE, I ALWAYS PICKED AMERICAN.

IT'S NOT A FANCY CHEESE, BUT IT IS THE BEST ONE FOR A CHEESEBURGER.

IT'S NOT A STAND OUT FLAVOR & YOU CAN'T HIDE BEHIND IT. IT'S COMPLIMENTARY & WHEN MELTED IS CREAMY & DIVINE.

THANKS, LOUIE.

ALRIGHT, I'M ALL SET TO GO! I'M STARTING ON THE WEST END OF WEST 7TH & HEADING EAST TOWARDS DOWNTOWN ST. PAUL.

IT'S CHEESEBURGER TIME!

WEST 7TH STREET

McDONALD'S AGAIN?!

KEENAN'S 620 CLUB

GLOCKENSPIEL — JA, IST GERMAN

CHRIS & ROB'S

DAY BY DAY CAFE — WHATEVER YOU ORDER, ENJOY IT ON THEIR PATIO.

Panel 1:

I WILL GIVE McDONALD'S CREDIT FOR HEADSPINNINGLY FAST SERVICE & A VERY CONSISTENT PRODUCT.

IT'S A SHAME ABOUT THE PRODUCT THOUGH...

①

Panel 8:

KEENAN'S IS ANOTHER DIVE BAR ENTRY WITH A FIRM GRASP ON HOW TO MAKE A GREAT CHEESEBURGER.

NOTHING FANCY HERE, BUT EVERYTHING DOES ITS JOB VERY WELL.

A SOFT, TOASTED SEEDLESS BUN, A MILDLY JUICY ⅓ POUND BEEF PATTY (THE PERFECT SIZE), & JUST ENOUGH CHEESE (AMERICAN) SO EVERY BITE IS AWESOME.

HAPPY BELLY!

AND WHILE YOU'RE THERE, TRY ONE OF THEIR DELICIOUS CONEY DOGS, THE 2ND BEST IN TOWN!

⑧

Panel 7 (left):

THE MOST BASIC CHEESEBURGER YOU CAN GET AT THE GLOCKENSPIEL HAS BACON GROUND INTO THE BEEF PATTY...

LETS PUT MORE MEAT INTO THE MEAT!

THERE IS NOTHING WRONG WITH BACON. EVER. HOWEVER, I AM SURPRISED IT DIDN'T HELP OUT THIS BURGER.

IT WAS ONLY A MINOR ADDITION OF FLAVOR, BUT NO HELP IN MAKING IT JUICIER, & IT NEEDED SOME HELP...

STOP PICKING ON ME, LOUIE...

THEIR USE OF CHEDDAR, WHILE WELL MELTED, ONLY EMPHASIZED THE DRYNESS OF THE CHEESEBURGER. IT WAS SERVED WITH A FINE MUSTARD ON THE SIDE, WHICH WHEN ADDED, DID MAKE FOR A FINE MEAL.

⑦

Panel 3:

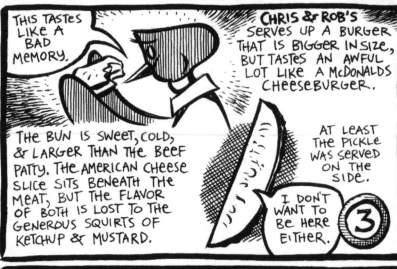

THIS TASTES LIKE A BAD MEMORY.

CHRIS & ROB'S SERVES UP A BURGER THAT IS BIGGER IN SIZE, BUT TASTES AN AWFUL LOT LIKE A McDONALDS CHEESEBURGER.

THE BUN IS SWEET, COLD, & LARGER THAN THE BEEF PATTY. THE AMERICAN CHEESE SLICE SITS BENEATH THE MEAT, BUT THE FLAVOR OF BOTH IS LOST TO THE GENEROUS SQUIRTS OF KETCHUP & MUSTARD.

AT LEAST THE PICKLE WAS SERVED ON THE SIDE.

I DON'T WANT TO BE HERE EITHER.

③

Panel 7 (right):

DAY BY DAY CAFE IS GUILTY OF OVER DRESSING THEIR CHEESEBURGER, BUT STILL HAS THE BASICS DOWN TO MAKE A GREAT ONE.

THEIR "HAMBURGER ROYALE" HAS UNSEASONED JUICY BEEF & FILLS OUT THE BUN WHICH IS SEEDLESS & TOASTED & COMES WITH ALL THE FIXINS ON TOP.

A HAMBURGER ROYALE WITH CHEESE?

THEY USE CHEDDAR CHEESE HERE, & IT WORKS ONLY BECAUSE OF THE TWO THICK SLICES OF TOMATO WHICH ADD MORE MOISTURE. WHILE THE TOMATO WAS GOOD, THE LETTUCE WAS A WASTE OF SPACE, THOUGH IT WAS NICE TO SEE SOMETHING GREEN. IT ALSO CAME WITH BACON ON TOP WHICH I ATE SEPERATELY & VORACIOUSLY...

⑦

GRAND AVE

GRAND 7 SALOON

TOM REID'S

DOWNTOWNER WOODFIRE GRILL

BURGER MOE'S

PATRICK McGOVERN'S

YES, BY THIS POINT I AM EXPERIENCING CHEESEBURGER FATIGUE.

THERE IS SOMETHING BEAUTIFUL ABOUT GRAND 7 SALOON'S CHEESEBURGERS

A THICK SLICE OF AMERICAN CHEESE IS WELL MELTED ON TOP OF A PEPPERY SEASONED BEEF PATTY.

YEAH!

THE PERFECT BEEF TO BUN SIZE & FLAVOR RATIO IS IN EFFECT. NEITHER GETS IN THE OTHER'S WAY, THEY JUST HELP EACH OTHER TO GREATNESS.

A LITTLE PEPPER GOES A LONG WAY.

NOT DRY, BUT NOT SUPER JUICY. BIG CHAR FLAVOR WITH A TOUCH OF SMOKINESS &, OF COURSE, A TOASTED SEEDLESS BUN. ALWAYS THE BEST WAY TO GO.

8.5

ARE YOU GUYS SERIOUS ABOUT THIS OR NOT?! C'MON!!

HEY MAN, YOU SHOULD LIGHTEN UP.

TOM REID'S CHEESEBURGER STRUCK ME AS ODD. THE TEXTURE OF THE MEAT WAS OFF. KINDA THICK & BREADY. IT WAS CHEESE HEAVY TOO, WITH 2 SLICES OF AMERICAN, BUT THE BUN WAS WELL TOASTED & THE BEEF WAS JUICY.

5.5

THE DOWNTOWNER TRIES TOO HARD, & THINKS IT'S MUCH FANCIER THAN IT ACTUALLY IS.

THE SEEDLESS BUN IS LIGHTLY TOASTED, THE BEEF IS A WELL DONE, HEAVY ½ POUND PATTY THAT IS PLASTERED WITH TWO PIECES OF CHEDDAR CHEESE, LETTUCE, TOMATO, ONION, & AFTER ALL OF THAT IS STILL A DRY CHEESEBURGER.

5

AT PATRICK McGOVERN'S, THE BEEF IS BIGGER THAN THE BUN, & THE BURGERS ARE VERY JUICY. HOW JUICY, YOU ASK? SOGGY BUN JUICY.

LIKE A VEGGIE BLANKET.

A THICK BEEF PATTY WITH A TOUCH OF PINK IN THE MIDDLE IS COVERED IN CHEESE, LETTUCE, TOMATO, & RED ONION ON A SEEDLESS BUN.

I WAS HOPING FOR MORE OUT OF A PLACE WITH `BURGER' IN ITS NAME... EXCEPT FOR BURGER KING, OF COURSE...

HUH?

THERE WAS NOTHING BAD OR WRONG WITH BURGER MOE'S CHEESEBURGER, BUT NOTHING THAT STOOD OUT EITHER. I GUESS SOMETIMES HAVING NO OBVIOUS FAULTS IS DOING PRETTY GOOD.

6

LIKE THE 90'S TENNIS PRO PETE SAMPRAS...FLAWLESS, BUT BORING.

IT'S A GLORIOUS, SALTY, JUICY, CHEESY, BEEFY MESS WITH TOO MANY FLAVORS GOING ON FOR ANY ONE OF THEM TO SHINE. AS THE SAYING GOES, "LESS IS MORE", I'D LIKE THIS CHEESEBURGER A LOT MORE IF THERE WAS LESS ON IT, & I ALREADY LIKE IT PLENTY.

PASS THE NAPKINS, PLEASE.

8

CHAPTER 6

THE NINE CIRCLES OF HELL'S KITCHEN: A JOURNEY TO THE HEART OF MINNESOTA'S BUSIEST BRUNCH

WRITER: CHUCK TERHARK :: **ILLUSTRATOR:** ANDY STURDEVANT

The busiest brunch in Minnesota is served in a basement in downtown Minneapolis decorated to look like a pit of despair. An odd choice for a business looking to attract a crowd, perhaps, but it has, by every measure, worked: Since Hell's Kitchen opened 11 years ago, it has grown into one of the nation's most successful restaurants*, trading on its magical mixture of mass appeal and niche allure, and drawing out-of-towners and locals alike into its dark depths with all the inevitability of a whirlpool sucking down Greek sailors.

By the time this is published, some 360,000 people will have eaten at Hell's Kitchen in 2013 alone. That's nearly 1,000 diners every day for an entire year. How does one restaurant serve so much food to so many people? Sitting in one of Hell's Kitchen's many dimly lit dining rooms, having navigated the huge space's labyrinthine red-and-black hallways, one imagines the restaurant's mercurial and foul-mouthed founder, Mitch Omer, ruling his lair from deep inside its kitchen, chewing on the heads of rival chefs while magically conjuring Benedicts and Bloody Marys for his loyal minions. (This is particularly easy to imagine if you've ever heard one of the many tall tales about Omer, easily Minneapolis's most Bunyanesque chef.[1])

If only it were as simple as magic. While it's tempting to think of your meal's life beginning when the plate appears at your table and ending as you scrape it clean, the truth is that the organizational machinery required to deliver the 1,000 dishes typically consumed during one Hell's Kitchen Sunday brunch service is as reticulated and unfaltering as a Swiss watch. From the time the plate that holds your meal travels from the dishwasher to your table, no fewer than eight different people will have touched it. And that doesn't include the host who sat you, the server who took your order, the bartender who made your drink, the band who entertained you while you waited for your food, the "brunch back" who made your coffee and filled your water, the managers who ensured everything ran smoothly, or the crack marketing team that got you through the door in the first place.

To illustrate the voyage that one plate of food takes through Hell's Kitchen, let's travel, like Virgil and Dante, through the restaurant's many operational rings. The scenario: Sunday, 11 a.m. You should be at church, but instead you've opted to indulge in some gluttony with the rest of the sinners. You've read about Hell's Kitchen in your Minneapolis guidebooks and you've decided to order their most popular brunch dish. Temptation, thy name is huevos rancheros.

Sitting in the restaurant and ordering your brunch, you've already passed through the restaurant's first three rings:

1. Management

2. Hosts

3. Servers

The Management Circle contains the owners, Omer and wife Cynthia Gerdes, their co-owners, and their team of managers. On most Sundays there are two managers on duty.

The Hosts are the first people most diners encounter in the restaurant. There are typically seven on staff, and consist of greeters, who welcome you to Hell; runners, who show you to your table; and the "Board," who manages the table assignments, keeps tabs on the servers' availabilities and workloads, fields reservations over the phone (and calmly explains to an endless stream of callers that Gordon Ramsay — the celebrity chef and host of TV's *Hell's Kitchen* — is not affiliated with the restaurant), and fields to-go orders from Bite Squad. She is the lord of Hosts, and most employees agree that she has the hardest job in the building.

The Servers place the food orders. At Hell's Kitchen brunch, they have a reputation for being sharp and efficient, if a little surly. They also wear pajamas.

You order you brunch from a waitress named Shelly wearing blue snowflake flannel. You ask for the huevos with homemade sausage, plus a side of guacamole. She takes note of your table number (703) and your seat location (1), then zips off to a nearby computer to enter your order. You lean back to enjoy the sounds of the Church of Cash, a Johnny Cash tribute band that regularly plays Sunday brunch.

Meanwhile, deep within the bowels of the restaurant, steam pours out of an industrial dishwasher as its doors open.

4. The Dish Pit

This is where someone else's meal ends and yours begins—ashes to ashes, dish pit to dish pit. Your plate is on a rack of freshly cleaned dishes, still hot and damp from the washer. The plates are stacked and carried to the kitchen by a dish pit assistant.

Meanwhile, preparations for your huevos rancheros have already begun.

5. Prep Cooks

Earlier that day, five Hell's Kitchen's prep cooks made the sausage, shredded the cheese, hashed the potatoes, mixed the guacamole, and cooked the beans that will combine to become your huevos rancheros.

They pile all these ingredients into plastic containers and move them from the prep area to the kitchen, where a printer called "The Wheel" is churning out a never-ending cascade of order tickets, one of which looks like this:

TABLE 703
SHELLY
1 – RANCHEROS
   – GUAC
   – SAUSAGE

A sous chef grabs the ticket and calls to his line cooks for a huevos rancheros with sausage and guacamole.

6. Line Cooks
7. Sous Chef

There are between three and seven line cooks working three stations: the fryer, the grill, and the sauté pan. The sauté cook cracks eggs into the pan while the fryer tosses a tortilla into the smoking oil. The grill cook tosses a handful of hashbrowns and sausage on the hot griddle. Once the tortilla is crispy, the fry cook places it on your plate and passes it to the sauté and grill cooks, who add their ingredients and shepherd it along to the sous chef. He puts it in the window and throws the order ticket in a basket, where an expeditor, or "Expo," pulls it down to the counter.

8. Expo

The Expo's job is to be the intermediary between the servers and the cooks — they're basically the U.N. of the restaurant world, only more useful. They make sure a table's orders come out at the same time, hot and ready to eat.

The Expo grabs your plate of huevos rancheros, finishes it with generous helpings of salsa, sour cream and guacamole, and passes it to a food runner.

9. Food Runners

In many restaurants, your server will deliver your food — hence the job title. At Hell's Kitchen that job falls to the food runner, the last hand to touch your plate before it reaches its final destination. He looks at the order ticket, notes the table and seat number, and drops off your huevos rancheros just as the band wraps up "Folsom Prison Blues." Shelly stops by soon after to make sure everything is as it should be and to ask if you need anything to drink. (Don't worry — she will also share your tip with that food runner.) You pick up your knife and fork and hungrily dive in.

Once you're finished, the food runner returns to bus your dishes, carrying them back to the dish pit, where a dish scraper deposits any organic material into one garbage can (which will later be delivered to a local pig farmer), any inorganic material into another. Having completed its journey, the plate passes once again through the dishwasher, ready to be reborn as the bearer of another brunch.

You, meanwhile, have paid your bill ($11.75, plus tax and tip) and prepare to ascend back into the world, happy and full, along with the thousand or so of your brunch compatriots, like Dante emerging from the darkness. And you walk out once more beneath the sun.

[1]A favorite Mitch Omer story: A 6-and-a-half foot blonde with bipolar disorder and obsessive-compulsive tendencies, Omer is always an imposing presence. But prior to a gastric bypass surgery that trimmed his weight considerably—as well as a marriage to Hell's Kitchen co-owner Cynthia Gerdes that has similarly shrunken his erraticism—Omer was pushing 400 lbs and behaving as unpredictably as ever. At one particularly dark winter, he isolated himself in northern Minnesota, where he took to running, completely naked, through the woods at night. Not coincidentally, the area saw a spike in Sasquatch sightings that year.

*Eveve, the software company that manages Hell's Kitchen's online reservations, ranks them among the top 10 independent restaurants in the country in terms of total reservations and sales.

Any Given Sunday: A typical Hell's Kitchen brunch by the numbers
Total meals served: 1,100
Diners in the restaurant at any given time: ~200
Employees on hand: ~50
Employee-to-guest ratio: 1:4[2]
Total revenues: $19,000

[2]Many restaurants carry a large staff in order to be as attentive to their diners as possible, but Hell's Kitchen's ratio is particularly low, especially considering how many people dine there. A more typical ratio would be in the neighborhood of 1:7 — which also happens to be the state-mandated daycare provider-to-toddler ratio.

CHAPTER 7

A DINER'S SURVEY OF SOUTH PARK STREET

WRITER AND ILLUSTRATOR: JOHN KOVALIC

South Park Street — Madison, Wisconsin's southern gateway — is a mostly uninspiring stretch of road, running from the Beltline northwards to the University of Wisconsin-Madison campus. It's two miles lined mainly — at first glance, anyway — with strip malls, storage installations, vacant lots, construction equipment and, eventually, modern medical facilities.

Few epic adventures appear promising, at their outset.

As any fan of fairy tales can attest, looks are often deceiving. While much of South Park Street appears culinarily inauspicious and unessential, it is home to restaurants that are as dynamic, diverse, and delicious as any in the region. It is Madison's great food adventure, less staid and more unpredictable than better-loved areas around town: Capitol Square's nouveau-Wisconsin restaurant sensibility is sophisticated but grounded; Williamson Street, dotted with delicious, eclectic East-side offerings, revels in a funkier vibe, yet still a safe one; State Street, with its shambling student chic, can be loud and enjoyable. But the thrill of discovering an incredible meal at an unexpected South Park Street gem is second to none.

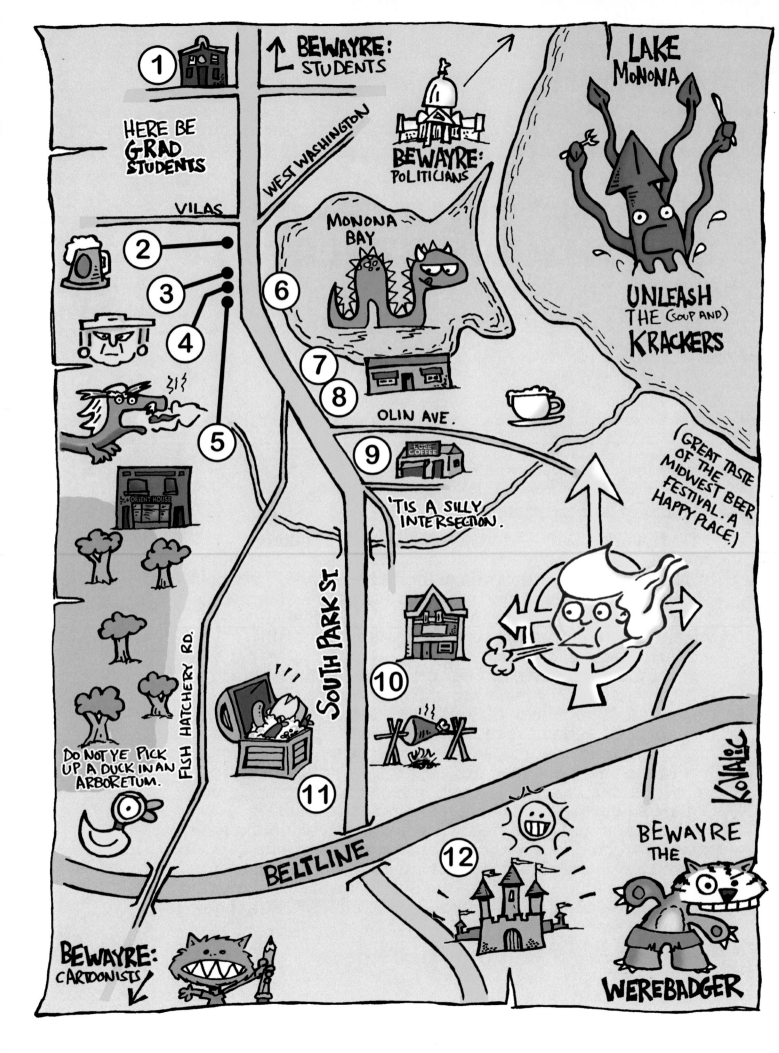

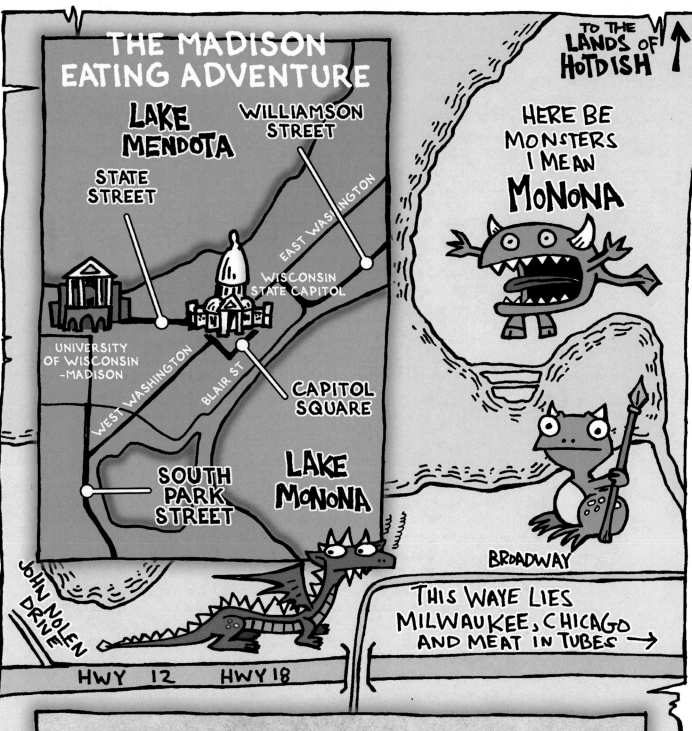

THE MADISON EATING ADVENTURE

LAKE MENDOTA

WILLIAMSON STREET

STATE STREET

EAST WASHINGTON

WISCONSIN STATE CAPITOL

UNIVERSITY OF WISCONSIN -MADISON

WEST WASHINGTON

BLAIR ST

CAPITOL SQUARE

SOUTH PARK STREET

LAKE MONONA

JOHN NOLEN DRIVE

HWY 12   HWY 18

TO THE LANDS OF HOTDISH

HERE BE MONSTERS I MEAN MONONA

BROADWAY

THIS WAYE LIES MILWAUKEE, CHICAGO AND MEAT IN TUBES →

HERE BE FLAGONS!
THE SOUTH PARK STREET AREA

1 - GREENBUSH BAR 914 REGENT ST
2 - MASON LOUNGE 416 S. PARK ST.
3 - INKA HERITAGE 602 S. PARK ST
4 - ICHIBAN 610 S. PARK ST.
5 - ORIENT HOUSE 626 S. PARK ST.
6 - THE CURVE, 653 S. PARK ST.

7 - BARRIQUES 961 S. PARK ST
8 - TAQUERIA GUADALAJARA 1033 S. PARK ST.
9 - CARGO COFFEE 1309 S. PARK ST.
10 - JB'S EAT-A-BITE BBQ 2209 S. PARK ST.
11 - YUE-WAH ORIENTAL FOODS 2328 S PARK ST
12 - MELLY MEL'S 313 W. BELTLINE

South Park Street doesn't offer up a dining "scene" so much as a patchwork of wide-ranging, generally non-Anglo eateries that may occupy the same street, but are separated both literally and figuratively by blocks or even miles. This is an area to drive down, not stroll around (again, both literally and figuratively).

As you're motoring, you'll notice that things can change quickly here. Restaurants seem to come and go faster; the food industry is unforgiving to hopefuls lacking training, financing or simply luck. It's culinary Whack-a-Mole in an area where rent can be cheap enough to tempt amateurs to ply their wares alongside the pros. New kitchens continually pop up: a Mexican bakery you never noticed before here, a Filipino buffet where a Colombian one once was there; even some guy just selling shave ice from the back of his truck on a summer's day.

The Villager Mall (2234 S. Park Street), a symbol of the south side's economic potential, is also symbolic of Park Street's culinary heterogeneity. Pop into **Yue-Wah Oriental Foods** (2328 S Park Street), and you can leave with some Armenian cheese or Portuguese sausage alongside your Indian spices, Mexican sauces and Chinese eggplant (braided Armenian string cheese is delicious, by the way). Similar finds are to be discovered in the street's several other grocery stores.

> It's culinary Whack-a-Mole in an area where rent can be cheap enough to tempt amateurs to ply their wares alongside the pros.

The cultural diversity of South Park Street echoes its past, with its roots in the district still affectionately known as "the 'Bush": the Greenbush neighborhood, Madison's Little Italy of the last century. Jewish, Irish, and German immigrants added to its integration, as did African Americans later on. The Ku Klux Klan marched through the area in 1924, to protest its ethnic mix. In the end, city planning, misguided urban "renewal" and the outward expansion of a giant land-grant university accomplished what the Klan could not: the 'Bush was bulldozed in the 1960s, its communities uprooted and scattered.

During prohibition, the Greenbush neighborhood also had a reputation for bootleg liquor and violence. This whiff of danger clings to South Park Street. It's a misguided conceit, though, reflective of realities a decade or two past. Still, it lingers, and it keeps some overly cautious types away.

Unfamiliar cuisines and "odd" ingredients, likewise, turn off others. Tongue, tripe and cartilage can strike fear into a timid culinary heart. They shouldn't. Strange and foreign words on a menu will send others into a panic. They oughtn't. But the staff at most southside restaurants will helpfully walk newbies through potential menu minefields, finding something less challenging but equally delicious, should that be the diner's preference.

There are pitfalls and traps along any road to high adventure. Not everybody's grandma's recipes keep well under buffet heat-lamps at the end of a long lunch service. Fringe food aficionados may leap at the opportunity to sample a dish a server expressly warned them away from. Deliciousness can result. But sometimes, the nasty bits can be, well, just plain nasty.

More often than not, however, eating outside of your comfort zone, discovering a taste that's genuinely new to you, is simply one of life's true joys. A great meal on South Park Street can be comforting and familiar or — to many Midwesterners, anyway — mysterious and exotic. Either way, you'll leave filled and happy.

GREENBUSH BAR | *914 Regent Street | 608.257.2874 | greenbushbar.net*
The Greenbush Bar — about a hundred feet off of South Park Street, located in the
basement of the Italian Workmen's Club — is firmly planted in the area's historic past. But
the food here is forward-thinking: the Greenbush takes sustainability seriously, and the
commitment to quality ingredients makes it irresistible. Some consider its pizza to be the
best in town, a stand that's hard to dispute, if your preference is for thin crusts that get the
mix of crispy and chewy just right. The hot Italian sandwich is delicious, should your tastes
tend toward the assertive flavors of Pecatonica Valley Farm coppa ham, banana peppers,
marinated tomatoes, and provolone. The low-ceilinged, noisy, holiday-light-strewn bar is
constantly packed and service can be dodgy, but a great selection of Scotches and
bourbons make the wait for a table happier. A decent range of tap beers is supplemented
by a smart selection of bottled ones and hey, with both pizza and beer that's second to
none, perhaps that is amore.

MASON LOUNGE | *416 S. Park Street | 608.255.7777*
From time to time, the subject of Park Street gentrification pops up in conversation.
Possibly the sleek, young Mason Lounge spurs it on. The Mason sits in the space
once occupied by the decidedly seedier Bennett's on Park (a bar best known for "Smut n'
Eggs" — pornos screened during breakfast) and the troubled Azzalino's Bar and Grill.
Replacing them, the Mason is chill and relaxing, its coziness belying the proto-hipster guilt
you may get staring at the taxidermied chicken behind the bar. The craft beer selection is
terrific, easily the best on Park Street, and the rival of many in Madison. There's no set
closing hour ("12-ish" most days), no website, and no cocktail list, but the bartenders
mix a mean Old Fashioned. If you're peckish, you can always order a pizza from Falbo
Brothers, two doors down: they'll deliver it right to your seat at the bar. So sit back,
enjoy a great Midwestern brew out of — yes — a mason jar, and take your mind off of
gentrification for a while.

INKA HERITAGE | *602 S. Park Street | 608.310.4282 | inkaheritagerestaurant.com*
That a city of Madison's size would have a Peruvian restaurant was once a big deal.
These days, it has three, along with other South- and Central-American joints. Inka Heritage
hit the figurative beach early in this little wave of Latin restaurants, and was proclaimed
by the *New York Times* as "one of the brighter spots" in Madison's culinary scene a
couple of years ago. Despite Inka Heritage's almost legendarily slow service, there's still
plenty to love about it, especially if cilantro is your bag: the arroz con pollo is served
with an unfeasible amount of tasty cilantro rice, and the aguadito de pollo is rightfully
described as a "revitalizing cilantro soup." (Bonus to midday patrons: a cup of aguadito
de pollo is on the house with any item on the lunch menu). The ceviche is a must, as
is a pisco sour, a now nationally trendy cocktail so delightful both Peru and Chile claim
it as their own.

ICHIBAN | *610 S. Park Street* | *608.819.8808* | *ichibanmadison.com*
Ichiban Sichuan is a cavernous restaurant behind an unassuming storefront in a building that once housed an autobody repair business (repurposed car shops are a Park Street leitmotif — the area was known as "Gasoline Alley" in the 1940s). It's a large space that can seem empty during off-hours, or when university is out of session. Take advantage of these times: Ichiban is the real deal, with outstanding Szechuan and Hunan dishes, and the restaurant can be busy. The fragrant, numbing heat of the Szechuan peppercorn can be unsparingly employed, but the waitstaff will guide you to milder dishes, should setting your mouth ablaze in an inferno of pure peppery pleasure somehow not be your thing. For every dish of ox tongue and tripe with chili sauce that captivates those of us with a thirst for delicious, spicy danger, there's an equally worthwhile plate of savory dandan noodles (a steal at $4.95) to keep those with subtler palates enthralled. The hot pot, bubbling and spicy, is ridiculously life-affirming, and can be ordered spicy or mild. Ichiban can blow your mind or your taste buds, if you're not careful. HINT: it's OK not to be careful.

ORIENT HOUSE | *626 S. Park Street* | *608.250.8880* | *orienthouseonline.com*
For years, the Orient House employed two menus — one of blander, Americanized dishes, the other of more authentic Cantonese and Mandarin fare. These days, the menus are combined into one. Possibly the staff simply got tired of Madison foodies bugging them about the "secret" menu. In any case, the native offerings are both the far more interesting and far more successful of the two. The hot and spicy shredded beef is terrific, with full, balanced flavors. It is savory but not scorching, a pile of tender, aromatic strips of beef. Ho Fun — thick, flat rice noodles — are a house specialty, and arrive with just a touch of char from the frying. Spicy string beans are fresh, sweet and delicious, with plenty of snap, due to a deft touch on the part of the cooks. Vegetarians will want these served without the ground pork: anyone else would be foolish to forgo the salty, meaty addition. To top it all off, your wallet will love you: a recent feast for seven topped out at just $20 per person, drinks and tip included.

THE CURVE | *653 S. Park Street* | *608.251.0311*
The Curve is a Madison institution, a quintessential, unapologetic greasy spoon best known for its lack of frills and hefty portions. Lunch is served, but it's the breakfasts that keep us coming back. The bacon is hearty and the American fries buttery. Order the corned beef hash on the weekends, when it's homemade (other days, sadly, it comes out of a can). The pancakes are substantial things, with just the right amount of chew to them. One should be enough for most appetites, but why stop there? Almost too conveniently, there are heart specialists located in the hospitals nearby.

BARRIQUES | *961 S. Park Street | 608.819.6787 | barriquesmarket.com*
The ideal coffee shop experience, one imagines, includes laconically watching the world pass by, while coddling a good cup of dark roast. Possibly you're contemplating your first novel. The sixth Madison location of Barriques is a fine cafe... it's just not a place to stare, daydreaming, out of the windows. The intersection of South Park Street and Fish Hatchery Road makes for a pretty miserable vista. Fortunately, the interior of this pleasant spot is well designed, employing a kind of rustic-cum-industrial aesthetic that actually works. The coffee is well-brewed, the sandwiches smartly thought-out and solidly executed, and the cookies sinful. Topping it all off, the soups are terrific — try the Cream of Carrot, if it's on the menu. Beer and wine are served throughout day. And like all Barriques locations, the "Wall of 100" — a hundred recommended bottles of wine, each costing $10 or less — gives patrons something to stare at other than the vacant lots or muffler shops across the street. Pick up a couple of bottles on your way out, and get going on that novel.

TAQUERIA GUADALAJARA | *1033 S. Park Street | 608.250.1824 | lataqueriaguadalajara.com*
In February, 2013, a kitchen fire caused nearly a quarter of a million dollars in damages to the Taqueria Guadalajara, closing it. When it reopened six months later, you could almost hear the collective unclenching of Madison foodies. Gone is the gaudy pink exterior from before — in its place is a classy brick frontage that's far more inviting. The interior is brighter and larger, giving off a fresher and more welcoming air. But the important bit — the critically important bit — is, the food is the same as always. Which means it's the best Mexican food for miles around. I mean, lots of miles. Like, we're talking Interstate miles, here. Patrons rave about the $2 tacos for good reason. Even if carne asada is your safety zone, at two bucks you can afford to give the tongue or the tripe a try! The Platillo Guadalajara (grilled skirt steak, cactus, onion, jalapeno and refried beans) costs $10, but if you're leaning in that direction, grab some friends and go for the the Parrillada — a massive mound of grilled meats (steak, ribs, chicken and chorizo), with onions, cactus, jalapenos, rice and beans — it serves four for a ridiculously reasonable $32.

CARGO COFFEE | *1309 S. Park Street | 608.268.0597 | facebook.com/pages/Cargo-Coffee/ 126726134024035*
If South Park Street is anything, it's a series of brilliant, bizarre moments that can be snatched from unexpected places. Take Cargo Coffee, a charming, sunny cafe created from the shell of a Jiffy-Lube station. The sight is odd, to say the least, but inside, there are good beans and great service. The sandwiches and wraps are honest and tasty, and the WiFi's as strong as the coffee. When the weather's pleasant, sit in the old service bay area: the giant garage door is opened, and a cool breeze can trip through the service-station-cum-cafe. As the traffic streams by in front of you, you'll never mistake this for a Champs-Élysées moment. Yet in its own way, it's really kinda cool, and we'll take it.

JB'S EAT-A-BITE BBQ | *2209 S. Park Street | 608.251.2209 | jbseatabite.com*

Proprietor James Brown wants you to try the okra. No. He really wants you to try the okra, so he brings over a sample, even though you're really not an okra fan at all, because it's slimy and stringy and greasy and... hey... hey... hey... this stuff is delicious! What'd you do to it? Pan fry it? Wow! And he asks your daughter if she'd like to sample the gator — flown in from Louisiana — as you're waiting for your order to come up. JB's Eat-A-Bite BBQ does mostly a take-out business, but there are a few tables to be grabbed, and we'd recommend that, for the samples and conversations alone. The menu is varied, ranging from satisfying Chicago Italian beef and Polish sausage sandwiches to ace rib tips, catfish (filets or steaks, for those who prefer bone-in), red beans and rice and jambalaya (family recipes abound). Fans of chicken livers, gizzards and giblets won't be disappointed. Dip them in Brown's homemade hot sauce, which is fiery, vinegary and one of the best in town.

MELLY MEL'S | *313 W. Beltline Highway | 608.270.9512*

If the Greenbush Bar is an excellent starting point for any expedition down the magnificent, flawed, rambling, self-contradictory but frequently outstanding South Park Street dining corridor, then Melly Mel's, the beloved Madison soul food restaurant, is the quest's perfect conclusion. The small restaurant and catering business is only a quarter mile from South Park Street, as the crow flies...but that's a couple of miles away, as the Subaru Forrester weaves around dreary Beltline frontage roads. Finding it is an adventure in itself. Look for an unremarkable doorway on the side of a soulless commercial building. Descend a depressing flight of stairs and step quickly through the drab hallway. Once inside, you won't want to leave. The fried chicken, cooked to order (this will take time — you're warned) is impossibly moist. The catfish fillets and nuggets are succulent and steamy. The homemade desserts will vary, but the peach cobbler is a perennial favorite. Best of all, you're sure to be treated to a smile or — if you're lucky — a story from owner Carmell Jackson, to whom everybody coming through her doors is family. Family is important here. Though the restaurant's rave reviews are up on the walls for all to see, pride of place goes to many, many photos of family and friends. There's great food down those bleak stairs, to be sure, but also there's joy, laughter, passion and community. You can't possibly leave Melly Mel's without feeling better about the human race, let alone chicken and waffles.

CHAPTER 8
EAST LAKE STREET

WRITER: SUSAN PAGANI :: **ARTIST:** ANDY DUCETT

"We all have hometown appetites. Every other person is a bundle of longing for the simplicities of good taste once enjoyed on the farm or in the hometown left behind."
— **Clementine Paddleford**

There are only a few, flat miles of city street between the Marshall Avenue Bridge and Interstate 35W. To the casual observer passing through, this stretch of East Lake Street may seem like an unexceptional collection of small businesses. Yet those of us who live and work here know it to be full of gems — hardworking local shops that keep the surrounding neighborhoods vibrant, livable, and well stocked with car parts, furniture, art supplies, printing materials, tools, groceries, gas — and, yes, great meals. In fact, contained in this short distance is the cuisine of no less than 12 countries and four continents.

When we mention that fact, people will always ask, "Where can I get the most authentic such and such dish?" To which we reply, "Who are we to say?"

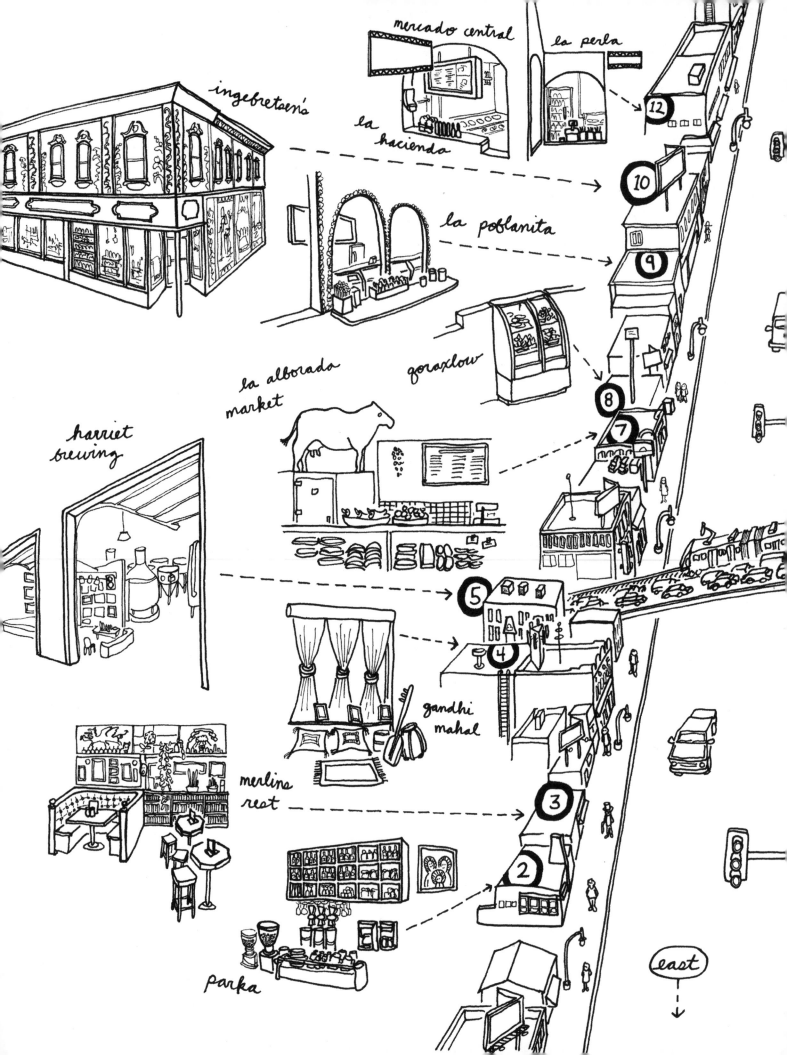

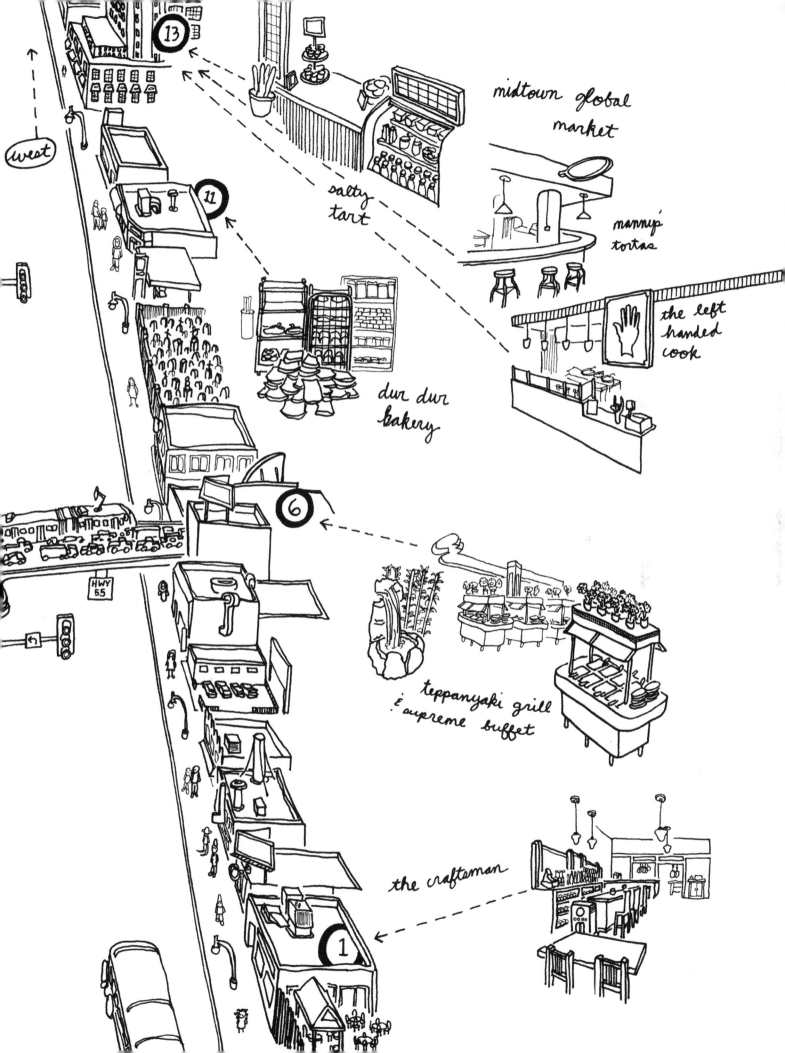

In talking to chefs, bakers, and producers, it seems as though recipe creation is all about food memories. There may be the classic interpretation, but when it comes to flavor and texture, chefs are forever trying to recreate the full, sensual experience of their best meals. Manny Gonzalez of Manny's Tortas once told us that he had vivid memories of going out to the movies with his father as a kid in Mexico City. More often than not, they punctuated their dates with a sandwich. Manny based his famous tortas on those meals, and people who have lived or traveled in Mexico City may recognize them as authentic — others may not.

For the diner, a meal can be like coming home or it can be a brief adventure. The awesome thing about living on the East Lake Street corridor is that we have the best of both.

THE CRAFTSMAN RESTAURANT | *New American*

What to expect:

The dining room at the Craftsman is likely the most elegant spot on East Lake. Here you'll find the eponymous tables and high-backed chairs arranged around shelves of glimmering mason jars packed with housemade pickles and booze-y fruits. This spare yet comfortable aesthetic suits the menu, which features all that is good about recent trends with an emphasis on regional game meats, charcuterie, lake fish, and seasonal vegetables. The food is rich, no doubt, but it is also seasoned simply to let the flavors of the ingredients shine, which gives every dish a certain pleasing freshness.

The drink menu deserves a note, too. Seasonal offerings feature the aforementioned infused fruits and house-made bitters and liqueurs layered in classic and original cocktails that run the gamut from dry to sparkling to sweetly dangerous.

What to eat:

At brunch, we like poached eggs with a side of thick-cut bacon and creamy, creamy grits and a Bloody Mary. If you favor sweets in the morning, try the brioche French toast, which is custardy on the inside without being soggy, and light enough that it won't kill the rest of your day — unless you combine it with the Summer Thyme, a refreshing, herby citrus vodka concoction that goes down like juice but packs a punch.

Now, about dinner: the Craftsman's charcuterie absolutely sings, so meat eaters should start the cocktail hour or meal with a plate, sampling such delights as rabbit rillettes, duck prosciutto, pickled ramp, and lardo on toast. For entrees, we think the pork chop is the best in town — tender, succulent meat served with a satisfying side of mashed potatoes and greens — and it's a staple of the menu. That said, if it's being offered as the special, we'll always take the lake herring, a delicate but meaty fish prepared with only a modicum of fuss to preserve its clean flavor and earthy sweetness. Vegetarians might want to start with the hummus plate — which features house-made crackers and a nice selection of pickles — and then move on to any of the housemade noodles.

What to pack:

Bring along a light throw or jacket: the Craftsman has a pleasant patio with very pretty, vine covered pergolas that keep the sun out of your eyes during the cocktail hours, but also make it a wee bit cool on spring and fall evenings.

4300 E. Lake Street | 612-722-0175 | craftsmanrestaurant.com

PARKA | *New American*

What to expect

You may find yourself wandering through a haven of mid-century lamps, low-slung couches and laminated nut dishes and into white space. You may find yourself seated at a glowing neon bar. You may find yourself ordering pot roast off a limited yet abundant hot pink menu. And you may find yourself presented with ribbons of sweet gel and savory foam under a great chalk drawing of an Eskimo family. And you may tell yourself: This is not my beautiful dinner. Oh, but it is.

At Parka molecular gastronomy is used wondrously, separating out the basic tastes of a dish and then bringing them back together in a way that is surprisingly harmonious. Mild wasabi foam, carrots candied like sweet tarts and potpourri, and a cube of succulent beef can actually equal pot roast. Same as it ever was.

What to order

Parka is a partnership between Rustica Bakery, Dogwood Coffee, and Victory 44 restaurant. If you are looking for a beautiful pastry, a loaf of bread, or a sublime cup of coffee, you'll find them here.

Despite its otherworldly presentation, the menu is a fair representation of Minnesota's farms, fields and streams — with fish, rabbit, cow, pig, chicken, and plenty of seasonal veggies — and its cooking. For starters, we have enjoyed a luscious smoked white fish, playfully delivered in a pop-top tin can and served on twists of housemade cracker so thin we could see through them. We liked that crunch in the mix with the dish's pickle-y condiments, sweet yuzu gel, spicy jalapeño foam, and briny roe. For entrees, we recall an elegant cube of beer-can chicken nested in a bed of popcorn-flavored polenta, fresh greens and sweet piquillo, and surrounded by speckles of hot sauce gel. Oh yes, and little chicharron, a delightfully crunchy companion to the incomparably moist chicken. At dessert, there was a banana cream pie, deconstructed but with all the flavors present and accounted for: Imagine the rich creaminess of chevre mousse amongst tangy-sweet gelatinous cranberry, offset by the gentle vegetal flavor of celery and the crunch of apples and pecan. And then wafers of chevre meringue, hard and flat like little river stones.

What to pack:

Bring your allowance because Forage Modern Workshop, the store next door, is filled with beautiful bespoke furniture and gently used retro items you will immediately recognize — this is your beautiful home.

4021 E. Lake Street | 612.886.1585 | Parkampls.com

MERLINS REST | *English Pub*

What to expect:

Here is everything you might hope for in a pub with the name Merlin attached to it. The walls are lined with county shields from England, Ireland and Scotland, hunkering gargoyles, and commodious booths — which face out, so you can watch locals of every age wander in, grab their beer steins from over the bar, and enjoy their neighbors of an evening.

In an age when local is king, Merlins Rest offers the best of the British Isles import taps, single malt Scotch, and Irish whiskeys. The pub is often host to musicians, but the sound is kept to a dull roar, making it one of the few spots in town where you can hear yourself and the merry chatter of the locals as they enjoy a wee tipple or a pint or two. Best of all, there is no television!

What to eat and drink:

In addition to the above, the pub offers a few specialty drinks. We find the Merlins Ginger, a ginger-infused Jameson's whiskey layered with ginger ale and bitters infinitely quaffable — well balanced with a ginger kick and a nice herbal twist from the Angostura.

The menu is pure English pub food. With beer, we like the Scotch egg: a hearty meatball encasing a hardboiled egg, and then fried and dunked in wasabi. Huzzah! The pies are surprisingly light, with tender pastry and a fair amount of gravy, which is lovely over the side of mashed potatoes. A standout is the speyside, which combines herbed white beans and mushrooms in a rich béchamel. That said, we will always order the fish and chips — the fish light, flaky and tender, the fries crisp on the outside, light and potato-y on the inside.

What to Pack

Bring your encyclopedic knowledge of everything: Merlins Rest hosts highly competitive yet very convivial trivia nights. Mind like a sieve? Bring your wool and needles, there's also a knitters night.

3601 E. Lake Street | 612.216.2419 | merlinsrest.com

GANDHI MAHAL | *North Indian*
What to expect

The dining room of Gandhi Mahal is so warm and aromatic it is as if you have climbed into the tandoor. Great loops of pink and green silk hang from the gold tin ceiling, skimming richly painted orange and yellow walls festooned with mirrored elephants, whose trunks are frozen in time yet seem to sway.

If you are there on a weekend evening, there may be a sitar player and a drummer tucked into the restaurant's front window. Their repertory of ragas is so peaceful, so energizing, so perfectly expressive of the depth and richness of the Mughal-style sauces and the fiery complexity of the chutneys — you may feel more than content to settle into your basket of warm, housemade naan and stay awhile.

What to eat

At lunch, there is a buffet we like very much. There you'll find fragrant rice pilaf — peas, onion, and a light yogurt — over which you can layer channa chat masala, a miraculously tender chickpea curry that will set your nose running. We are also fond of the crisp potato pancakes, which are sweet and soft on the inside, and the ideal vehicle for the spicy cilantro chutney.

In the evening, the menu is bespoke, and you may specify the protein — fish, fowl, hoof, or soybean — and spice index of any sauce. The Bombay korahi featured chunks of tender goat tossed with green peppers and onions in a luxurious red curry, faintly sweet and redolent with ginger and chilies. Also intoxicating, the moghal saagwalla, a dish in which relatively simple ingredients, spinach and mint, are combined with spices to create a light, rich sauce with a gorgeous texture. Buy a basket of garlic naan so you can mop up every last bit of it.

What to Pack

Be forewarned: The gifted saucier at Gandhi Mahal will not condescend to your Minnesota palate. Hot is hot. Bring your arthritis, fever, common cold, vertigo, and congestion; all will be healed by the mighty capsicum pepper.

3009 27th Avenue S. | 612.729.5222 | gandhimahal.com

HARRIET BREWING | *Microbrewery*
What to expect

From the outside, Harriet Brewing looks like nondescript warehouse, but roll up the loading dock door, and inside you'll find a mash-up of man cave, psychedelic art fair, and tasting room.

Although the brewery has earned a reputation for its beer, people also just like to hang out there — not like you do at a bar, like you do at a friend's house. It's a very sweet, community kind of place. Resident artist Jesse Brödd has filled the space with same sort of art he created for the Harriet labels: vibrant, colorful pieces that seem to swirl in space.

Most evenings, there's a woman making glass beads in the corner and a band playing some bluesy, funk, jazz folk. And sometimes, there's just a bunch of people hanging out on the couch, listening to vinyl records, and sharing a pint. It's all good.

What to eat

In the summer, various and sundry food trucks park in the lot next to the warehouse, and dish out everything from pulled-pork tacos to spiced donuts. Otherwise, there are no bar snacks.

For beer, we once fell hard for the seasonal Sol Bock, a beer as sweet and bright as the sun itself, with plenty of malt. Of the regular offerings, we like the West Side for its citrus and cinnamon notes. Much like the heavier herbal ice teas, it's tasty but refreshing. On the flip side, we go for the Elevator Doppelbock, which comes off bitter at first, but then melts into cocoa, toast, and bananas — it's like dessert.

What to pack

In winter, bring an admirably long beard or an awesome knit cap. You'll fit in like a native and you'll be warm — not a lot of heat at the warehouse. In summer, take it all off and bring an umbrella; by 4 p.m., the sun hits that loading dock door like a laser beam.

3036 Minnehaha Avenue | 612.315.4633 | harrietbrewing.com

TEPPANYAKI GRILL & SUPREME BUFFET | *Asian Buffet*

What to expect

Suspend your disbelief or this will never work out. You must believe that there is a grotto paradise where triceratops, black adders, and miniature monkeys live in peace, cavorting among waterfalls and miniature Dutch windmills. They eat plentifully from an arbor of green grapes and crimson chili peppers, and do not think to explore beyond their own bamboo forest.

But you will venture out of the restaurant's waiting area and beyond the grotto because you are not afraid to face the Supreme Buffet. You know that General Tso's chicken, wakame salad, and kielbasa can also live in timeless harmony. You trust that in nearly 100 feet of warming tray, there is something you want to eat. It may have traveled a million frozen miles to get here, but you are determined to find it fresh, steaming hot, and delicious. And despite all of the humanity — the hundreds of tiny, snotty fingered kids –who have peered into it, sampled it, and slopped it onto their plates, you know it will be safe to eat. You will inhale ten dollar's worth of it, and you will feel content.

What to eat

Eat whatever calls to you. In keeping with a buffet that defies all order and logic, our list is rather random. A cold cucumber salad dressed with Szechuan peppers was fresh, bright, and lip-burning hot. It was lovely with a donut hole rolled in sugar. The sushi rolls were all palatable, and a five-spice teriyaki chicken kabob was moist and tasty. The prime rib and mashed potatoes recalled TV dinners we have thoroughly enjoyed.

Our advice: Though their glowing red sauces beckon from across the dim dining room, do not eat the crawfish or the glazed bananas. If you must eat seafood, focus instead on the 14 (14!) shrimp dishes.

For dessert, there is ice cream. Although they are next to the sprinkles, don't be fooled into putting a crouton on your mint chocolate chip — the garlic undermines anything you gain in crunch. Do try the mocha torte: it is deeply satisfying to slip your fork through the layers of cake and cream, and the whole is melt-in-your-mouth, box-cake delicious.

What to pack

Bring a helmet, kneepads, and your motion sickness bracelet — the parking lot is completely gonzo, and you will be lucky to find and exit your space without incident.

2216 E. Lake Street | 612.728.3838

LA ALBORADA MARKET | *Mexican*
What to expect

At midday, La Alborada is bustling. Staff is already restocking displays — glass bottles of Coke, cactus paddles, piles of bananas, and bolillo rolls — and there's a line out the door for antojitos Mexicanos (Mexican street food). If you ask the owner, Orlando Cruz, he'll tell you that the folks here are coming for more than their groceries, they are coming for tradition, to get a little bit of home. Accordingly, along with the fresh produce and baked goods, he stocks a fair amount of imported goods, candy, spices, horchata, and the like.

The market has an Old World ambience: Murals depict women in rustic kitchens, embroidered blouses slipping from their shoulders as they roll tortillas, and arched transitions, wooden display boxes and wagon wheels suggest an outdoor market. In the tiny Antojitos Mexicanos, you'll find just a few tables, but look up — above the door is a full-size buggy hitched to a fiberglass cow.

What to eat

There are plenty of good sweets in the panaderia, but we're here to talk about Antojitos Mexicanos and snacks. The barbacoa taco offers a sweet, mildly hot, very tender shredded beef. Add a dollop of green salsa and a few slices of radish, and it's possible to polish off three in a matter of seconds. The carne asada taco delivers a rich texture and char flavors, just right with a heap of bright, sweet cilantro and grilled onions.

Of the classic corn-husked tamales, we like the jalapeño-cheese, filled with a deceptively hot, smoky red salsa, slices of pepper — and, surprise, a squeaky chunk of curd-like añejo cheese. The pork oaxaquenos tamale is heaven in a banana leaf, featuring a mildly spicy, pulled pork and unbelievably creamy white polenta. It goes down like a savory pudding, the ultimate comfort food.

What to pack

Bring your Spanish speaking skills, as there are few English speakers working at the market. Otherwise, bring your patience. The folks at La Alborada are warm and helpful; you will get your snacks.

1855 E. Lake Street | 888.311.1671

LA POBLANITA | *Mexican*
What to expect

The quintessential hole-in-the-wall, La Poblanita will never draw you in with its ambience. The charm of its wall mural — where a fellow gazes out from beneath his hat, ever hopeful of the pretty lass sitting on his flower-laden raft — is overwhelmed by the proximity of the galley kitchen. Fluorescent lights illuminate a laminated menu of plated botanas Mexicanas and a radio announcer's lightning fast trill introduces a blast of musica, musica, musica.

But close your eyes: in the steam wafting out of the kitchen is corn, toasty and sweet. Here the chefs make each tortilla to order. Cooked on the grill, they are thick, imperfect circles that add a tender, less chewy texture and a robust flavor to everything. Who needs white tablecloths and moody lighting? Let's eat.

What to eat:

Every taco has its pleasures, but here we especially like the chorizo, which has a wonderful heat, smoky paprika and cumin flavors, and a rich, unctuous texture — yet is not as oily and salty as is typical of the sausage.

We'd like to live in a papusa. Essentially a handmade tortilla pouch filled with refried beans and mozzarella cheese, it is deeply satisfying with a generous heap of salsa (we like to mix the mild tomatillo with the smoky, mouth-searing red stuff). It comes with a warm coleslaw of carrots and cabbage, which adds a piquant note to the meal and cuts some of the papusa's fried goodness.

What to pack:

Bring your most woeful day. Fresh corn tortillas are comfort food extraordinaire, a wonderful if fleeting cure for heartbreak and enmity.

1617 E. Lake Street | 612.253.8898 | lapoblanitamn.com

INGEBRETSEN'S | *Scandinavian Deli*
What to expect

Surely, Ingebretsen's is the most cheerful sight on East Lake Street. With its pale blue and yellow facade, it resembles a giant Scandinavian hope chest decorated with folksy rosemaling flowers and scrolling hindeloopen — it's so inviting, you want to take a peek.

Inside, it's cozier than a Danish pancake. Here is everything you love about Scandinavian homes, from the understated Danish candlesticks to wonderfully complex, brilliantly colorful textiles. Looking for a critter? Here are round-nosed and admirably bearded Swedish nisser and Finnish Moomintrolls — plus some really fabulous felted cats. Viking helmet? Yes. Whittling kit? Yes. Stieg Larsson? You betcha.

There's something for everyone: How better to express your Scandihoovian dog's snowbound lament than a "Woof Da!" water bowl?

What to eat:

Ingrebretsen's deli is piled high with canned fish balls, boxes of Korni flat bread, and blankets of lefse. In the refrigerator, you'll find a fine assortment of prepared foods, such as baked beans, Swedish meatballs and pickled herring. We like the fruit soup, a stew of prunes, peaches, apricots, and raisins that tastes like pie filling and gives our oatmeal and yogurt a renewed sense of life.

The fellows behind the meat counter are rather famous, having dedicated almost a hundred combined years to butchering, smoking, and curing meats. While many will avow their hams are the best in town, we favor the Danish wieners. Twenty-five percent pork, 75 percent beef, they are linked in long strands and produce a deeply satisfying snap when you bite into them. Also commendable: The lamb loaf, which bakes up juicy, with a nice caramelized mustard crust across the top. It has a savory, sausage-like flavor that holds its own at dinner but is especially good in sandwiches the next day.

What to pack:

Bring a snack: There's no dining in at Ingebretsen's, and to shop there on an empty stomach would be a mistake. If you do arrive hungry, bring a commodious bag.

1601 E. Lake Street | 612.729.9333 | ingebretsens.com

QORAXLOW | *Somali*
What to expect

Were it not for the friendly fellows behind the counter and a pastry case filled with sambusa, one might think the dimly lit restaurant had long been closed. Its booths and tables hold nary a napkin, table tent or condiment, and the walls are simply adorned with a shadow box papered in tropical fish.

Don't let this spare aesthetic or the lack of menus turn you away. Approach the counter and one of the staff will ask you to choose a protein: goat, chicken, or beef. He'll tell you that it comes over rice and is served with soup, a fresh banana, and your choice of drink, sodas, or mango juice.

You may not be offered sambusa — delectable, fried triangles of ground meat and chili peppers — so speak up if you want some. And then find a table: you're in for a treat.

What to eat:

We were served a very simple beef stew. It had a spicy kick, but was otherwise reminiscent of the stuff we grew up with here in Minnesota. It came with a wedge of lime, which helped to cut the salty richness of the broth — as did the giant pitcher of mango juice that arrived with our meal.

The meats came on large platters, heaped with well-nigh addictive rice that was turmeric yellow and wonderfully aromatic with cumin, cardamom, and sage. Slivers of dried apricot and whole peas added texture and sweetness. The waiter announced with a sly smile that the chicken was better than chicken because it was chicken steak — and so it was! Beautifully charred, it was millimeters thick and yet still juicy and flavorful. We also enjoyed chunks of bone-in goat. Basted in a spicy, coriander-tomato sauce, it was fork-tender and delicious.

The banana was a surprisingly nice addition to these savory delights, providing another starch, slightly sweet and perfectly ripened.

What to pack:

An open mind. No menus means no prices; however, our generous meal for two came to a very reasonable $20. If you are female, Somali or otherwise, you may be asked to eat in a separate space. Non-Somali couples may also be sequestered. And it is quite possible that if you dine at dusk, one or two Muslims might roll out mats and perform the evening prayer. Feel free to set your fork down — the prayer ends in mere moments, and your food will still be warm.

1201 E. Lake Street | 612.822.4480 | qoraxlow.com

DUR DUR BAKERY & MARKET | *East African*

What to expect

The aisles of Dur Dur market feel something like an East African Costco, stripped down and utilitarian — and filled with the staples of home cooking that are useful to have in bulk.

Explore rows and rows of safflower oil, ghee, mango pulp, French lentils, East African spices and milk powder in family size containers. There is honey, so much honey, for your tea and your health — restore mirth, increase hemoglobin, prevent osteoporosis! At the back of the store is a butcher, offering a variety of halal meat; though, perhaps not for consumers because the display case is empty and there is no signage.

You might like to take home a burlap sack of basmati rice, imprinted with lions or flowers. They have handles and zippers and are the perfect size for carrying a pocket novel and sandwich to the park. Etsy will be mad with envy.

What to eat:

Every day, various and sundry East African bakers deliver fresh bread and pastry to Dur Dur. We tasted the influence of Italian East Africa, a briefly existing colony that included Ethiopia and Somali in the late 1930s, in some of the pastries. Tender, crumbly shushumow cookies are deep fried and coated in sugar syrup. They taste like fried Italian shortbread and go down easy with a cup of coffee. We also enjoyed korsanyo, a super soft egg bread that is folded like a croissant and filled with vanilla pudding.

Dur Dur also sells locally made hombasha — a slightly sweet Ethiopian flat bread, which is lovely at breakfast — and injera, a gluten-free, sourdough bread that resembles a porous crepe and is delicious wrapped around salads and saucy stews.

What to pack

A notepad: If you are looking for a specific spice or ingredient and don't speak Somali or Amharic, it can be enormously helpful to write down what you need.

1552 E. Lake Street | 612.721.9449

MERCADO CENTRAL | *Mexican*

What to expect

Created as a place for Latino entrepreneurs to make their start — such as the popular Manny's Tortas — Mercado Central has transformed what was once a row of dilapidated buildings into three floors of successful businesses, including folk art, fashion, candy, and some of the city's best Mexican food.

Along the way, the Mercado has become a cultural center for the community. Most weekends, it is packed with milling shoppers. Around meal times, folks line up to buy tacos, tortas, tamales and other assorted goodies, winding through the tables and into the corridors. In the dining room, every wall is painted a different color. On a sunny day, it fills with light, and there's a celebratory din about the place as families visit and sit down to a meal together.

What to eat:

We like to start with a bowl of pozole from La Perla. Here, the hominy is submerged in a sublime chicken soup, which much like pho can be doctored up with sides of fresh onion, jalapeños, lime, radish and cilantro. While you are there, buy some corn and flour tortillas to take home (if they are warm, eat a few before sticking them in the refrigerator).

Next, we'll wander over to La Hacienda for alambre carnitas, which is a plate of mini corn tortillas smothered with a concoction of smoky pulled pork and bacon, sautéed onions and green peppers, and cheese. It is glorious, but huge; one serving will feed two people.

What to pack:

Bring some of that green, folding money as many of the vendors do not accept plastic or checks.

1515 East Lake Street | 612.728.5401

MIDTOWN GLOBAL MARKET | *Variety*

What to expect

Walking through Midtown Global Market, it's possible to get very turned around. Even a person with a reasonable sense of direction can spend a fair amount of time looking for a booth they visited once before and end up never finding it.

You could ask someone, but where's the fun in that? Wander a bit, and you will stumble upon all kinds of good eats, tucked in amongst the perfumeries and mirrored pashminas.

An egg the color of latte, plucked from the nest of a happy Minnesota chicken. Beef tongue lovingly marinated in peppers and then tucked into a corn tortilla. A beady-eyed lobster, madly waving his red limbs and rubber bands. Here a plate of fried sambusa; there a cardamom-laden krumkake cone.

You may get lost, but you won't go hungry.

What to eat:

Such is the wealth of good food that you must develop your own progressive approach. From Manny's Tortas, we fancy the special: a French roll spread with chipotle mayo and refried beans, and then layered with ham, steak, cheese, chili peppers and grilled veggies. It sounds unwieldy, but it's actually remarkably balanced.

At the Left Handed Cook, we love the orange-y overtones of the Brussel sprouts, which are braised with garlic and bacon. The poutine looks a mess, but is in fact amazing. In a small, checkered to-go boat, curried gravy, poached egg, and cheese are combined to create a pungent, creamy sauce that, when combined with crispy pork and French fries, is as delicious as it is weird.

For dessert, we go to the Salty Tart. If we are stuffed, a wee coconut macaroon — toasty, chewy, dense, and tender — is just right. If we have space, the bakery's chocolate brownie is best in class, with a crisp crust that gives way to a moist, cocoa interior. And of course, the cream-filled brioche is a magic trick: a slightly salty, very light bread, filled with custard cream and coated in sugar.

What to pack:

Bring your kids! In the center of the market is a stage that, at any given time, may be occupied by highly entertaining bands, mimes, or poets. And a bib for yourself: the juices from the Torta at Manny's are guaranteed to roll down your chin and wrists.

Midtown Global Market | 2929 Chicago Avenue S. | midtownglobalmarket.org

It may happen to any of us ... you're cavorting across the Driftless region, the North Coast's non-coastal arcadia, when all of a sudden, BAM! You're in the Hawkeye State. Luckily, the western side of the river road~ a winding two-lane stretch going up, down and through the bluffs ~ is my choice for the loveliest drive in the tri-state region. And isn't every drive better with some victuals to anticipate? ¶ Just as you cross Hwy. 26 from the north, stop at the **City Meat Market** ★ in New Albin. I've never availed myself of its butcher offerings ~ locals say it's a grillmonger's paradise~ but if I drive past I must stop in for cured meats. Their hot beef jerky ($13/lb.) elicits oaths of fealty from all who try it. The turkey ($8/lb.) and sweet pork ($13/lb.) portions are as thick as your thumb~ the pork is practically a whole chop, and the turkey is juicier than you'd find on a blue-plate special. ¶ Prefer your beef cooked? Perhaps a 1 lb. patty on a bakery bun loaded with all the fixings, plus bacon and fried mushrooms? Try the legendary Gunderburger. ("Legend" here is a euphemism for "cholesterol".) ★ **The Irish Shanti** in Elgin has nothing Gaelic on their menu except Guinness, but that burger is a pot of gold. ("Gold" is also a euphemism for "cholesterol.") ¶ Do international dignitaries visit Elkader annually to eat at ★ **Schera's**? Probably, although they've got a great cover story~ an annual forum dedicated to cross-cultural understanding in honor of the town's namesake, 19th century emir Abd el-Kader. At Schera's, the couscous ($17) and harissa pork ($16) entrées delighted, tender and robustly spiced. It may not be the well-traveled gourmand's favorite Mediterranean joint, but it's the area's best dinner spot, and a remarkable institution for a town of 1,300. But even if it didn't have a great kitchen, it would make this list just for its destination taproom ($6 for most pours), with a beer selection that, in its thoughtful curation, competes with any place I've been, without qualification. Plus, its sister company Abu Nawas Beverage, distributes breweries such as Jolly Pumpkin and Evil Twin; Schera's craft and import selection could not possibly disappoint. ¶ All these spots are less than 40 miles from a Great Lakes neighbor; a road trip making all three stops would be far too many good eats, so: Better make three trips, eh?

South of the Border

CHAPTER 10
A TRIP ALONG THE MEKONG

WRITER: JOSHUA PAGE :: **ILLUSTRATOR:** ADAM TURMAN

This place is special, though you might not know it by driving through. That market on the corner sells some of the best bánh mi in town. That old Burger King? It's now a Thai restaurant slinging tasty curry. Deep within that Hmong supermarket is a deli that sells delicious sausage, caramel pork, and whole tilapia. Over there, a nondescript storefront is actually an authentic Cambodian restaurant full of locals slurping noodle soup and drinking fresh coconut water. Tucked behind another building is a tiny Vietnamese restaurant that's invisible to the uninitiated. And that white building with the small red sign dishes up mouth-*and* eye-watering Szechuan food, while the fire-engine red spot down the block has lip-smacking Laotian larb. Oh yeah, that place, that place, that place, and *that* place all have damn good pho. *This* is Little Mekong.

Between Mackubin and Galtier streets, this half-mile stretch of St. Paul's University Avenue is home to over a dozen Southeast Asian eateries (if we include the delis in Ha Tien market and Wung Lee market — and we must, because they're fantastic). The gradual development of Little Mekong began in the late 1970s and early '80s as refugees coming primarily from Laos, Cambodia, and Vietnam began to set up small businesses, catering mainly to fellow first-generation residents, especially St. Paul's large Hmong population (the largest of any U.S. metropolitan area). In the decade between 1981 and 1991, the total number of Asian businesses on this strip of University Avenue increased from one to 22, and by 2005, the total had jumped to 61.[1] This "incubator for immigrant entrepreneurship," as economist Bruce Corrie calls this corner of capital city, has become *the* place for Southeast Asian food in Minnesota.

The core audience for these restaurants remains the local immigrant population. Although popular with a fair share of non-locals (especially state workers who come a few blocks west from the Capitol for lunch), the area enjoys nowhere near the notoriety of other concentrations of Twin Cities ethnic restaurants, such as Eat Street in Minneapolis. The St. Paul-based Asian Economic Development Association's effort to brand "Little Mekong" is part of a larger initiative to draw new visitors and boost local businesses negatively affected by construction of the Light Rail corridor along University Avenue — uprooting the thoroughfare temporarily made driving and parking in the area a major headache. Locals are hopeful that the train, which starts rolling in 2014 and stops right in the heart of the business district, will bring a whole new set of movers, shakers, and eaters to Little Mekong.

Named after the Mekong River, which winds its way through China, Burma (Myanmar), Laos, Cambodia, Thailand, and Vietnam, the district offers (more or less) traditional Southeast Asian cuisine without the need to travel 8,000 miles.

CHINA: LITTLE SZECHUAN

Our first stop is China — Szechuan province in the southwestern part of the country, to be exact. Bold, fiery, and pungent, the food here is not for the faint of heart or weak of stomach. Since 2006, Little Szechuan (between Arundel Street and Western Avenue North) has dished up authentic cuisine, and it has expanded to a second location in St. Louis Park, a western Twin Cities suburb. Owner Rong Bai grew up in Szechuan before immigrating first to North Dakota and then to Minnesota. The food served at her restaurant is purposefully traditional — especially in its chest-thumping spiciness. "If the customer wants to reduce the heat, they need to tell us," says Ms. Bai with a bit of Szechuan pride.

There are many examples of traditional Szechuan dishes on the menu, but two provide a particularly revealing window into the region's food. The first, Ma-Po Tofu, is all about the chili pepper. Served in a casserole dish that could pass for a cauldron, soft cubes of tofu bob in a ruddy sauce flecked with scallions, fermented black beans, and chili flakes. A thin layer of chili oil flows around the rim of the dish, and dashes of white pepper coat the tofu. Eaten with rice, the mixture is definitely spicy, but not inedibly so. Savory, salty, earthy, and just a touch sweet, this flaming dish shatters bland misperceptions of tofu.

In its liberal use of chili oil and deep pepper flavors, Ma-Po tofu is quintessentially Szechuan. However, it lacks one of, if not *the*, most distinctive ingredients of the region's famed cooking: the Szechuan peppercorn (actually a dried berry from the prickly ash tree). The spice imparts a subtle lavender aroma and a surprising (at least to greenhorns) numbing sensation. Little Szechuan's kitchen uses the peppercorn sparingly because, Ms. Bai says (again with a touch of pride), "a lot of people cannot handle it. Szechuan people, originally from Szechuan, love it. *I* love it!"

While sparse on the menu, the berry asserts its power in fish fillet and peppercorn soup. Featuring tender flounder and sturdy, tangy greens in a clean broth, the soup sounds tame. It's not. Chunks of light orange habanero chili and the tiny peppercorns produce a wild combination of spice and tingle (talk about mouthfeel!). As occurs with many dishes at Little Szechuan, we quickly move from "That's intriguing..." to "Wow, I want more!"

LAOS: FAMILY LAO-THAI

From China, we move south along the Mekong to Laos, where the food is savory, herbal, and spicy — but not as in-your-face hot as Szechuan fare. Family Lao-Thai is a newly renovated, bright-red establishment on the western edge of the Little Mekong district. As its name indicates, the restaurant also serves Thai food, largely because owner and chef Saykham Sengmavong, an immigrant from Laos who cooked in a well-known Thai restaurant in Minneapolis before striking out on his own, believes more people are familiar with (and less intimidated by) Thai than Laotian food. Along with his daughter, Annee, who runs the dining room and will soon take over the restaurant with her fiancé, David Simoukdalay, Sengmavong views Thai as a "gateway food," bringing their customers to Laotian cuisine.

There's no better menu item for such an introduction than larb (or laab), considered the national dish of Laos. Eaten as a salad or main course and featured at Laotian gatherings, larb is deceptively simple: it revolves around finely ground spiced meat. The flavor combination, however, is anything but plain. Lime, fish sauce (a staple in Lao cooking), cilantro, scallions, and chili give the dish an unmistakable brightness, while rice powder (made from toasted rice grains), kaffir leaves, and lemongrass provide hints of nuttiness and smokiness. Savory ground beef and ribbons of tripe (chicken larb is also available) combine with the other ingredients to produce a complex yet cohesive dish. Like most Laotian dishes, larb is eaten with sticky rice ("You *have* to eat it with sticky rice," Annee instructed), which serves as both utensil and sponge for the slightly astringent, aromatic liquid that remains on the plate after the meat soaks up its share.

With its clean, fresh flavors, the larb is characteristic of Chef Sengmavong's cooking. According to David, Annee's father is "very particular, very precise about what he wants. Sort of like a perfectionist." Family Lao-Thai's signature dishes — the larb and a beef soup called Gaeng Kaolaou — give the chef nowhere to hide; there aren't fatty sauces or anything else to cover shoddy ingredients or technique. What you see is what you get: straightforward, soulful food.

THAILAND: THAI CAFÉ

For those seeking Thai cuisine, there are several choices available in Little Mekong, including Bangkok Thai Deli, a former Burger King that has been transformed into a purveyor of spicy curries, stuffed chicken wings, and, our favorite, tender pea-tips. But we're docking at one of the new kids on the block, Thai Cafe, for a couple of destination dishes. We're talking hot car, no A/C, long-drive dishes.

Just east of Western Avenue, Thai Cafe is a humble storefront with just a couple dozen seats. In the two-person operation, owner Ya Poophakumpanart does all the cooking and manages the restaurant, while her precocious teenage daughter, Aun, does everything else — when she's not in school. When asked why she opened her restaurant, Ms. Poophakupanart said simply: "To show Minnesota people Thai food, to bring in the real Thai food."

As examples of the "real" Thai food and her style of cooking, the chef served us green papaya salad and sour pork ribs. The latter featured small pieces of pork rib, soured through a five-day fermentation process and then fried with whole pieces of garlic and lime leaves — they have a crusty exterior and tender interior. The slightly sour, deeply rich pork hits the palate with a superhero-size punch. Pow! Bam! Wham!

A fitting foil for the sour pork ribs, the papaya salad, comprised of shreds of green fruit (not the sweet yellow variety), chili, fish sauce, sugar, and lime, is refreshing and balanced.

It's an ideal entree on a hot summer's day, and it counterbalances rich, savory food. In blending sweet, spicy, and sour components, the papaya salad is very Thai.

A central reason Ms. Poophakupanart chose this location for Thai Cafe is because she wanted to keep the operation small. With a limited number of seats, she can do all of the cooking herself. Like Saykham Sengmavong at Family Lao-Thai, she wants complete control in the kitchen to ensure that each plate of food meets her standards.

CAMBODIA: CHENG HENG

For our penultimate stop, we head south to Cambodia. There's just one place in Little Mekong for Cambodian, Cheng Heng, and it's one of the oldest restaurants in the business district. Owned and operated by Kunrath Van and her family, who came to the states in 1983 as war refugees, Cheng Heng serves food that's tame, at least compared to some other restaurants on the avenue. It's "not too oily, not too sweet, not too spicy," says Ms. Van. That way, "You can taste all the ingredients." True, flaming chilies are in short supply here, but there's plenty of curry, lemongrass, lime, galanga, and basil, so the food is appetizing and approachable, even for normally spice-adverse Minnesotans.

Take, for example, Pahok Ktiss — red curry with ground pork, lemongrass, and peas served with an array of fresh veggies (including an adorably small globe of green eggplant we wanted to take home with us) for dipping into the curry mix. This Cambodian "fondue" is an interactive, appetizing version of the typical meat and vegetable curry.

Cheng Heng's take on surf and turf is called Chean Chuen. A large piece of crisply fried, moist sole is paired with ground pork and topped with cilantro, scallions, and a light, zesty (though not spicy) sauce flavored with lemongrass and ginger. This Cambodian classic would steal the show at a Friday night fish fry.

For us, the restaurant's signature dish is Ho-Mok (also called Amok) — curry fish steamed in a banana leaf. Opening the large green wrapper unveils custardy, aromatic salmon, perfumed by generous amounts of lemongrass and kaffir lime leaf.

Cheng Heng has remained in business for 16 years on the strength of entrees like Ho-Mok — we suspect that fresh coconut water (served in the shell) and a wide variety of delectable Cambodian pastries made fresh each morning might also have something to do with its enduring popularity.

VIETNAM: TRIEU CHAU

Our last stop along the Mekong brings us to Vietnam. The Twin Cities is awash in Vietnamese restaurants, from favorites like Quang and Jasmine Deli in South Minneapolis to Ngon in St. Paul (just a few blocks west of Little Mekong), which uses primarily local and sustainable ingredients. Little Mekong alone boasts a half-dozen Vietnamese restaurants and one market deli, Ha-Tien (which, in our opinion, makes the best bánh mì in the entire region, with a roasted pork sandwich that's the definition of succulence).

Many of the spots in Little Mekong are welcoming, as the large numbers of regulars that frequent the various restaurants attest, but Trieu Chau puts hospitality front and center. If you want to go where everybody knows your name (and they're always glad you came), you're in the right spot. The small staff runs the cafe like a neighborhood tavern, with a knack for remembering names and favorite orders.

When it comes down to it, though, if Trieu Chau didn't have good food, the staff likely wouldn't have many names to remember. While we've enjoyed soups, sandwiches, and stir-fries at this cheery joint, it's a salad (Bún Thập Cẩm) that stole our hearts. With an egg roll, two different preparations of pork, and rice noodles, this "salad" is a meal in itself. The star of the show is a skewer of luscious pork meatballs, flash fried and then quickly grilled for a slight char and subtle smokiness. A crisp egg roll and thinly sliced BBQ pork play supporting roles, and the extras bring the dish together: pickled carrot and daikon, cilantro, fried onions, crushed peanuts, and nuoc cham (slightly sweet fish sauce).

The salad mirrors Trieu Chau's overall atmosphere, which took years to develop. After taking over the troubled restaurant from his sister in 2003, Minh Nguyen focused his attention on quality service. In about five years, Trieu Chau had a steady flow of regulars, says Nguyen. The little place is now one of the more popular restaurants in the area, and customers commonly wait for tables during peak hours. Nguyen has toyed with the idea of expanding, but he's decided against it.

"I don't want to expand, because I want to get to know all my customers," he says. "When you have 200 customers in your restaurant, you're not going to know all of them. At our restaurant, 45 is the maximum, and that's really cutting it close. Thirty people in my restaurant and it's full. At 30 people, I have a better chance of remembering most of the customers. And so, I want to keep it at a more intimate level. I get to know them."

[1]David H. Kaplan, 1997, "The Creation of an Ethnic Economy: Indochinese Business Expansion in Saint Paul," Economic Geography 73(2): 214-233. Bruce P. Corrie et al., 2012, "The Transformation of University Avenue by Immigrant Entrepreneurs from 1981-2005: A Report."

CHAPTER 11
HIDDEN GEMS
KICKSTARTER CONTRIBUTORS

Kickstarter contributors :: **CARTOGRAPHER:** MATT DOOLEY

We asked the $100+ Kickstarter backers of this book to each contribute a "hidden gem" — a restaurant somewhere in the Upper Midwest that was special, and worth discovering. We framed it as a reward for backing the project, but the real beneficiaries turned out to be us — and the readers of this volume. The restaurants, cafes, saloons and bowling alleys that our backers contributed to these maps represent a glorious spread of Upper Midwestern eats — everything from high-brow farm-to-table to down-n-dirty humble small town diners. There's a road trip here — hit each of the gems, and come back well-versed in some of the region's best and best-loved spots. And probably several dozen pounds heavier, but that's between you and your diet plan.

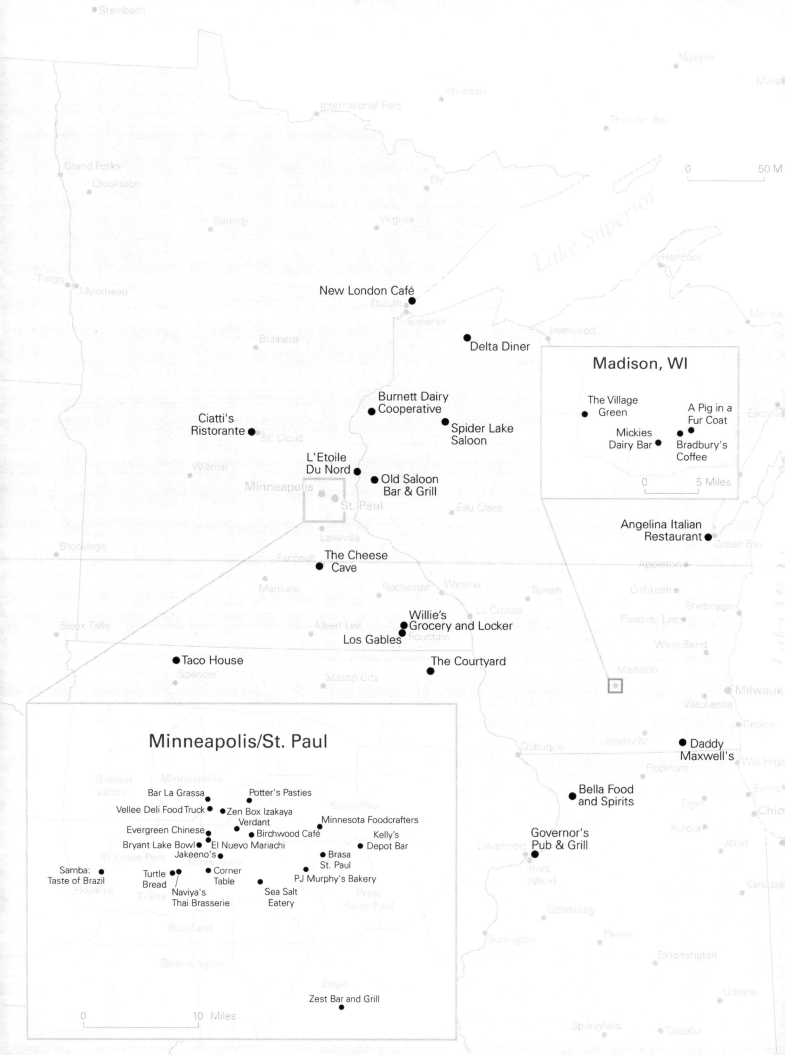

New London Café

Delta Diner

Madison, WI

The Village Green

A Pig in a Fur Coat

Mickies Dairy Bar

Bradbury's Coffee

0   5 Miles

Burnett Dairy Cooperative

Spider Lake Saloon

Ciatti's Ristorante

L'Etoile Du Nord

Old Saloon Bar & Grill

Angelina Italian Restaurant

The Cheese Cave

Willie's Grocery and Locker

Los Gables

Taco House

The Courtyard

Daddy Maxwell's

Bella Food and Spirits

Governor's Pub & Grill

0   50 M

Minneapolis/St. Paul

Bar La Grassa

Potter's Pasties

Vellee Deli Food Truck

Zen Box Izakaya

Verdant

Minnesota Foodcrafters

Evergreen Chinese

Birchwood Café

Kelly's Depot Bar

Bryant Lake Bowl

El Nuevo Mariachi

Jakeeno's

Brasa St. Paul

Samba: Taste of Brazil

Turtle Bread

Corner Table

PJ Murphy's Bakery

Naviya's Thai Brasserie

Sea Salt Eatery

Zest Bar and Grill

0   10 Miles

MINNESOTA (TWIN CITIES)

BAR LA GRASSA | *800 N Washington Avenue, Minneapolis | barlagrassa.com*
Nominated by: James M. Shultis
Why? Variety of small plates.
What should I order? Like all.

BIRCHWOOD CAFÉ | *3311 E 25th St, Minneapolis | birchwoodcafe.com*
Nominated by: Diana McKeown
Why? The food is made with the freshest, local, and sustainable ingredients and is so tasty! Chef Marshall Paulsen and baker Sandra Sherva are easily the best at what they do. I love the staff and the way Birchwood owner Tracy Singleton is such a big part of our community. We feel lucky to have this as our neighborhood café!
What should I order? So hard to choose, but our family just LOVES the scones for breakfast. The specials are great but the turkey burger is always on the menu with changing toppings and is simply delicious. We often make a run for dessert, the best in the city.

BRASA SAINT PAUL | *777 Grand Avenue, St Paul | brasa.us*
Nominated by: Mikael McLaren
Why? Most of the menu is gluten-free comfort food, making it a perfect choice for our entire family. It has become our go to place for special occasions, visiting family and even holiday meals.
What should I order? The pork is tender joy on a plate.

BRYANT LAKE BOWL | *810 W Lake St, Minneapolis | bryantlakebowl.com*
Nominated by: Julianna Simon
Why? It's hardly hidden, being known and loved by many, but you could literally write our lives in the meals we've had there. The turkey BLT on our first date, the bad-breath-burger now that we're married, the amazing Rueben because it's Thursday and that's special too, right?
What should I order? The bloody marys — with an array of infused vodkas — are a great way to start a Saturday.

CORNER TABLE | *4257 Nicollet Avenue, Minneapolis | cornertablerestaurant.com*
Nominated by: James Norton
Why? Corner Table is the very model of a farm-to-table restaurant, neatly incorporating seasonality, a sense of place, and a cosmopolitan awareness of the most delicious way to cook food.
What should I order? You can't go wrong, but the loving way in which Corner Table handles anything and everything pork-derived merits appreciation. Pork belly and pork skin, in particular, shine like diamonds here.

EVERGREEN CHINESE | *2424 Nicollet Avenue, Minneapolis | evergreen-chinese.com*
Nominated by: Joseph Howell
Why? For 10 years, this basement-level gem has been offering vegan Minneapolitans exquisitely prepared Asian favorites.
What should I order? Try the moo shu mock pork. The accompanying pancakes are handmade in-house, the vegetables are fresh, and the flavor is wonderful.

JAKEENO'S PIZZA AND PASTA | *3555 Chicago Avenue S, Minneapolis | jakeenos.com*
Nominated by: Paul Dennis
Why? It's a great Powderhorn fixture for pizza and Italian sandwiches and pasta, even a New Jersey transplant approves of their fare.
What should I order? Jakeeno's makes a fantastic thin crust pizza with a delicious

housemade sauce that allows for a number of different toppings and specialty pies, the best of which is the Chicago Super. Instead of slices, the chefs at Jakeeno's slice their pizza in a tic-tac-toe pattern allowing for each piece of the Super to have an assortment of the following toppings: onions, green peppers, mushrooms, olives, pepperoni, and sausage. Delicious!

KELLY'S DEPOT BAR | *241 Kellogg Boulevard E, Saint Paul* |
facebook.com/pages/Kellys-Depot-Bar/149585945071219
Nominated by: John Hines
Why? Family-owned, serving a great burger and coney.
What should I order? The burger.

MINNESOTA FOODCRAFTERS | *865 Pierce Butler, Saint Paul*
Nominated by: Thomas Ruhland
Why? A culinary workshop for local food producers and a retail store that highlights the fruits of the labor of those who work here.
What should I order? Products from anyone who crafts food there.

NAVIYA'S THAI BRASSERIE | *2812 W 43rd Street, Minneapolis* | *naviyas.com*
Nominated by: Julie Ingebretsen
Why? Great fresh food, nice location, lovely ambience (even quiet, sometimes!), neighborhood-oriented.
What should I order? Love the Rama Thai.

EL NUEVO MARIACHI | *2750 Nicollet Avenue, Minneapolis* |
facebook.com/pages/El-Nuevo-Mariachi-Restaurant/257091570996342
Nominated by: Sam Carlsen
Why? Great meats, music, and prices. Everyone we've taken there has been blown away.
What should I order? Carnitas.

PJ MURPHY'S BAKERY | *1279 Randolph Avenue, Saint Paul* | *pjmurphybakery.com*
Nominated by: Colin McFadden
Why? Donuts without the pretense. Full of happy children and happy children at heart.
What should I order? Buttercream filled raised donut. It will blow your mind.

POTTER'S PASTIES | *1828 Como Avenue SE, Minneapolis* | *potterspasties.com*
Nominated by: Fiona Carter
Why? It is the only pasty shop in town. And it is really fucking good. And lots of people think so in a short amount of time
What should I order? Market Special. Forever changing and amazing!

SAMBA: TASTE OF BRAZIL | *922 Main Street, Hopkins* | *sambatasteofbrazil.com*
Nominated by: Evan Pedersen
Why? The antithesis of urban eye-sore chain restaurants claiming to be true Brazilian cooking, family-owned Samba is the real deal.
What should I order? Start your meal with a Caipirinha made properly with Cachaza rather than light rum. Follow that up with a few different types of their Pastels, empanada-like pockets of joy; we recommend ones filled with hearts of palm or carne seca and cream cheese. Do not miss the Feijoada, a traditional Brazilian pork and bean stew. Served with a side of rice and farofa, follow owner Jose Luiz Pantano's instruction of taking a little bit of rice and some of the stew onto your fork or spoon, then lightly dipping the mixture into the farofa. The end result being a extraordinary concoction of flavor, texture, and comfort.

SEA SALT EATERY | *4825 Minnehaha Avenue, Minneapolis | seasalteatery.wordpress.com*
Nominated by: Kevin Winge
Why? Good food. Great venue for summer dining.
What should I order? Fried Oyster Po Boy

TURTLE BREAD | *Various locations in Minneapolis | turtlebread.com*
Nominated by: Faysal Abraham
Why? Great coffee, pastries, and wonderful light to start your day.
What should I order? Salmon scramble. The dish reminds me of my trip to see my family in Paris.

VELLEE DELI FOOD TRUCK | *Find its location online at velleedeli.com*
Nominated by: Vellee Deli
Why? Flavor fusion unlike anything else around town. And the adventure is trying to track it down.
What should I order? The Korean BBQ Burrito: luscious BBQ beef short ribs, kimchi, fresh romaine lettuce, smoky salsa and lightly seasoned rice. It's the crowd favorite and winner of the 2012 Best Burrito of the Year!

VERDANT TEA TASTING ROOM & TEA BAR | *2111 E Franklin Avenue | minneapolis. verdanttea.com*
Nominated by: David Duckler
Why? Creative partnerships and inspiring food collaboration are at the heart of Verdant Tea. You'll taste artisan tea sourced from real farmers whose photos and stories are featured on the teahouse walls. Right alongside, you can enjoy Real Deal Chocolate, a vegetarian farm-to-table menu from the Birchwood Cafe, and all-natural small batch ice cream from Sweet Science Ice Cream.
What should I order? Try the Tea Tasting Flight and spend an afternoon comparing four teas, back to back, for an introduction to tea or a guided tour of a region, a style of tea, or a single family farm.

ZEN BOX IZAKAYA | *602 Washington Avenue S, Minneapolis | zenboxizakaya.com*
Nominated by: Dale Yasunaga
Why? It's an excellent representation of authentic Japanese izakaya cuisine and craft ramen.
What should I order? Tonkotsu ramen.

ZEST BAR AND GRILL | *525 Diffley Road, Eagan | zesteagan.com*
Nominated by: Kevin Diepholz
Why? Great Service. Fresh unique dishes.
What should I order? Zesty Goddess Salad. Grilled Sushi grade tuna, with Green Goddess dressing make this truly unique.

MINNESOTA (OUTSTATE)

THE CHEESE CAVE | *318 Central Avenue N, Faribault | cheesecave.net*
Nominated by: Becca Dilley
Why? One of Minnesota's best cheese plants also has a great stand-alone shop – around the corner from Faribault Dairy, the Cheese Cave does a ton of cheese sampling, a classy sit-down lunch, and even sells fresh curds from time to time.
What should I order? The Blue Pear pizza is more of a dessert than a main dish, with local honey, candied pecans, blue cheese, and pears — it's different, and it's delicious.

CIATTI'S RISTORANTE | *2635 W Division Street, Saint Cloud* | *ciattisristorante.com*
Nominated by: Patricia Schnobrich
Why? It was 'our' favorite place, (my husband and I). He has passed away and being at there brings back memories.
What to order? Chicken fettuccine Alfredo with vegetables.

L'ETOILE DU NORD | *41 Judd Street, Marine on Saint Croix* | *letoiledunordcafe.com*
Nominated by: Eric Schneider
Why? Like The Bikery in Stillwater, L'Etoile Du Nord is a bicycle-centric bakery and coffeehouse that also operates as a full service bike shop. But unlike its progenitor, L'Etoile Du Nord offers a quainter locale for cyclists and a food truck that shows up at various festivals.
What should I order? The bread pudding or the Belgian waffle.

LOS GABLES | *122 U.S. 52, Fountain* | *losgables.com*
Nominated by: Tim Gihring
Why? It looks like something out of rural Mexico, a truck-stop in the middle of nowhere, among the hills and hollows of bluff country. But it's authentic Mexican, with local grass-fed beef.
What should I order? The mole chicken. The sauce incorporates more than 20 ingredients — a rich dish.

NEW LONDON CAFE | *4721 E Superior Street, Duluth* | *newlondoncafe.com*
Nominated by: Rick and Ann Garland
Why? Reliably good homemade breakfasts, good service, and good prices. Just what you want for a hearty breakfast.
What should I order? Any of the eggs and potatoes — simple and good!

WILLIE'S GROCERY AND LOCKER | *92 Main Street, Fountain*
Nominated by: Marjorie Kelly
Why? Skip the groceries, go directly to the meat counter. The refrigerators and display cases are from the 1930's. The owners Willie, his wife Beezy, and son Darran are helpful and friendly.
What should I order? They make great brats, summer sausage, ring baloney (I've had all these) and from what I've hear jerky.

ILLINOIS

BELLA FOOD AND SPIRITS | *110 Market Street, Mt. Carroll* | *facebook.com/Bellafoodandspirits*
Nominated by: Kevin Platte II
Why? An intimate setting with a constantly perfected menu, live performers, and even cobblestone streets ensures your return.
What should I order? Chef Tucker's daily special. Inspired by ever-changing seasons and celebrations, every visit assures you taste something unique.

IOWA

THE COURTYARD | *421 W Water Street, Decorah*
Nominated by: Nathan Matter
Why? Large downtown beer garden with a surprisingly vast bottle selection, bent towards sours and farmhouse ales. Bring your own food, or order from the adjacent BBQ!
What should I order? A 750 of a good Belgian saison or a fresh IPA from the local brewery, Toppling Goliath. Bonus: all of the spendier bottles come with a free Hamm's.

GOVERNOR'S PUB & GRILL | *3470 Middle Road, Bettendorf | govsqc.com*
Nominated by: Scott Kuhlman
Why? Governor's is where construction workers sit next to business men who sit next to college kids all to enjoy ice cold beer, endless peanuts, towering nachos, and their famous pretzel stack.
What should I order? Pretzel Stack. This sandwich elevates the basic turkey sandwich by layering tons of high quality hardwood smoked turkey, melted cheese, lettuce, and tomato on a fresh pretzel roll. While not a fancy sandwich, the Pretzel Stack has stood the test of time and pairs well with a frosty mug of beer.

TACO HOUSE | *Old Hwy 71, Arnolds Park | yelp.com/biz/taco-house-arnolds-park*
Nominated by: Kelly Ingstad
Why? You might have to stand in line awhile to order but its worth it... You'll be hooked immediately once you get your food!
What should I order? Soft shell taco, nachos and don't forget to load up on their homemade sauces.

WISCONSIN

ANGELINA ITALIAN RESTAURANT | *117 N Adams Street, Green Bay | angelinarestaurant.com*
Nominated by: Stephanie Kuenn
Why? Take a break from typical Titletown fare and step into this romantic hideaway with delicious Italian food, made with love by the family who owns the restaurant.
What should I order? The ravioli — it changes each day and it's always freshly made.

A PIG IN A FUR COAT | *940 Williamson Street, Madison | apiginafurcoat.com*
Nominated by: Dan Norton
Why? Fun cozy space, helpful staff and some of the best food in Madison.
What should I order? Foie Gras Mousse, crazy and indulgent and delicious.

BRADBURY'S COFFEE | *127 N Hamilton Street, Madison | bradburyscoffee.com*
Nominated by: Jessica Forbess
Why? Third wave espresso from local and national roasters. Skillfully made crepes with seasonal veggies.
What should I order? Piccolo: slightly less milk than a cappuccino so you can appreciate the espresso, but still enjoy the sweetness of the milk. On Wisconsin!

BURNETT DAIRY COOPERATIVE | *11631 Wisconsin 70, Grantsburg | burnettdairy.com*
Nominated by: Michael Gordon
Why? Recently remodeled, the BDC has a great selection of cheeses, small (but good) selection of wines, lots of specialty food products and delicious soft serve ice cream and malts. BDC is an oasis in a retail food desert.
What should I order? 14 year cheddar; Soft serve ice cream. The 14 year cheddar is rich and sharp — as good or better than Hooks, and the soft serve is simply delicious.

DADDY MAXWELL'S | *150 Elkhorn Road, Williams Bay | daddymaxwells.com*
Nominated by: Karsten Steinhaeuser
Why? This igloo-shaped "Antarctic Circle Diner", located in a one-stop-sign village in Southern Wisconsin, is loved for its take on tasty diner fare and unique decor. From fresh made donuts to Sunday "clucks", Daddy's is a must-try for anyone visiting the Lake Geneva area!
What should I order? 60 Second Pile-Up, the perfect diner breakfast plate: a stack of hash browns, American cheese, grilled ham, and two eggs your way, served with a choice of toast (we recommend cinnamon swirl with a side of peanut butter!)

DELTA DINER | *14385 County Highway H, Mason | deltadiner.com*
Nominated by: Heather Wilkie
Why? Always good!
What should I order? Friday night fish fry.

MICKIES DAIRY BAR | *1511 Monroe Street, Madison*
Nominated by: Deb Diepholz
Why? Great for breakfast, people watching and worth the wait on weekends. The anticipation of getting seated as you get closer to the wonderful smells can't be beat.
What should I order? The scrambler. Awesome for both the early riser and the "still up" college student.

OLD SALOON BAR & GRILL | *145 S Knowles Avenue, New Richmond*
Nominated by: Jill Miller
Why? This is a genuine Saloon (been there for decades) featuring a beautiful Brunswick back bar with original booths and liquor cabinets. This hidden page from the past also offers up made to order, tasty American fare and served by a friendly, energetic staff.
What should I order? Hard to pick just one but the Big Island Fish Tacos with pineapple / ginger/chili dressing tossed with a shred of napa / carrot / scallion and cilantro are really good. But then there is the homemade soup like the artichoke / mushroom / sun-dried tomato with fresh thyme or the more obvious Hot Chicken Wings served with Blue Cheese Dip (good enough to dive into). I know that's three... so you'll have to decide.

SPIDER LAKE SALOON | *2586 Spider Lake Trail, Birchwood | spiderlakesaloon.com*
Nominated by: Julie Pearson
Why? It's quaint and has a timeless atmosphere in the north woods.
What should I order? The Bloody Mary on Sunday Bloody Sunday, complete with a sausage and asparagus spear.

THE VILLAGE GREEN | *7508 Hubbard Avenue, Middleton | thevillagegreenmiddleton.com*
Nominated by: Tim Ikeman
Why? In a state loaded with small-town bars, Middleton's Village Green combines timeless charm with straightforward and delicious bar food. Over the past 30 years Middleton has changed a lot, but inside this family-run joint the food tastes just as good today as when I started eating there in the early 1980's. Bonus: the Village Green is just a short walk from two other Middleton destinations, the Capital Brewery Bier Garten and the National Mustard Museum.
What should I order? Two hamburgers with fried onions and a side of cheese curds. The made-from-scratch patties really shine when you add ketchup, mustard and a few cheese curds before devouring. It's not haute cuisine, but it sure hits the spot with a cold beer.

CHAPTER 12
THE CURIOUS HISTORY OF NORTH COAST WINE

WRITER: JOHN GARLAND :: **CARTOGRAPHER:** NAT CASE

The pioneers who first laid eyes on the future Midwestern United States found grapes. They were growing in dense clusters along streams and rivers, in masses similar to those that had been documented along the Eastern seaboard. It was a sign of hope for the European nations colonizing the continent. Grapevines in the New World represented not only a symbolic extension of their culture, but also an important economic opportunity. England especially dreamed of a day when its colonies would produce enough wine to make trade with the French a thing of the past.

It seemed self-evident that a continent with such a natural bounty of grapes would one day make world-class wine. Instead, winemaking in North America got off to a dreadful start. Colonists as early as those who settled Jamestown in 1610 learned that France's finest grapevine cuttings wouldn't thrive here, even when tended to by expert *vignerons*. They would take root in the perfect soils on hills with just the proper aspect. The vines would grow, maybe for a year or two, before dying without warning and no one could explain why.

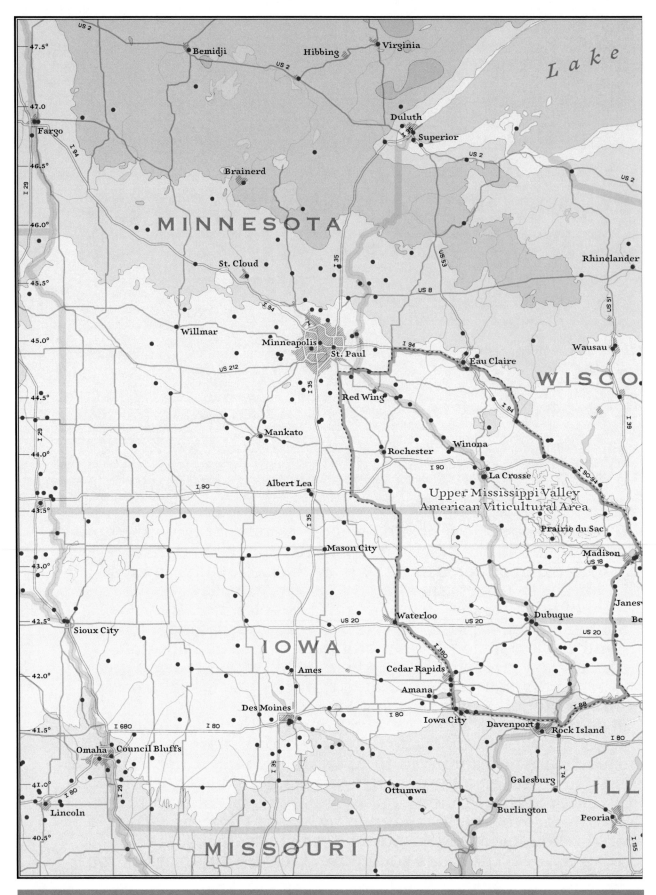

The Norton Grape [Southern Iowa]
Sometimes called the Cabernet of the Midwest, Norton is a *Vitis Aestivalis* hybrid with a deep, inky character. It was the most promising grape at the center of the Missouri wine industry that was the country's largest in 1870. In 1873, a Norton bottled from Hermann, Missouri won a gold medal at the prestigious *Weltaisstellung* wine competition in Vienna. It's currently a grape on the fence in Southern Iowa. Some vintners consider it a prime candidate for their best red wines. Others consider it too late-ripening to be effective year after year for their vineyards.

Marquette and La Crescent [Saint Paul, Minnesota]
Of all the grapes developed at the University in Minnesota, these two grapes have made the finest cold climate wine to date. They make modern tasting wines with finesse and polish. Marquette is the genetic granddaughter of pinot noir. Its

Wineries of the Upper Midwest

Superior

Marquette
Sault Ste. Marie
Iron Mountain
Escanaba
MICHIGAN
US 2
I 75
Marinette
US 41
Traverse City
Green Bay
Appleton
Oshkosh
Fond du Lac
Sheboygan
NSIN
Lake Michigan
West Bend
US 31
US 10
Muskegon
Saginaw
I 94
Milwaukee
Grand Rapids
I 96
Waukesha
I 96
Racine
I 43
Lansing
US 131
Battle Creek
Rockford
Waukegan
I 69
Benton Harbor
I 94
Kalamazoo
I 94
Elgin
I 88
Evanston
Chicago
Elkhart
Aurora
Gary I 94
South Bend
I 80-90
I 80-90
Joliet
INDIANA
OHIO
I 39
Kankakee
I 65
Fort Wayne
Lima
INOIS
I 55
I 57
Kokomo
Marion
I 69
Bloomington
I 74
Lafayette
Muncie
I 75
Beloit
ville
loit

47.5°
47.0°
46.5°
46.0°
45.5°
45.0°
44.5°
44.0°
43.5°
43.0°
42.5°
42.0°
41.5°
41.0°
40.5°

USDA Growing Zone	Average Annual Extreme Minimum Temperature 1976-2005
6b	-5 to 0°F
6a	-10 to -5°F
5b	-15 to -10°F
5a	-20 to -15°F
4b	-25 to -20°F
4a	-30 to -25°F
3b	-35 to -30°F
3a	-40 to -35°F

Comparable wine-growing latitudes:

McMinnville, Oregon .... 45.2° N
Queenstown, New Zealand .... 45° S
Minneapolis, MN .... **45° N**
Asti, Italy .... 44.9° N
Bordeaux, France .... 44.8° N

Chateauneuf-du-Pape, France..44° N

Greve in Chianti, Italy ....43.6°N
Aix-en-Provence, France ...... 43.5° N

Prairie du Sac, WI .... **43.3° N**
Niagra-on-the-Lake, Ontario. 43.2° N
Montalcino, Italy..................... 43° N

Logroño (Rioja), Spain .... 42.5° N
Ithaca, NY .... 42.4° N

Amana, IA .... **41.8° N**
Aranda de Duero, Spain .... 41.7° N

Martinborough, New Zealand. 41.2° S

• Wineries registered with the U.S. Alcohol and Tobacco Tax and Trade Bureau

---

wines are complex and fruity with delicate tannin that takes well to oak aging. LaCrescent may be the grape that has the greatest combination of cold-hardiness and promise for wine. It can be made dry, like an austere chenin blanc, or perhaps better as an off-dry wine where it echoes a good riesling.

Lake Michigan [Lower Peninsula]
In the same way that the Atlantic Ocean imparts a temperate climate to France's coastal regions, Lake Michigan provides a pocket of shelter for *Vinifera* vines to grow on Michigan's Lower Peninsula. Wineries around Traverse City produce multiple *Vinifera* wines, including rieslings that compete among the best

in America. The same lake effect traps warmer air between Lake Ontario and the Niagara Escarpment, making the Niagara Peninsula the largest winegrowing region in Canada.

So they tried to make wine from the hardy, native grapes and the results were disheartening. Native grape wine tasted roughhewn, unpolished, and ill-considered. It was far too acidic to have any finesse and not worth sending back to Europe in any significant quantity. It would be nearly two hundred years before North American winemakers figured out how to make native grapes into better wine and how to grow French grapes so they wouldn't die.

Meanwhile, Americans took to brewing beer and hard cider. They distilled whiskey and imported Madeira. By the time the Midwest's first vineyards were planted the early to mid-1800s, there had been few successes in American wine and little interest in wine among Americans in general. Still, farmers emigrated from winemaking nations and planted vineyards in the Midwest. Newly formed universities and horticultural societies in the area began experimental vineyards as well.

But anyone who's tasted Midwestern wine, even in the 21st Century, knows that it doesn't compare to the best of California, France or Italy. The Midwest has become famous for agriculture, so why can't good wine grapes grow here? Why, for the vast majority of its history, has the Midwest made such awful wine?

THE VERY RAW MATERIALS

The success of any wine region hinges on its growers identifying the right grapes for their climate. The Midwest is a precarious spot for wine grapes because it lacks the thermal influence of a large body of water. The Atlantic Ocean, for example, keeps the temperature stable in Bordeaux, France through the changing seasons. Despite occupying almost the exact same latitude, Minneapolis is exposed to the prairie winds and drastic swings in seasonal temperature, making its growing season shorter and more unpredictable. This effect of water on winemaking can be seen locally in how Lake Michigan provides shelter to the wines of the Lower Peninsula [see side bar, page 83].

Thus, the Midwest's center-of-the-continent climate is too cold to ripen cabernet sauvignon, chardonnay and the other varieties of the species *Vitis Vinifera*, the Asiatic wine grape, the source of all the world's finest wines. *Vinifera* is a delicate plant. Its vines will usually die when temperatures dip between 0° and -15° F, a yearly occurrence in the Upper Midwest. *Vinifera* is also susceptible to Phylloxera, a North American aphid that loves feasting on vine roots (this was the invisible problem that sidelined those early vineyards in Virginia). Native American grapevines, on the other hand, have a natural immunity to the pest.[1]

So Midwestern winemakers would have to start with the grapes species noticed by early explorers. The most significant was *Vitis Riparia*, often called the "frost grape" or "riverside grape." It's an early ripening species that can survive temperatures as low as -40° to -50°F. Also important was the hardy *Vitis Labrusca*, the "fox grape" of the Southern US, a species that makes peculiar tasting wines. Some use the term *foxiness* to describe its signature musk, which, at its worst, is like some haunting combination of a mossy fen and moldy basement.

As it became clear that the right grapes didn't yet exist for American wine, scientists and home gardeners alike began to experiment with hybridization.[2] Dr. Daniel Norton engineered his most famous grape [see side bar, page 82] in Virginia in the 1820s. Perhaps the most famous hybrid is the Concord, the great Eastern blue grape. It has made a significant amount of American wine since being developed in 1849 and was the most cultivated variety in Iowa until the year 2000[3].

These new grapes were being produced at the same time the Midwest was becoming more populated, so the region's first vineyards would fair better than those at Jamestown. But a host of other problems for Midwest wine was on the horizon.

A TROUBLED HISTORY

The agricultural promise of the Midwest made it a beacon for Europeans in search of traditional living. Tired of political instability back home, Germans were responsible for many of the Midwest's first important vineyards. They settled Hermann, Missouri in the 1830s after being lured with the promise of a farmer's Eden and the chance to begin a new Fatherland. They made Missouri the nation's leading wine producer up to and shortly after the Civil War.

Germans were chief among the settlers of the Amana Colonies in the 1850s. These villages along the Iowa River ran on a communal lifestyle in which all families tended to the vines in exchange for a share of the wine at harvest. Attractive land prices in Iowa also appealed to members of the Icarians, a socialist French society, who established vineyards near Corning, Iowa by 1860. They planted Concord, having learned their lesson from a previous settlement in Nauvoo, Illinois a decade earlier, where they had grown European grapes only to watch them wither and die.

In Minnesota, vineyards were reported around Lake Minnetonka and in Minneapolis as early as 1855. The state's first important grape grower was Louis Suelter, a German homesteader, who in the 1870s engineered numerous hybrids that would become important genetic material for the region's future grape scientists. And though Wisconsin was slower to adapt to winemaking than its neighboring states, it contains a notable regional landmark: the first American stop in the legendary winemaking life of Agoston Haraszthy [see sidebar].

The quality of Midwest wine was improving but it hadn't captured the nation's attention. Instead, it was a different group of Germans slaking the thirst of the Midwest. Men like Frederick Miller, Frederick Pabst, Eberhard Anheuser and Adolphus Busch found the region populated by amber waves of grain and citizens thirsty for beer. Wine production in the Midwest began declining in the late 1800s, thanks especially to the new transcontinental railroad and the advent of commercial refrigeration. These factors made the prodigious output of grapes from California (a place warm enough to grow Vinifera) available nationwide. Few vineyards in the region could still turn a profit once Prohibition went into effect; many were ripped up and converted to other crops.

Other than vineyard destruction, Prohibition wasn't unkind to wine drinking nationwide. A loophole in the Volstead Act, affirmed by an Internal Revenue ruling,

Agoston Haraszthy

Agoston Haraszthy left behind a groundbreaking resumé: first Hungarian to settle in the United States, first sheriff of San Diego County, father of California winemaking. He was commissioned by that state to travel through Europe, collect vines and document the best growing practices. He grew zinfandel on his estate in Sonoma, being among the first Americans to experiment with the grape. His 1861 book Grape Culture, Wines, and Wine-Making, was considered a seminal work of viticulture for decades.

But he first settled along the Wisconsin River, laying out a city he called Szeptaj ("beautiful view") that would eventually become Sauk City. He had found an advantageous microclimate for grape growing, one with steep hills enjoying the thermal protection from the river below. His vineyard is now the site of Wollersheim Winery, a now 40-year old operation that neatly illustrates the evolution of Midwestern wine — a one-time object of derision that grew out of its stereotype thanks to technology and better grapes.

He's often described, like other notable European immigrants of the time, as idealistic, driven and ambitious. Though, in his case, there's a darker undercurrent to his travels. He left Hungary afraid for his life after political winds shifted. His gold rush fever led him to California, but left behind over-extended finances in Wisconsin. He was charged, though not convicted, of embezzling $150,000 from the new US Mint in San Francisco through his capacity as assayer.[5] After the trial, he somehow raised enough money to attempt development of a sugar plantation and rum distilling operation in Nicaragua, where he died after slipping in a river and being consumed by crocodiles.[6]

essentially legalized home winemaking. It allowed a person to manufacture 200 gallons of "non-intoxicating cider and fruit juice" per year. The wine could exceed the 0.5% legal limit for an intoxicating beverage but no upper limit was defined, save for the vague directive that the beverage should not intoxicate when used. As one might imagine, vineyard acreage *increased* during Prohibition, as did per capita consumption.[4] But it was West Coast vineyards that reaped the benefits.

After Prohibition was repealed, there was very little commercial and scientific interest in Midwest winemaking. Instead, the region was focused on the crops that would make it famous; soybeans, sugar beets, corn and other cereal grains. These crops took to the ultra-fertile soils that blanket the Midwest, which the grapevine doesn't need. In fact, the best wine comes from stressed-out vines that receive only *just enough* water, sunlight and nutrients. Not so for corn, which now grows in Iowa at three times the volume of Mexico's entire crop.

The few Iowa grape growers that remained or replanted after Prohibition received another setback courtesy of the state's new dominant crop. Beginning in 1949, an herbicide called 2,4-D had been popularized to target broad-leaf plants in the cornfield. Unfortunately for winemakers, grapevines are broad-leaf plants. The herbicide drifted out of cornfields and, within five years of its introduction, 2,4-D had devastated almost every vineyard in the state.

So for most of the 20th Century, Midwest wines were stuck in the realm of novelty. They were something people might politely sip at the state fair with a nod and a grimace. Since good wine grapes were elusive, wine was more often made from the region's prominent fruits, including apples and cranberries. These fruit wines tasted unbalanced, alcoholic and unserious. They are to grape wine what backwoods moonshine is to a fine bourbon. Despite any promise grape wine once held, the region became best known for rhubarb wine in the Amanas and cherry wine in Door Country, Wisconsin.

MODERN RESURGENCE

Midwest wine has improved more in the last thirty years than in the previous two hundred. During that recent history, winemaking technology and grape science were advancing. Public consciousness of regional and farm-direct products was percolating. Still, the region would need better grapes, and the most important advancements began on Elmer Swenson's dairy farm in Osceola, Wisconsin. He began experimenting in the early 1940s, using Louis Suelter's grapes, French hybrids, and grapes from the University of Minnesota. He joined the U of M staff in 1969, and in ten years had produced thousands of cultivars that are still grown all over the region today. They include delicate white grapes like Edelweiss and Brianna and deep reds like Saint Croix and Sabrevois.

The University of Minnesota has grown grapes since its inception, but only since 1996 have they engineered the four grapes now making the best wine in the history of the Midwest. LaCrescent and Marquette are respectively the finest white and red grapes [*see side bar, page 82*]. The other two are Frontenac, which shows best when made into rosé or fortified wine, and Frontenac Gris, which can be made like a bracing sauvignon blanc and shows promise as a sparkling wine.

With better grapes came better wine and the chance to grow a viable industry. Several vineyards were established in Minnesota in the 1970s, mostly by hobbyists making wine for home consumption. The state's first commercial wineries were established in 1976-77. The Minnesota Farm Winery bill was passed in 1980, reducing the annual fees and excise taxes and allowing growers to make and sell their own wine. Vineyards and wineries have exploded since 2000 in both Iowa and Wisconsin. Both states went from a handful of wineries at the beginning of the decade to over 100 at present.

Though wines made in a dry style have improved, the region still prefers sweet wine. A great percentage, if not a majority, of Midwest wineries has a sweet wine as their leading seller. The raw materials inform this stylistic decision: cold climate grapes are far more acidic and less tannic than *Vinifera,* and can be balanced by a hefty sugar content. Marquette is the region's finest grape for dry red wines that, though it's too early to say for sure, have the potential to compete with the best in the country. A grape has yet to surface with the same promise for dry white wines.

In wine-loving cultures, there's a notion that each region's wine is special for the most basic reason: *because it's regional* and emblematic of the place itself. To not promote a region's wines is to dismiss its cultural identity. Midwest wine has finally established itself as something worthy of such encouragement almost two hundred years after it began. While it may never reach the heights of California, it's found a solid footing in just a short period of time. Along with micro-breweries and distilleries, Midwest wine is on track to becoming a justifiable source of regional pride.

[1] Since Phylloxera has now spread nearly worldwide, grape growers everywhere plant native American rootstock in their vineyards. They will then graft traditional Vinifera vines onto these roots so they can grow unaffected.

[2] The process involves cross-pollinating different varieties and species, then selecting genetic offspring that express the most advantageous traits of the parent plants. This type of work with plant hybrids was happening on an informal basis some 40 years before Gregor Mendel used pea plants in his famous research on the same subject.

[3] Manischewitz, the famous kosher wine, is perhaps the most prominent use of the concord grape in wine today.

[4] This can also be explained by the fact that wine drinking wasn't altogether popular before Prohibition, and during which, it was a lower priority for law enforcement efforts than beer and liquor. Still, in the years leading up to 1922, wine was a drink tolerated by the temperance movement. Many anti-alcohol Dries adopted the French attitude that wine is a drink of moderation, and represented an agreeable alternative to the lascivious saloon culture fed by an overindulgence of whiskey and brandy.

[5] A prominent Jeffersonian Democrat, he was appointed to the position by President Pierce without having to give up his stake in a precious metals refining company that, unsurprisingly, received contract work from the small new mint after his appointment. A grand jury investigation was centered on Haraszthy's personal wealth and what the State's Attorney thought was a discrepancy between the amount of gold dust being delivered and the value of currency actually minted in coin. He mortgaged nearly all of his assets to pay for his defense, and though he was acquitted, his reputation and finances never quite recovered.

[6] Most likely, anyway. There were no eyewitnesses, and his mule was found near a crocodile-infested stream. No body was recovered.

Author's Recommendations for Good Midwestern Wine

The amount of great LaCrescent wine seems to multiply every year. I particularly enjoy the **Saint Croix Vineyards LaCrescent** from Stillwater. The winery is co-owned by Peter Hemstad, the grape scientist at the U of M that originally engineered the grape. Frontenac Gris is also coming on strong, and there may be none more delicious and unique than **Parley Lake Winery's Parley Vu Rosé** from Waconia. They steep the skins of the white grape in its juice to make a refreshing, orange-tinted wine that's one of the best cold climate rosés I've ever tasted. For reds, track down the **Indian Island Marquette** from Janesville, Minnesota — a velvety, young wine that invites comparison to Merlot. Most cold climate wineries still bring in juice from the coasts, and one of the best of those wines is **Wollersheim Winery's Prairie Fumé,** a refreshing Sauvignon Blanc-like sip made from Seyval Blanc grapes from Upstate New York.

CHAPTER 13
THE SENSES ON CENTRAL

WRITER: PETER HAJINIAN :: **CARTOGRAPHER:** MATT DOOLEY :: **ICONS:** ANNE ULKU

When you ask someone how a restaurant was, they'll usually tell you what they ordered, whether it was good or not, how the service was, and then give a random jumble of details that they found important while there: the decor was nice, there was easy parking, it was quaint, they played crappy '80s metal. A restaurant is a sum of its parts: the building, the tables, the service, the food, the atmosphere. All of these things work together to affect our mood, the way a rocking burger joint can be energizing and satisfying, or going to an empty bar early in the day feels like a theater with all the lights on, contemplative (and depressing).

Central Avenue is the main artery in my neighborhood in Northeast Minneapolis. From south to north, it's studded with a galaxy of restaurants and groceries. The reasons I walk into them vary. Sometimes a sign intrigues me, or I need a quick bite. Sometimes I've got some time to kill before going out, and sometimes I need a place to sit and think some stuff through. And in a place like Central Avenue, sometimes I just want to find a little bit of the extraordinary in the ordinary. To feel adventurous close to home. Each one of these reasons led me into a different restaurant in my neighborhood. Let me tell you what happened.

 • Chimborazo

17th Ave NE

East Side Coop

• Central Liquors • • Holy Land

Sen Yai Sen Lek • Sabor Latino

Lowry • Subway

• Durango Bakery • Karta Thai

Taco Riendo • • Adelitas

• Crescent Moon

• La Colonia

Bombay • • Rzaaq

Maya • • Patel's

Diamonds •

Central

0   ½ Mile

Ideal Diner •

• 612 Brew

AFGHANISTAN

COLOMBIA

EAST AFRICA

ECUADOR

INDIA

MEXICO

MIDDLE EAST

THAILAND

USA

DIAMONDS COFFEE SHOPPE

Some places are good places to eavesdrop. I had an hour to kill before a party, so I went to see what people were saying at Diamonds Coffee Shoppe.

The cafe is a maze of rooms, each leading deeper and deeper into the large white building. To the right of the entrance is a bright yellow room populated by a few small tables, and plenty of potted plants; it has the comfortable room tone of a living room. A good place to take a quiet date. Or to set up shop and study while scowling at everyone who peers inside. Back the other way is the main chamber and kitchen. The blare of rock-n-roll and the whine of a coffee grinder bounce off the walls and high ceiling, giving the room a cavernous feel. The art is eclectic: part atomic age, part motorcycle, part sci-fi. The food is portable. I think that's to encourage picnics and forays into the deeper tunnels. So I order a sandwich and a coffee, and continue on like a caffeinated spelunker.

Just off the main chamber is a corner of plush chairs. A college dorm in a cave. For all the social noise coming from the main cavern, it's cozy and relatively quiet here. I move on to the next chamber. The walls are coolly painted brick, the ceiling dim, the lighting pale or white. It should be an echo chamber, but instead it inspires the lush hush of a library, making the six small tables arranged along the walls feel like the kind of places at which you could get some real work done. Which is what you want out of a coffee shop. Unless you're looking to relax or talk or eavesdrop, which you could do here, but there are definitely better chambers of this maze for that.

Like the next one, which is the largest and serves as an annex for the rest of the building. Around the room are wooden doors with small business cards announcing which artist, which nonprofit, which startup wants to make sure you don't block their entrance with your chair. This is the space that's best for group meet ups or working sessions. For conversations at normal voice levels. When I get there, a group was finishing up a meeting, and a young couple who weren't a part of the meeting sat at a table across the way. I take an empty spot on the far side, eat my sandwich and listen.

Too far away to hear what the group on the couches are talking about, I focus on the young couple. She's wearing a pink tank top and jeans. He's wearing a baseball cap and a Harley-Davidson pull over hoodie that is way too big for him. She talks about tattoos and getting caught driving without insurance. As she talks, he throws on a pair of expensive-looking reading glasses and studies his smart phone. There are plastic bags of clothes, and a takeout coffee cup not from this establishment.

As I finish my sandwich and start on the coffee, she goes into the bathroom and returns dressed in business attire. The thought pops in my head that they're on the lam. Or a couple of scam artists. This is their staging area. But that's as far as I get. I can't think of a good scam for them to be pulling, so the fantasy dies. I finish the coffee as I make my way back through the chambers and galleries back to the front entrance and its natural light. Then it was out onto the street to walk off the buzz.

CHIMBORAZO

There's something exotic about going to a restaurant in another city, another country. And then there's something exotic about trying a place in your neighborhood that you see all the time but never venture into. Like finally reading that book you've been shuttling around to various apartments and houses for years.

And so for lunch I walk into Chimborazo. I'd heard the owner was Ecuadorian, and which gave a little context to the pipe flute music and pictures of the Andes mountains on the walls. I sit at a table in the dimly lit restaurant, pick up a menu, and order.

"What's good here?" I ask the waitress.

"You been here before?"

"Nope."

"I'd recommend the llapingachos. They're awesome."

The menu describes llapingachos as a potato pancake. The dish comes with rice, chorizo, fried egg and peanut sauce. What's not to like about that? I sip my Inca Kola, which alternates between tasting like pineapple and bubble gum, and place my order.

The rice reminds me of a trip I took to Ecuador years before to visit an exchange student from my high school. Between the sounds of South American rock and the breathtaking views of Incan ruins, I remembered the effervescence of the food. The rice, yes, but also the way they'd put sliced cucumber in the water jugs, the way they'd lightly sauté flowers as a side dish. Things that played to the airy part of the palate. The chorizo and fried egg bring me back to earth. Salty, hearty, and with just enough spice. I mix in the peanut sauce, and my mind went back to Ecuador again. I thought about bombing down the highway over the paved mountain passes that cut through the Andes, stopping for lunch in a small town and eating the kind of food people find at food trucks these days.

And then I eat the llapingacho. True, they were a potato pancake, slightly smaller in circumference than the fried egg. But the menu didn't mention they were stuffed with cheese and incredible. If the Earth was ever under attack from an alien species that had any taste buds or appreciation for chemical change that comes over someone when they eat something amazing, then surely the llapingacho will be our salvation.

The first one I eat by itself. The second I cover in peanut sauce, and that was like being in a cover band, and playing your favorite song from your favorite band, and having people come up to you afterward and tell you they prefer your version. The third one (they give you three!) I break apart into three bites. The first bite I take with a bit of egg and chorizo, and it rivals the best breakfast I've eaten at any greasy spoon diner. The second I eat with the rice and peanut sauce and feel like an Incan warrior. The third one I eat by itself. It could be its own meal.

And that was it. The meal was over. I was full. My taste buds had travelled to South America and back for an hour. I paid the check and walked home full and carrying a deep feeling of satisfaction.

AL RAZAAQ RESTAURANT

The sign intrigues me. It says "RAZAAQ EASTERN AFRICAN CUISINE" and has a tagine on it. It used to be a Moroccan restaurant, and I wonder if the tagine is left over from that. Next to the faux wood roof, the sign hangs over a mural of a courtyard somewhere in Saharan or Sub-Saharan Africa. Between the street and the dark front entrance is a small gated courtyard, and because the restaurant is set back from the street, it appears possibly closed. But the sign reads OPEN.

It's dark inside, the shades drawn to block out the evening sun. Tables are roughly arranged in rows, and stretching out in front of me is pale tile leading to a display case that's nearly empty and obviously barely used in the first place. At the small counter, a woman in a deep purple abaya takes my order. I don't feel hungry enough for some of the more involved dishes in the menu, so I order a couple of samosas, pay, find an empty table and wait.

Sporting Chinese characters and ink paintings of birds and fish, the tables are obviously left over from a Chinese restaurant. Fake flowers with their hot glue water droplets stand proudly in narrow vases, serving as centerpieces. There's a TV, but it's not on. The tan walls are covered with pictures of Al Aqsa mosque, the Kaaba, Hagia Sophia, and posters touting your chance to rent out the restaurant for your next banquet.

Imagine what it could be like inside, with people, with a party, with a banquet. The tables cleared off one side, the curtains completely drawn and special party lights setting the mood. Even though it'd be dim, everyone would be dressed in their best, so when the laser lights passed over them on the dance floor they'd look glamorous.

My samosa is crispy and buttery and packed with piping ground beef and onions, and comes with hot sauce and yogurt dip. As the heat dissipates and the spice fills my head, I went back to the party. I imagine the space would be perfect for a smoke machine, a mirrorball, and a DJ who knows how to get people on their feet. The buffet or dessert table would be on the opposite side of the room, stuffed with the kind of food that makes you want to walk up and down it once just to look and see what's there so you can plan the best way to fill your plate.

Outside, a pair of old ladies stop me.

"We saw you coming out of there, and we've never seen anyone come out of that restaurant," they sat. "What's it like?"

I tell them, but I leave out the party part. Unprompted, they told me their own visions of what could be there. "It should be a gelato shop, with tables out front! And a guy playing a concertina!"

I nod and eat my second samosa.

"That smells good," one of them says. "I think I'll try it. Do you know their hours?"

I look back at the building. Next to the OPEN sign, clearly marked, are the hours.

"Nine AM to nine PM, it says."

MAYA CUISINE

When I open the glass front door of Maya, I have the need to get to the bottom of something. And as soon as I step in off the street I forget what that something was. The walls are painted bright yellow, red, green. The ceiling high, lights and fans adding to the light drifting in from the windows along the front. But the real attraction is the heart of the restaurant. Like a museum piece, a long tiled roof hangs over the long counter. A woman waits to take my order at one end, and a woman waits to take my money at the other. Between them a glass sneeze guard stands over an array of sides and garnishes. Behind the counter I can see into the kitchen, the smell of grill and fryer making its way out. It was immediately relaxing. I could have been peering into the kitchen of someone's home. Someone's home built in the middle of an industrial space just off Central Avenue.

I order, then make my way down the counter, pointing out toppings: cebollas, cheese, some of that, a pinch of the cilantro, yes salsa please, medium, no wait pico de gallo. How much? OK, here you go. Thanks. Could I get a soda, too? Coke. In the bottle. Thanks.

It's a Tuesday night, and the restaurant isn't busy. I have my pick of the wooden booths in back. When a place is quiet like this, I like to take a booth for myself. Spread my meal out on the smooth table, pinch a couple of silky paper napkins out of the holder, then sit and soak in the atmosphere. At the far end of the restaurant, a music channel plays on a TV. From the kitchen come sounds of spatulas on metal. A few empty tables over, a man speaks languidly into a cellphone, his mouth half full of rice and beans.

There is space there. To spread out on the table of a booth. Or stretch your legs under one of the four tops, six tops, or under the bar out front where you can sit and look out the windows at the traffic on Central. The kind of space where people leave you alone to enjoy your meal. Space to disappear in public. Space to think. Space to read. Space to take as little or as much time as you'd like. Space to drink Coca-Cola from a glass bottle and to eat a couple of ground beef tacos. And on any given Tuesday night, after a long day, who couldn't use that kind of space?

DURANGO BAKERY

Bakeries are a bit like flowershops. They're both places you visit right before you're off somewhere to celebrate. They're emporiums of celebrations. But I'm not here to celebrate, I'm here to eat something, and I don't want tacos or Thai. Right after Sen Yai Sen Lek, just before the Taco Riendo awning, is the portal to Durango Bakery. Compared to the size of the building and the restaurants on either side, it's not much when you walk in for a quick bite. A couple of coolers and slanted shelving stuffed full of all kinds of baked goods, and a nothing-fancy coffee pot in the corner.

But what it lacks in visual appeal, it makes up for with aromas. Yeast. Sugar. Coffee. It reminds me of grandma's kitchen. A place where your nose is too big for your stomach. They might just be a couple of coolers, but every tray has some sort of baked delight that's been twisted, puffed, folded over, filled, stuffed, deep-fried, or sprinkled with sugar. And then there're the cookies.

The only thing I can smell is sweet. I use the tongs and grab an apple turnover, an elephant ear, a heart-shaped baked goodie with cream and raisins, and a croissant because it looks too good to leave alone and my bag feels too light. I want to eat them all, but I know I can't do it. A woman comes out of the back and a blast of freshly baked bread enters the small room. If they ever get a handle on smell-o-vision technology they should set every movie in a bread factory or a bakery like Durango. It'd be amazing.

My bag of goodies costs me under four dollars, which makes sense but also seems like a crime. How could something that smelled this good cost so little? Outside on the curb, I bite into the turnover. Again, how could something that tastes this good cost so little?

I eat the turnover and keep walking. When I finish that I eat the croissant and plot a return the next morning to get it even fresher, and have a cup of coffee, too. It must have been a revelation, the first time humans baked bread. They smelled it and thought: "What is this?", and then immediately knew where they'd be returning to. They say city-states rose up in our distant past as places to store and protect grain harvested from the fields. As I finished the croissant and toyed with tasting the elephant ear, I wondered if it had just as much to do with what was coming out of the ovens.

CHAPTER 14

ROAD TRIP EATING BETWEEN THE CAPITALS

WRITER: JOHN GARLAND :: **CARTOGRAPHER:** NAT CASE

I don't take road trips like they used to. Who *they* are I can't exactly say, but I've heard a great deal about them. They used to call sightseeing its own reward. They used the suffix "cents per gallon." They didn't endure travel, they enjoyed it. Now, long jaunts down the highway are reserved for some unfortunate practical purpose. You *have* to drop your undergrad at school. You *have* to visit the relatives from *that* side of the family.

But if being on the highway is a punishment, you can still suffer through it the right way. Instead of being defeated by the drive, redeem it with a good meal. Navigating between the North Coast capitals, you'll be surrounded by its agricultural bounty for hours on end. You'll spend the better part of your day staring at vast tracts of food. So why not plan for a few extra minutes of drive time to taste some of the region's finest?

This food will not be advertised on the blue signs that point to the exit ramp. The interstates aren't concerned with your comfort and none of the worthwhile food is convenient to the highway. You won't find Pierre's Organic Farm-To-Table Bistro at the bottom of the ramp next to the BP and the Pizza Ranch.

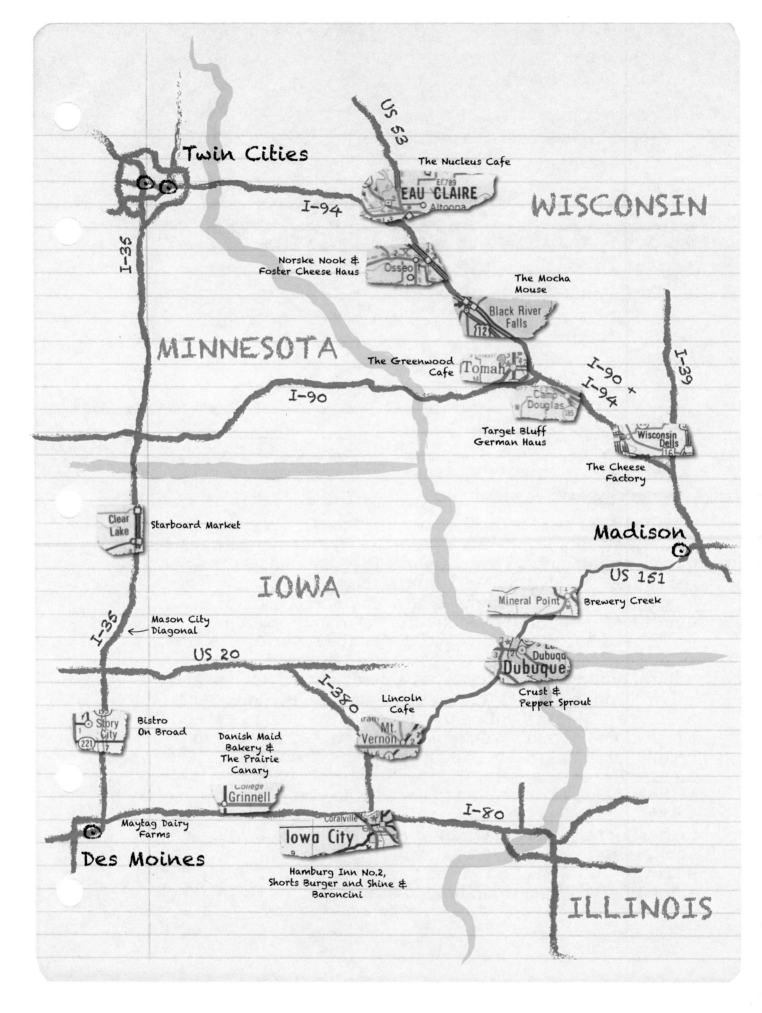

Twin Cities

The Nucleus Cafe

EAU CLAIRE

WISCONSIN

I-94

US 53

Norske Nook &
Foster Cheese Haus

Osseo

The Mocha
Mouse

Black River
Falls

MINNESOTA

The Greenwood
Cafe

Tomah

Camp
Douglas

I-90 +
I-94

I-90

I-39

Target Bluff
German Haus

Wisconsin
Dells

The Cheese
Factory

I-35

Madison

Clear
Lake

Starboard Market

US 151

IOWA

Mineral Point

Brewery Creek

Mason City
Diagonal

I-35

US 20

Dubuque

Dubuque

I-380

Lincoln
Cafe

Crust &
Pepper Sprout

Bistro
On Broad

Story
City

Mt.
Vernon

Danish Maid
Bakery &
The Prairie
Canary

Grinnell

Coralville

I-80

Maytag Dairy
Farms

Iowa City

Des Moines

Hamburg Inn No.2,
Shorts Burger and Shine &
Baroncini

ILLINOIS

Instead, it's found farther into the towns you might pass without a second thought, beyond the motels and fireworks stores, where the cornfields give way to little league ball fields in places where the main street is called Main Street. There, you'll find a killer deli, a quaint cafe or a winery with a pizza oven.

Not only will you find good food, you'll be smitten with small towns that beg you to walk around for an hour. The essence of the great American road trip was discovering the hidden gems buried in your own backyard. So don't settle for Butter Burgers and Blizzards when you can search out cheese curds among the bluffs of Southern Wisconsin. Don't pass up a hunt for old-fashioned doughnuts in Iowa. In short, don't get drawn in by the golden arches. The next time you're on the road, let the region's unique sights and bites lead the way.

SAINT PAUL TO DES MOINES

Interstate Highway 35 is a long, straight path that motors through cornfields with a sense of expediency. It's also a food desert, brushing up against few towns, leaving limited options for a decent meal. So get breakfast before you leave the Cities because things get rural in a hurry once you're southbound. The first truck stop is at exit #69, which leads to Northfield. Crops already enclose the road at mile #66.

Road trippers would be wise to write off the Southern Minnesota stretch of I-35 altogether. You won't get hungry in the one hour it takes to approach Owatonna. The same is true for Faribault, a town that Highway 35 used to go straight through before the new interstate was built to bypass it. Hold your hunger until exit #194, an intersection that exemplifies the road tripper's dilemma.

That's the exit to Clear Lake, Iowa which greets travelers with an onslaught of fast food only a few blocks from the exit ramp. There's a Culver's, McDonald's, Arby's, Pizza Hut, Subway, Taco Bell, KFC, Dairy Queen and Wendy's (*note: woefully incomplete list, edited for brevity*). Their multitude suggests that you are in the middle of nowhere and you have no other options. *I am the great and powerful rest-stop. Pay no attention to the city behind the curtain.*

But not a single mile farther from the highway, you'll find a tranquil town nestled on the northeast shore of Clear Lake. The streets are lined with two story buildings with brick facades. City folk will appreciate the abundance of parking. Since it wouldn't be a road trip without seeing a dubious piece of Americana, check out the Surf Ballroom — the last venue played by Buddy Holly, Ritchie Valens and the "Big Bopper" J.P. Richardson on February 2nd, 1959, the night before The Day the Music Died.

You'll find the Starboard Market on Main Street. It's the kind of sandwich shop you wish was always around the corner and nearly a dead ringer for Nelson's Cheese & Deli in St. Paul. Among their mayo-based pasta salads (requisites for any Iowa deli) get the one with big chunks of cornbread in a creamy sage dressing. If you want to make it a picnic, grab a bottle at Back Alley Wine behind the market. Across the street is the Cabin Coffee Company, a homespun Caribou clone that's a great choice for java and a scone.

August is the best month to drive through Iowa, during its agricultural apex when the corn is just reaching elephant eye-level. It's when the state seems to have been painted with an inexhaustible palette of green — dark hunter green in clumps of forest between the fields, the striking emerald of the corn stalks, the dark shamrock in the soybeans and rough artichoke-tinted grasses in the culverts and ditches.

The road strikes an angle through Wright and Franklin counties, a section sometimes referred to as the Mason City Diagonal. I-35 was supposed to run straight north from Des Moines until business leaders in Mason City lobbied that it be moved closer to their town. Farmers rebelled, claiming their fields would be less productive if carved into triangular plots. After a drawn out period of litigation, the final piece of I-35 in Iowa, now about ten miles closer to Mason City, opened in 1975.

Just south of the diagonal is Story City. Its main drag is Broad Street, so named as if it was measured to allow a team of pack animals towing a wagon enough room for a U-turn. The Bistro On Broad looks as if someone put a handful of tables in his living room and called it a restaurant. The kitchen looks like your kitchen, maybe even less equipped. It's decorated with a mashup of small town Iowa and French art nouveau. Regulars gather, drinking coffee, nibbling on pie. The sandwiches are simple and satisfying.

The last town of note before Des Moines is Ames. But just as Owatonna is too close the Twin Cities, there are too many worthy places in Des Moines to waste stomach space in Ames. It's easy to get hypnotized by this stretch of road. With seemingly nowhere to eat, you can breeze by the mammoth wind turbines, get lulled by the Zen-like precision of row crops, and find that a few hours have passed. Keep your eyes open. There are better eats down the road.

DES MOINES TO MADISON

On my last road trip through Iowa, I ran into a friend I hadn't seen in years. We had reservations for the same time, at the cafe in her hometown that I'd never visited before. She was with her husband and I asked him about moving to the town. "Back home, and in Boston, you can barely see past the next building over," he said. "I never realized how big the sky is until I came to Iowa."

Iowa is like that — blue sky and utilized earth and not much in between them to complicate matters. The fertile expanse between the nation's two greatest rivers produces more corn, soybeans and pork than any other state. So before leaving the Des Moines area, indulge in one of the state's finest farm products. Make a quick stop in Newton to sample cheese at the Maytag Dairy Farms and buy a slab of the famous blue cheese to slice thin on your next sirloin.

Twenty miles east on I-80 is Grinnell (exit #182), home to the renowned college of the same name. Get a cream-filled coney and perhaps another one or three doughnuts from the Danish Maid Bakery and your morning coffee around the corner at the Saints Rest Coffee House. Then walk a few blocks to campus and have a relaxing breakfast lying out on MacEachron Field.

If you'll be anywhere near Grinnell during lunch or dinner, be sure to plan an hour for a meal at the Prairie Canary. Chef Carly Groben's sleek, airy space has a basement bar and a menu full of refined Midwestern fare. The grilled salmon on toasted challah is a damn near perfect sandwich, between the moist fish, crunchy pickled onions, and tangy dill-goat cheese spread.

One third of the way to Madison is Iowa City (exit #244), home to the largest variety of good restaurants in the state. For breakfast, take a pilgrimage to the Hamburg Inn No. 2, a classic greasy-spoon that's become a legendary campaign stop during the Iowa caucuses. For lunch, burrow into the slender tunnel that is Short's Burger & Shine; the burgers are made from local beef and only Iowa craft beer is on tap. Go upscale for dinner — Linn Street Cafe for their pork, One Twenty Six for Midwest-meets-Mediterranean, or full-on Italian classics at Baroncini.

From there you'll need to find US-151 to get to Madison. You could take I-380 north and veer east near Cedar Rapids. Instead, take IA-1 north from Iowa City. It's a winding, wooded path with access to the Lake McBride recreation area, a nice place to stop and relax along the reservoir. It will also deliver you straight into Mt. Vernon for a stunning meal at the Lincoln Cafe. It's a revelatory find in such a small, out-of-the-way town. This homey diner has all the elegance and polish of a spendy trattoria. Get one of the three daily specials. On my last visit, I inhaled a bowl of spicy mussels and a divine fried quail with polenta and a jalapeno succotash. They also serve wood-fired pizza at their wine bar on the corner if you forgot to call ahead for reservations.

For a quick dose of Iowa lore before arriving in Dubuque, take IA-136 north from Cascade to visit the Field of Dreams outside of Dyersville. The diamond and the farmhouse still look as they did in the 1989 film. In the height of summer, the corn in the outfield will be tall enough that you can envision James Earl Jones and the 1919 Chicago White Sox disappearing into the unknown.

From there it's an easy half hour along US-20 to Dubuque. The city is set into the bluffs that line the Mississippi River and there's a funicular on 4th street with views of the three-state convergence at the top. On Main Street, you can take a snack break with a small pizza and glass of wine at Crust, a casual Italian kitchen. If you're in the mood for a more upscale dinner, there's Pepper Sprout down the street. They get plaudits for their bison among an enticing menu heavy on fish and game.

The river here is already significantly wider than it is in the Twin Cities. Enjoy the view from US-151 as you make your way into Wisconsin, and stop in Mineral Point for a cheese fix before you get to Madison. It's home to Hook's Cheese Company, makers of some of the world's best aged cheddar and a damn fine sharp blue cheese as well. The 12- and 15-year-old cheddar is not to be missed. Just a few blocks from their factory is the Brewery Creek Inn. On the ground level, their brewery is a comfortable den with sessionable beers made in Old World styles. Relax with a Vienna-weisse and some cheese curds, or the beer cheese spread made with Hook's sharp cheddar.

MADISON TO SAINT PAUL

After you've crossed the Mississippi and entered Wisconsin from Iowa, there's no gradual change in the landscape. The state announces its presence immediately with fields of grazing dairy cattle, highways hewn into the bluffs, and billboards for restaurants that end with "haus".

The cows and German-themed attractions continue on the road between Madison and Minneapolis-St. Paul. But there's not as much wide-open cropland on this leg of the journey and no sense of the dramatic topography nearer to the Mississippi, with the exception of the craggy Target Bluff. Instead, you'll weave through forests on your way back to the Twin Cities.

If you leave from Madison in the morning, you're probably not going to stop as early as Wisconsin Dells (and if you're actively trying to go to the Dells, well then God help you). The Cheese Factory had been our go-to in the city, until they closed in September 2013. They're working on plans to reopen somewhere else. For now, add one more to the myriad reasons to pass up the city altogether.

Instead, you can indulge in one of two quirky small town sights. Precisely in the middle of the drive from Minneapolis to Chicago is the Target Bluff German Haus, just off the highway outside of Camp Douglas, exit #55. It's a German beer hall that hits all the right campy Wisconsin notes. Get a Reuben and feel free to have a light macro beer at 11am because the guy who's playing horseshoes near his RV outside will be getting a round for his buddies. Never mind that it's Tuesday.

The other is in Tomah, in the tines of the fork where Interstates 90 and 94 diverge. In general, though I don't have multiple experiences to back this up, eating breakfast beneath a moose skull should be a lot weirder than it is at the Greenwood Cafe. The place is stuffed to the rafters with taxidermy. There are ducks over the doorway and two young bears guard each end of the dining room. A stately jackrabbit keeps his chin up over the kitchen window while a nearby ocelot looks ready to pounce. But there's nothing creepy about the stick-to-your-ribs breakfast you'll be in for: their biscuits and gravy are all the rustic deliciousness they should be.

After Tomah, you may start getting anxious for the Twin Cities. But maybe you forgot to pick up a gift from your travels, or maybe your friends have requested a mixed case of New

Glarus. You can get all that done at the Mocha Mouse, exit #116 to Black River Falls. It's right off the exit and not well advertised (the signs 500 feet from the building don't even point to its existence). They sell all kinds of Wisconsin wines and microbrews, along with cheese, jellies, salsas, and other canned goods from the area. Perhaps best of all: $2.50 pints of Spotted Cow.

Or you could bring back a pie from the famous Norske Nook off exit #88 in Osseo. Though it's worth noting that a lot of partisans claim a severe drop off in the quality of their food as of late, I continue to vouch for the pies. And you can't leave Wisconsin without cheese. Of all the cheese shops you'll see advertised between Madison and St. Paul, I'm partial to the immense selection at Foster Cheese Haus, farther up from the main part of Osseo, off exit #81.

Eau Claire is too close to St. Paul to stop on the way home. If you're on your way to, say, Milwaukee and you want to get an early hour and a half on the road before stopping, reward yourself with the lemon ricotta pancakes served on weekends at the Nucleus Cafe. If it's a weekday, opt for the delectable savory crepes.

All these suggestions are worthy pit stops, but it's by no means an authoritative list. That's the great thing about road trips. You could drive this triangle, stop in a dozen towns I didn't mention and return with an equally compelling list of bakeries, diners and supper clubs. So take that exit you've always driven by, explore that town you only know by name, and find something new to eat. And as you head back to the highway, take a good look at all the cars lining up for the clown, the king and the colonel, and be proud you're not one of them.

CHAPTER 15

PICNICKING ACROSS WISCONSIN

WRITER/ILLUSTRATOR: SEAN WEITNER AND THE WEITNER FAMILY

Cartoon maps of U.S. states blossomed in the 1930s — an era of economic distress where leisure time could be rescued in part by a burgeoning car culture, and recirculating dollars into the tourist economy was a painless way to do one's part. With car vacations peaking in popularity again, we offer this scribbler's-eye view of roadside Wisconsin, combined with an eating tour: the best kind of vacation meals — picnics — at their ideal locations — state parks.

1. DEVIL'S LAKE STATE PARK | Sauk County

In the same way that Devil's Lake, the most visited and most profitable state park in the system, ticks every box on the wishlist — a crystal lake with sand beach, excellent hiking through forests and along bluffs, broad lawns, and a central location — Baraboo's Vintage Port (3 miles from park entrance) turns out to be an exemplar of one-stop picnickery. It has a broad menu of salads and hot and cold sandwiches, a deli case of Carr Valley cheeses and freshly prepared sides including hummus and salsa, and a coffee shop serving Milwaukee's Colectivo (formerly Alterra) plus a refrigerator case of standbys like Limonata and Honest Tea.

The Pig & Goat ($8, with chips and salsa) has cherrywood smoked ham from Fort Atkinson's Jones Dairy Farm, apple and tomato slices, and one layer of goat cheese and another of cherry vinaigrette. It's meant as a panini, though for takeout purposes we took it cold, and it was wonderful — the only asymmetrical advantage of the panini version is that the crustless soft roll would gain some character for being grilled. (Even the kids' meal sandwiches featured Jones ham carved off the bone.) An even better benchmark of sound kitchen philosophy is their potato salad, with an abundance of dill and a scarcity of mayo — that is, the exact opposite of the norm.

2. PENINSULA STATE PARK | Door County

This jewel is as grand as any Wisconsin park in its beauty and cornucopia of trails and sights, but it is not well served by picnic purveyors. In the summertime, Door County is bumper-to-bumper with visitors to its tiny towns, and those towns are in turn chockablock with places who'd be happy to provide you with table service. If you're not after whitefish Oscar, however, you'll be up a creek without a picnic — Fish Creek, to be specific. It's the town nearest the park, and we only found some undistinguished deli fare. (Or, worse, badly distinguished — one otherwise commendable toasted sandwich was capsized by a tidal wave of mayonnaise).

If you're headed to Peninsula, then, your best bets are the markets. On the west side of the peninsula, try Wood Orchard Market in Egg Harbor (6 miles from park entrance); on the east side, Koepsel's Farm Market in Baileys Harbor (7 miles). Forget about trying to cobble together an entree; just go for chips with homemade cherry or corn salsa (Wood Orchard), or pretzels with your choice of a dozen mustards (Koepsel's). Both have cheeses, jams, jellies, fruit butters, and cherry everything. Wood Orchard has a large selection of pies; Koepsel's, local beer by the bottle ("local" here includes the Upper Peninsula). Koepsel's has a meat counter, but if you're not going to be grilling, then smoked fish is your only option. Our one unforgettable purchase was a quart of tiny yellow plums, though of course availability changes with the season.

3. GOVERNOR DODGE STATE PARK AND TOWER HILL STATE PARK | Iowa County

These parks lie a dozen miles apart on Highway 23, accompanied by two towns that are worth your time. On the Spring Green side, Tower Hill is mostly a campground, but nearby attractions include Frank Lloyd Wright's Taliesin, American Players Theater, and The House on the Rock; on the Dodgeville side, Governor Dodge is in the running for the greatest playground in the park system, not because of its swingsets but because of its size and the breadth of fun on offer.

On both ends of the highway, your best bet for a spur-of-the-moment meal is a specialty grocer on the edge of town. Schurman's Wisconsin Cheese Country (3 miles from Governor Dodge) is the retail front-end of a long-lived dairy, and while their selection leaves something to be desired for both cured meats (mostly a selection of landjäger) and crackers (good but few choices), the cheese is an excellent anchor for a picnic platter. We couldn't resist the smoked Cheddar, which gustatorially fulfilled both the role of meat and cheese in our micro-sandwiches, and Schurman's may also be the place nearest any

Wisconsin state park to get fresh, incredibly squeaky salt-bomb cheese curds (fresh on Mondays and Fridays). Schurman's sells others' cheese as well, plus pints of Chocolate Shoppe ice cream (a Madison-based purveyor that crops up all over Wisconsin, we're happy to note).

By contrast, Spring Green's Driftless Depot (3 miles from Tower Hill) is both hoity and toity; instead of well-sourced ice cream, homemade gelato. You could stock a heckuva pantry shopping here, and while their somewhat limited produce selection won't do much for your crisper, your cheese drawer will be happy. (One provision they have in common with Schurman's: Pleasant Ridge Reserve, an Alpine-inspired farmstead cheese that is one of the state's best loved, amid a pack crowded with popular options.) Driftless Depot also has a cafe, with plenty of sandwich options: the egg salad got the seasonings just right, and the signature smoked trout with cream cheese on pillowy stirato was a scarfable delight, hors d'oeuvres flavor at entree proportions. Paired with an exceptional selection of drinks — Blue Sky, DRY Soda, and even Q beverages (NYC imports which include a wonderful tonic) — the Depot vies with Schurman's in a culinary personality test with no wrong answers.

Also of note: The Kitchen at Arcadia Books in Spring Green primarily stocks a refrigerator case with sandwiches and small plates, and while you never know what you're going to find if you stop in, it's intended for grab-it-and-go customers — culminating in pre-boxed picnic lunches, although for these your best bet is definitely to call 48 hours ahead. And Quality Bakery in Dodgeville makes a pasty with as delectable a crust as any we've found, with other wares that will leave no sweet tooth wanting.

4. HIGH CLIFF STATE PARK | Calumet County

High Cliff State Park on Lake Winnebago serves as the collective backyard for the Fox Valley area, and there are many points of entry. If you're coming from the south, Mud Creek Coffee in Stockbridge (11 miles from park entrance) has the kind of sandwich menu you'd expect from a coffee shop. The turkey crunch wrap ($8.50) sidesteps the bland-sandwich-fixin's-in-a-bland-tortilla snare; the meat and spinach get familiar bonuses of red onion and bell pepper, but craisins and vinaigrette give the whole thing sweet and tangy life, and sunflower seeds are a greater textural blessing that you'd expect. The service was slow, but the shop was also remarkably busy with dine-in customers when we visited; their drive-in window may not be wise if you're putting in a food order.

If you're coming from the north, Kaukauna Coffee & Tea (10 miles from park entrance) has a bowl-you-over chicken salad sandwich on focaccia. There was relish to be had in every bite, and not just because they've learned the apparently uncommon lesson of how well complemented the dish is with pickle. The menu is, again, just about what you'd expect — the most left-of-field option is a grilled gouda asparagus sandwich — but a picnic basket can happily be filled here.

5. RIB MOUNTAIN STATE PARK | Marathon County

Those who know Wausau wouldn't consider it much of a metroplex, but it has dozens if not hundreds of dining options. Evaluating which picnic meal to take to Rib Mountain State Park — a ski hotspot in the winter and Wisconsin's highest point (1,940 ft.) year-round — becomes a question not of which one restaurant is good and right, but which one is pretty good and right around the corner. In this case, that's Becca's, two miles from the base of the summit on Rib Mountain Road, tucked into a reef of strip malls. It's a quick casual joint with clear inspirations in the world of chain restaurants (one that rhymes with "shmanera" in particular), and if you eat enough of the menu you might happen upon something truly exceptional, but their role is nearer to "curator of recipes" than "chef."

Still, it's definitely good enough. Its version of a sturdy staple like tuna salad ($7) impresses, and its execution of something oh-so-slightly offbeat like a sweet chili shrimp wrap ($7.50) is exactly what you'd expect, the sum of some fresh parts and also flyover-country shrimp. Consider their summer salad: watermelon, feta, mint leaves and a touch of honey ($2.50, less as a side). It's a familiar recipe that's hard to screw up, and, lo, Becca's version was a nice refreshment on a summer day. Furthermore, their entrees kept very well in an insulated case with some ice, should you plan to hike between arriving at the park and dining. It's not a foodie destination, but it is a savvy choice for a no-fuss picnic.

6. BIG BAY STATE PARK | *Ashland County*

The charmingly named "sand spit" at Big Bay State Park is the closest I have come in the Midwest to a Pacific Ocean beach experience, which, yes, means it was frigid and beset with black flies, although — advantage Midwest — there were no tar globules. But for that timeless combo of sandy shores and featureless horizons of still blue water, a visit to Madeline Island on Lake Superior is worth the ferry toll.

Picnickers best come prepared, though. There are plenty of places to eat on Madeline Island, including an outfit with a joint specialty in Hawaiian shave ice and waffles, but no one's got meal-caliber takeout in mind. Aside from locally sourced raw meat, the most intriguing provision I found at an island grocery was a $5 copy of *Fantastic Mr. Fox* on Blu-ray. Assuming that you have packed neither grilling equipment nor HDTVs for your picnic, then you should bring your kit onto the ferry.

This is tourist country, and you'll find a handful of cafes and delis in Bayfield, which is where the ferry launches, but we were most intrigued by Cafe Coco in Washburn (13 miles from the ferry), which is down the road a spell but en route for 99 percent of island visitors. I could try to couch this in leading statistics like the blueness of the voter rolls, but the short of it is that the Chequamegon Bay area is arguably even hippier than Madison. Thus Coco is one of the few venues in our survey to advertise copious gluten-free and vegan options, to the point where you look at the bakery case and wish more of the items were gluten-enslaved.

They'll make it to order or you can choose from an impressive array of cellophane-encased sandwiches. Our spanakopita ($7) was not the best I've had, but it was the best I've unwrapped — genuine spinach flavor and mild feta bite. Spelunk the menu and pack a basket of these sandwiches; just pack some ice too, so it all survives the drive/ferry trip to the beach.

7. PATTISON STATE PARK | *Douglas County*

It's unlikely that you're going to be visiting Pattison, with its lovely swimming beach and Big Manitou Falls, without also availing yourself of the many eateries of Duluth, or at least Superior, where we chanced upon Rich Cuisine's Wednesday Bakery (13 miles from park entrance), a pop-up which only operates one day a week and served us a nice if thin-skinned savory pasty ($4) — just beef, carrots and potatoes with a side of gravy, agreeably spiced.

But for as-the-crow-flies delectations that aren't pub grub, your best bet is Superior Meats (9 miles from park entrance), which is nearer to the park by virtue of being in the village, not city, of Superior. For best results, consider this a B.Y.O.B. operation, where the last B stands for "briquettes" — they've got everything you'd want on your grill, specializing in many shop-made varieties of bratwurst. (Offbeat varieties such as apple, french onion and "Minnesota," which is blueberry wild rice, were no better or worse than they sound, though I'd opt for their everyday brat.) If you don't want that much production, however, the market provides top-notch housemade jerky ($19/lb.) and beef sticks in more varieties of each than you can count on one hand; the whiskey jerky is smoky sweet, and Ben's Jerky has an especially good handle on robust spiciness without oiliness.

The market is a full-fledged grocery offering the breadth of sandwiching supplies, although the lunchmeat comes from outside and they only sell the kinds of crackers that have 23 ingredients. (Not that the roast beef on offer isn't delicious on a Wheat Thins Little Italy Roasted Garlic toasted chip: "natural flavor with other natural flavor," the packaging boasts.) And the cheese and beer selection showed bountiful state pride, with more Wisconsin brews on offer than the drive-through liquor store up the road.

Of note: We kept our secret identities under our hats while shopping, but upon identifying ourselves as first-time visitors, we were given four free brats in exchange for our address, and my three kids each got a beef stick — an impressive stratum of service.

8. LAKE KEGONSA STATE PARK | Dane County

Downtown Stoughton (6 miles from park entrance) offers a couple of good options for a cold lunch — Main Street Kitchen is a fine sub shop of the checkbox variety, though your best bet is their deli salads or daily specials; Fosdal Home Bakery is strongly recommended for the creme de la cream-filled, and they also offer a small lunch menu. But let's break with the cold lunch tradition to recommend grabbing a slice ($3) or pie to go from Famous Yeti's Pizza on the north side of town (5 miles from park entrance). Stoughton shares a county with Madison, which is no slouch in the pizza market, but Famous Yeti's is neck-and-neck with the best Madison joints (that also serve the home delivery market; let's put the Neapolitan brick-fireds in their own category). There's palpable basil brightness in the sauce, the sausage is house-made, fresh mozzarella is available, and no crust will be left behind in either the thin (though not crisp) or hand-tossed pies ($8 to $14, plus toppings). Their stuffed pizzas may be too much of an undertaking for eating at a picnic table, and may likewise prove too much of a digestive undertaking for anyone who subsequently hopes to tromp around the lovely park, but the garlicky Yeti Spaghetti ($15 to $21) is a local legend, indeed stuffed with spaghetti noodles and tiny meatballs.

9. FLAMBEAU RIVER STATE FOREST | Sawyer County

Upon entering Flambeau River State Forest from the west, via the town of Winter, it seemed possible that the forest wouldn't make this map because Winter's pickings were too slim, offering at best gas stations and co-op grocers that sell cheeses and cured meats from Wisconsin purveyors. (See Roche-A-Cri, below.) Fortunately, on the east side of the forest is Phillips, which, though its population is only 1,500, has a downtown with a bakery and multiple meat markets. More unexpected still is Lola's Lunchbox, a food truck whose generator chugs along noisily in its corner of a gas station parking lot. Ahead of us in line was a mom making her second trip because her encampment sent her back for another "ques-egg-dilla," and it's easy to see why the cart could inspire such repeat business, especially among tent-dwellers who have perhaps been a little culinarily deprived: Lunchbox's game is excess. The loaded "smashies" — American potatoes, served with cheeses, chives, sour cream and the house pulled pork — were impeccable, with a crispy char on the potatoes that evinces masterful griddlemanship. The pork, sweet and flavorful and with rind somehow in every bite, is the foundation for many Lunchbox dishes; the cart's marquee item, the Stacker, pairs the pork with slow-cooked beef for a salty wallop. (I doubled down on the umami by having the Stacker served "melt-style" on just-crisp-enough Texas toast.) This is wonderful junk food made with quality (and reputedly locally sourced) ingredients. Don't go to Lola's Lunchbox if you have any particular plans to eat later in the day, and don't go on the weekend expecting it to be there — the cart's hours are oriented on weekday lunches and Tuesday to Thursday dinners.

10. GOVERNOR KNOWLES STATE FOREST | Burnett County

Anyone who's out looking for Wisconsin's state bird, the mosquito, or the state xenomorph, the wood tick, will be well pleased with the hiking trails at Governor Knowles State Forest. The picnic vendor of choice is the Burnett Dairy Co-op in Alpha, Wis. (9 miles from park entrance), locally famous for its cheeses and staffed by not one but two certified master cheesemakers including Bruce Willis (yes, that Bruce Willis - Bruce Willis the rural Wisconsin master cheesemaker). If you want a salumi-style meal, the co-op provideth, and likewise if you have a lakeside cabin, you can get locally sourced sausages and frozen pizzas. For prepared food, the co-op deli serves many stripes of grilled cheese: Try The Wisconsin, with turkey and Burnett's Morning Sun cheese (a blend of Cheddar and Gruyere) on slices from a cranberry loaf. Thanks will be indeed be given.

11. ROCHE-A-CRI STATE PARK | Adams County

We visited this state park, site of Wisconsin's most significant petroglyphs, at the wrong time — nothing was open in any of the surrounding small towns, except those kitchens that revolve around deep fat fryers. This reveals a special feature of Wisconsin relative to other states, however — there are even good eats at the gas stations. We stopped by the BP station (2 miles from park entrance) and found local wares including beer and wine, but most notably selections from Carr Valley Cheese and Wisconsin River Meats, two purveyors headquartered in Mauston, which is 30 miles south. In 75 percent of the nation's gas stations, if you wanted meat and cheese your best bet might be a Lunchable; here, you can get delectable goat cheese and smoked Swiss sausages.

12. BUCKHORN STATE PARK | Juneau County

We were tempted away from other (admittedly non-existent, especially on a Sunday) options on this central Wisconsin peninsula by Sunday pig roast ($15, all you can eat) at Buckhorn Cafe (1 mile from park entrance). The many implications of "temptation" all apply: The thing that tempted you is more or less worth it, but there are all of these consequences that sap the pleasure. The pig (also from Wisconsin River Meats) is as smoky and good as you please, and the draft beer selection suffices, but almost everything that came out of the kitchen was once frozen, from the agreeably revived signature pierogies to the incredibly inedible iceberg salad. (One exception is the gravy on the mashed potatoes, which tasted more out-of-a-packet than frozen.) So if your party is happy with only meat and beer, Sunday nights from May to September are a fine time to visit the adjacent Buckhorn State Park.

13. INTERSTATE STATE PARK | Polk County

The Wisconsin side of this park is verdant bliss, but it's the Minnesota side that boasts trap rock "potholes," deep wells eroded by glacial meltwater; they're pretty boss. Back on the Wisconsin side, however, two downtown St. Croix Falls coffee shops will treat you right: Coffee Time and Dalles Bakery (2 miles from park entrance). Both assemble sandwiches Chinese-menu style, but with distinction. Coffee Time put homemade blackberry and strawberry jelly on a PB&J, and picked-on-the-way-into-work tomatoes on a tasty, hearty roast beef sandwich. That sandwich was definitely filling, so I'm not sure what adjective best describes the two pound sandwich we got at Dalles Bakery. It was distinguished by a house bread made with coffee for a sweet, dark quasi-pumpernickel. You'd have to order something pretty extravagant to pay more than $7 for a sandwich at either shop. We also have fond childhood memories of the broasted chicken at Al's Diner in Centuria (10 miles from park entrance); chicken is of course a classic American picnic meal, and Al's is worth a visit, a greasy spoon against which to measure others' grease.

14. AZTALAN STATE PARK | Jefferson County

This is an overlooked park, but as long as you go on a day whose weather respects the fact that most of Aztalan is shadeless lawn, it's a gem. The tree-lined walk along the Rock River is perfectly pleasant, but the park's real attractions are the mounds and timber walls of a thousand-year-old village, which are best contemplated by long walks up, down, around, and between them. There's a decent apple tree in the park if you visit when it ripens; for more reliable fare, consider bringing something from Jefferson's Bon Ton bakery, which is excellent in the sweets department and boasts not only deli sandwiches but a rotating hot menu as well. But the pro tip is to work up an appetite, then head to Wedl's (7 miles from park entrance), a not-quite-prehistorical but nevertheless storied hamburger stand across the street from the bakery. Orders are taken in the same tiny street-corner shack as the griddle, where gobs of beef are satisfyingly thwacked into flatness by a ceaseless spatula; I've never been there when fewer than eight patties were being cooked at once. These are the umami paragon of burgers; in theory, I prefer them medium rare and a little charred with some poncy aioli, but when faced with a greasy-griddled tile, heaped with onions fried in the same fat, layered in melted Swiss, and then squirted with mustard, all pretense falls away. Two dollars will get you a single cheeseburger plus some change; put that change toward their Chocolate Shoppe ice cream. If Aztalan becomes your favorite Wisconsin state park strictly because of its proximity to Wedl's, we understand.

AN ADDENDUM ON MALTED BEVERAGES: IF YOU THINK, YOU CAN

For the most part, Wisconsin only gets picky about the use of glass bottles at certain protected natural areas, but we can all agree that cans are a picnicking best practice in forests, lawns, and beaches, and there are some terrific Wisconsin microbrews in cans. Check out:

Lucette Brewing, especially Ride Again APA — I understand yowza hoppiness has become passe, but this is a delight on a summer's day.

Capital Brewery, especially Island Wheat — Supper Club's coppery taste doesn't score with me, so I opt for this lovely, unassuming weiss (has notes of: wheat), brewed with crops harvested from a Door County island.

Northwoods Brewing Company, especially Floppin' Crappie. If you're in a part of the state (the Eau Claire area) where you can get this for a buck a can, you win; it's a legit microbrew ale in macro clothing. Malty instead of hoppy, thin without being watery, it's a sci-fi brew, suggesting an alternate history where the top 20 best-selling beers were ales, not lagers.

Milwaukee Brewing Co. — Hop Happy is the epitome (not to be confused with the ideal) of the American IPA; look also for O-Gii, a wheat beer brewed with tea.

I didn't score ultralocal canned brews from others such as Stillmank and Lazy Monk, but scan the shelves when you're in country. For those for whom Point and Leinenkugels are still microbrews, you can get those in cans too.

CHAPTER 16

MEAT ME ON THE MISSISSIPPI

WRITER: JASON WALKER **:: CARTOGRAPHER:** MATT DOOLEY

You can tell by the wieners.

Old-fashioned meat markets have many virtues — quality service, unique products, and often unbeatable quality — but the most tell-tale sign can be eating a house-made wiener. A snappy bite into one of these humble sausages can transform the hot dog from the butt of jokes to salty gastronomic bliss.

Take the old-fashioned wieners at Mike's Butcher Shop in West Saint Paul. Long, curly, and properly encased in the small intestine of a sheep, these affordable homemade sausages have a snappy, meaty flavor that in no way resembles the wimpy mystery meat of the supermarket. What could be considered an afterthought, eaten only by children and at ballgames and the state fair, is transformed into something any right-thinking carnivore would devour straight off the grill. And when paired with one of Mike's expertly homemade coney buns, the experience of eating a simple sausage is turned into something both uniquely American and utterly satisfying.

Thielen's
Meat Market

St. Joseph
Meat Market

McDonald's
Meats

Osseo Meats

Ready Meats

Hackenmueller's

Stasny

Morelli's

Kramarczuk's

Clancey's

Mike's Butcher Shop

Everett's

WISCONSIN

MINNESOTA

IOWA

Holmen Meat
Market

City Meat
Market

Kickapoo Locker

Cremer's

N

0   25   50 Miles

Urban Area

Everett's Foods in Minneapolis offers two versions of wieners: a finely textured dog aimed at kids and those craving a more familiar experience as well as one filled with coarsely ground meat that packs more of a garlicky punch and is almost bratwurst-like. At a few bucks a pound, they're the deal of the century.

And that's what makes small, family-run meat markets so special — most take such pride in their product that even the lowly wiener is treated with care, respect and dedication to the craft of butchering. When the hot dogs are this good, imagine what they can do to a pork belly or a ribeye.

The Upper Midwest is not known for large-scale livestock production like the lower Plains states, but a nexus of German and Eastern European immigrant heritage has made Minnesota, Wisconsin and Iowa ground zero for meat quality. The origin of the Green Bay Packers, the sausage race at Milwaukee's Miller Park, the impeccably cured meats of La Quercia in Norwalk, Iowa, and the *New York Times*-lauded bacon at both Thielen Meats of Pierz, Minnesota, and Nueske's in Wittenberg, Wisconsin, are all examples of the region's phalanx of old-fashioned markets and also a general public that won't stand for a shoddy product.

> When the hot dogs are this good, imagine what they can do to a pork belly or a ribeye.

To take a trip down the mighty Mississippi River and visit old-fashioned meat markets along the way provides a perfect window into the mix of creativity, work ethic, and high quality standards that dominates food culture in the Upper Midwest.

Here, then, listed north to south, is a sampling of markets making a difference within a few miles of the river. At these gleaming markets, the meat is absurdly fresh, the selection is vastly diverse, and a friendly face in a white hat will say, "How can I help you?" before the door even closes behind you.

These are places with workers who brag about their use of sheep intestines, who aren't willing to settle for anything other than carnivorous perfection, who slice smoked pork belly into bacon as you order it… because why in the world would you do it any other way?

THIELEN MEATS | 310 N Main Street, Pierz, Minnesota 56364 | 320.468.6616

Massive meat case, family owned, nationally lauded, located in the heart of Minnesota beef country — if there's a flagship market in the state, it's Thielen Meats.

At Thielen Meats, third- and fourth-generation owners still cure their pork bellies like founder Phil Thielen did in the 1920s. The 2002 *New York Times* article featuring Thielen's bacon lauded as its best feature "… the smokiness, which is pronounced but not overwhelming, with just the right cure of salt and seasonings."

With an expert array of hams, sausages, jerkies, steaks, chops, and Amish-raised chicken, Thielen Meats is central Minnesota's go-to meat market.

In 1990, Joe Thielen splintered off from the original and opened his own meat market in Little Falls, also called Thielen Meats, creating a Carolina/Duke-like 12-mile meat rivalry. But the fussed-over bacon definitely came from the Pierz market.

SAINT JOSEPH MEAT MARKET | 26 1st Avenue NW, Saint Joseph, Minnesota 56374 | 320.363.4913

Offering a ridiculous array of brats and sausages and having won multiple national awards for its braunschweiger, St. Joseph Meat Market is as old-school as they come. Operating for more than 60 years in the quaint confines of downtown St. Joseph, the market emphasizes traditional virtues like cleanliness, service and quality, but it isn't afraid to innovate — new sausage varieties are constantly being developed, and in spring 2013 owner Harvey Pfannenstein won the Beef Backer Award from the Minnesota Beef Council for going "above and beyond to promote beef to their customers."

But about those brats: St. Joseph's varieties include BBQ rib brats, cajun brats with jalapeño cheese, taco brats, sloppy joe brats, Philly steak brats, and even "funeral hotdish" brats. Yep, it's worth a stop next time you're driving down I-94.

MCDONALD'S MEATS | 8601 Main Avenue, Clear Lake, Minnesota 55319 | 320.743.2311

The main attraction in tiny Clear Lake, McDonald's Meats is well-known in Central Minnesota not just for its impeccable butcher shop but for its livestock processing. Every farmer producing small-scale livestock knows the difference made by quality processing, and McDonald's attracts producers for miles who come for their dedication to quality as well as their creative nature.

From a wide array of unique brats (like the Everything Omelet With Hashbrowns) to locally raised chickens, multiple varieties of top-tier bacon, house-rendered lard, and a phenomenal braunschweiger sold in giant tubes that pound-for-pound has to be the state's best food bargain, McDonald's is a place meat enthusiasts can quickly fall in love with.

Locally baked buns are also available, as is Alpine Touch, a seasoning from Montana that takes garlic salt to new heights. Take a cooler and detour on a drive to cabin country; if you're lucky, they'll be barbecuing in the parking lot. The summer sausage and braunschweiger are both must-buys, and the staff is as friendly as the day is long.

OSSEO MEATS | 344 County Road 81, Osseo, Minnesota 55369 | 763.425.2215

A lunchtime visit is required at Osseo Meats, which boasts a full-service meat counter with an army of dedicated butchers but also a hot-food bar. It's sold by the pound and includes deli meats, house-made bratwurst and sauerkraut, and a daily hot lunch special of stick-to-your-ribs dishes like meatloaf or hot dog casserole, which would be homemade mashed potatoes mixed with wiener chunks and cheese, of course.

Battling Robbinsdale for the title of the metro area's most charming small town, Osseo is a city full of food surprises like the Olympia Cafe and Linde's Restaurant — but Osseo Meats is the true star. The steaks are superb and the prices are reasonable, and they even make homemade head cheese.

HACKENMUELLER'S MEAT MARKET | 4159 W Broadway Avenue, Robbinsdale, Minnesota 55422 | 763.537.4811

A butcher shop can make a quaint downtown into something truly great, and Hackenmueller's meat market fills that bill in downtown Robbinsdale.

The 120-plus-year-old shop claims to sell more than 600 pounds of bacon a week, and despite its small size packs a lot of inventory in its case and freezers. Hackenmueller's also sells 50- and 100-pound variety packs with beef, pork, and chicken — for those who like to fill a freezer, there's hardly a more affordable way.

Hackenmueller's Meat Market is the kind of place that, upon leaving and walking through Robbinsdale, makes you wonder how we got away from old-fashioned meat markets in the first place.

KRAMARCZUK'S | 15 E Hennepin Avenue, Minneapolis, Minnesota 55414 | 612.379.3018

Probably the quintessential shop on this list, Kramarczuk's has been around for decades in a visible spot just off the river in Northeast Minneapolis. Its sausages are available at nearby Target Field; it hosts an annual Kielbasa Festival; and though Kramarczuk's falls into none of its namesake categories it has been featured on that popular arbiter of culinary greatness, "Diners, Drive-Ins and Dives."

But Kramarczuk's is the increasingly rare place whose fame is completely justified. With a gleaming U-shaped meat case, more than 40 sausage varieties, a bakery whose pumpernickel and coney buns are unsurpassed, and an attached restaurant that serves some of the best Eastern European-influenced food in the city, Kramarczuk's is a true Minnesota landmark.

Where else would you look for three varieties of head cheese, Bohemian liver sausage *jaternice*, the blood sausage *kishka*, or a gigantic tube of Polish *Krakowska*?

EVERETT'S | *1833 E 38th Street, Minneapolis, Minnesota 55407*

Everett's, an old-school grocery with a dominant meat case that spans the market's west side, is the type of place you wish you lived near so you could shop there every day. They sell milk and bread, sure, but clearly the meat is the star, from the aforementioned two kinds of wieners to spicy porketta to homemade Swedish meatball mix and what could be the best steaks in the city, Everett's is a place where service is king.

An acquaintance who wanted to braise turkey for Thanksgiving told a story that she called several stores asking for a cut-up bird to no avail, until she reached out to Everett's. "That's what we're here for," said the butcher. Indeed.

READY MEATS | *3550 Johnson St NE, Minneapolis, Minnesota 55418 | 612.789.2484*

Tucked into a former 7-11, Ready Meats has for decades served Northeast Minneapolis with Scandinavian-, Polish- and Italian-influenced meats and sauces. Visit Ready Meats for hard-to-find items like ground veal and lamb, ready-to-roast braciole, porketta roasts or their ever-popular homemade red pizza sauce — co-owner Dave Carlson said they go through 40-to-80 gallons a week.

Carlson, who's been on the job since 1975, said Ready Meats was founded in 1946 when the three Ready brothers bought out an older meat market.

"We try to be full-service, and the neighborhood has changed," he said. "It used to be Swedish, Italian, and Polish; now we get a good mix of everybody from every country, so we have to be ready for what they want."

The veteran meatcutters here are quick with advice and are happy to customize your cut or packaging. Picture "old-fashioned meat market" — that image to a T is Ready Meats.

CLANCEY'S MEATS AND FISH | *4307 Upton Avenue S, Minneapolis, Minnesota 55410 | 612.926.0222*

A bit of an oddball on this list given its philosophy and relatively recent founding, Clancey's Meats and Fish opened about a decade ago in a southwest Minneapolis building that for decades housed a butcher shop. Clancey's, though, is driven by an absolute dedication to locally raised, organic meats and the highest quality seafood.

One of the nation's few organic butcher shops, Clancey's is not for the faint of pocketbook but its creative housemade sausages are everchanging; the service is friendly, patient and knowledgeable; and at lunchtime its sandwiches are better than you can possibly imagine. Taste Clancey's deli-sliced roast beef just once and you will never, ever turn vegetarian.

Clancey's also sells farm-fresh eggs and locally famous Rustica baguettes, which also make the bread for those sensational sandwiches.

STASNY'S FOOD MARKET | *1053 Western Avenue N, Saint Paul, Minnesota 55117 | 651.489.2171*

Tucked into the back of an unassuming corner grocery in St. Paul's weathered North End, Stasny's Food Market has lasted more than 90 years because of its commitment to variety. From frozen rabbit to Korean-style beef short ribs to frozen dago sandwich filling — the hot dago is a traditional St. Paul sandwich of Italian sausage with peppers and red sauce — Stasny's is the type of tiny place that you'd drive across town to visit. It's also like stepping back in time to when every grocery store was of the small, neighborhood variety and probably had a traditional meat counter in back. The butcher on my visit, Stu Gerr, said he'd been cutting meat for more than 60 years.

The store also sells a lunchmeat product called "Jellied Beef Loaf," which a patron described as "like beef that has gravy right in it."

Stasny's makes its own sausages and cures its own bacon that's available sliced to order. It also has a nice selection of Kansas City barbecue sauce as well as frozen fruit-filled "kuchen" that Gerr told me were "the real thing, they're made by old ladies over in North Dakota."

MORELLI'S | 535 Tedesco, Saint Paul, Minnesota 55130 | 651.774.5961

Morelli's is one of the few grocery stores in the state that also sell liquor thanks to being in business for nearly a century. A full-service meat market, its homemade flagship Italian sausages are footlong and key to making the type of authentic Italian dishes you picture a little old Sicilian lady fussing over every day of her life. Morelli's also offers the butter-knife steak, a special cut of beef that's both tender and affordable; at $10 a pound it's a budget stand-in for a filet.

There's also an array of deli meats and ready-to-cook dishes like meatloaf and beef and noodles. Giant house-made frozen pizzas are a terrific deal — made with that house-made sausage and high-quality mozzarella, they're worth a spot in your deep freeze for a last-minute dinner.

And for as small as the place is, man do they cram in the craft beer, wine and booze. Just don't bring plastic — Morelli's accepts cash or "approved checks" only.

MIKE'S BUTCHER SHOP | 1104 S Robert Street, West Saint Paul, Minnesota 55118 | 651.457.4821

Holed up in an unassuming strip mall behind a Dairy Queen, Mike's Butcher Shop is churning out the best wieners you'll ever eat in addition to a wide array of cuts. After four decades as a butcher, owner Mike Quast has clearly mastered the art and knows his customers by name — this is a shop that those who live nearby never abandon because of its quality and intimacy.

"We talk to every customer just to shoot the bull a little," Quast said. "They ask us questions on how to cook things and we give them recommendations. A big grocery store, you don't even find a butcher anymore. We are a small-town feel in a big town. West Saint Paul is not small."

Mike's also bakes top-notch burger and coney buns daily. Another top-seller is jerky, with versions including chicken and an especially sublime turkey jerky.

KICKAPOO LOCKER | 325 Main Street, Gays Mills, Wisconsin, 54631 | 608.735.4531

You could say that Kickapoo Locker's third-generation owner, Jim Chellevold, is a bit of a ham expert.

"I've won the State Fair grand championship five times in 10 years I was there," he said.

"I've won the ham classes at state conventions quite a few times, but I'm wore out. I don't do that anymore."

Their loss, apparently, but at Chellevold's meat market in downtown Gays Mills you can get his hams as well as six varieties of both summer sausage and snack sticks, multiple ring bolognas, eight flavors of bacon and 15-20 different brat varieties like gyro brats and spicy

Hungarian. As Chellevold said, "You name it, we've probably made it at one time or another.

"I had three uncles who were in the locker business and I have a cousin whose son has a locker now — it's in the family blood."

HOLMEN LOCKER & MEAT MARKET | *412 N Main Street, Holmen, Wisconsin 54636 | 608.526.3112*

Veteran meatcutter Scott Stettler is the current owner of the Holmen Meat Market, which was founded in 1944 on Main Streeet in Holmen. In the early 1970s the locker moved next door into a former creamery; a more recent expansion and renovation resulted in a 3,000-square-foot retail store that sells its signature meats alongside specialty foods, wine and craft beer.

That large size doesn't keep Holmen from having its specialties, though.

"You say the Holmen Locker, and I'll guarantee 95 percent of people will say we've got the best jerky," Stettler said. "We cut out of choice top inside round and each slice is just under an inch thick. Our spicy version is our original and we sell six-to-seven hundred pounds of that a week."

Another Holmen stalwart is hot dogs, which are made with natural casing in small batches in a state-of-the-art smokehouse, which Stettler says doesn't drain the wieners of moisture and ensures a good snap. Holmen is also known for its thinly sliced dried beef, which is popular on sandwiches or for making creamed chipped beef.

The city of Holmen is just north of La Crosse, which Stettler said in 1891 had 41 butcher shops but now has zero.

"Down through the 1960s and '70s, they still had butcher shops in La Crosse," Stettler said. "There were all kinds of them. That's the way it was in the good days where you just went down to the local butcher and you got your meat from him and your groceries from the grocery store."

CITY MEAT MARKET | *199 Railroad Avenue, New Albin, Iowa 52160 | 563.544.4236*

Just up in the tippy-top northeast corner of Iowa is City Meat Market, a fifth-generation market currently owned by Al Wuennecke, whose great-great-grandfather, Christopher Meyer, started the market when he immigrated from Germany. His son, Frederick, ran the place around the turn of the century and was known as Butcher Fritz.

Yeah, this place is old-fashioned.

"The ring bologna is our biggest seller and what we're most famous for," Wuennecke said. "Quality meat goes in it in the first place, and it's smoked the old-fashioned way with real wood fires. No artificial heat. Everything is cooked with wood."

Yet Wuennecke isn't afraid to innovate. He smokes plenty of ribs, brats and jerky but also smoked salmon, which he said was a big seller.

"I've had people come from Alaska and say this was the best smoked salmon they've ever had," he said.

Wuennecke, 53, lived above the store as a boy and began working at the market full-time after he graduated high school. He's got a photo from around 1900 that shows market furnishings that he still uses today, including a counter and butcher block.

"My son just got out of the navy; he's been in there for six years and he wants to take over," Wuennecke said. "Basically, we've been here forever."

CREMER'S GROCERY | *731 Rhomberg Avenue, Dubuque, Iowa 52001 | 563.583.6589*

In 1955, according to grocer Jeff Cremer, Dubuque had 110 family-owned grocery stores. Today, there's one: Cremer's, a small grocery dominated by its meat counter that opened in 1948 in a building that had housed a meat market since 1909.

"We're still around because we're hand-cutting meat and we're cutting a higher-quality meat," said Jeff Cremer, the third-generation owner. "The people I take care of know the difference between a good steak and a bad steak, but a majority of the people in the world don't. In the Midwest, we're more in tune with what is a good steak."

Cremer's does the trappings of a quality meat market but also offers sandwiches like a locally famous "Turkey 'N' Dressing" version. Holiday business is big — a few years ago, Cremer even opened a pop-up store in Dubuque's west side to handle the demand.

"My business is focused on people who are thoughtful about what they're eating and where they're buying it," Cremer said. "We're lucky in Dubuque — we have a community that likes to support local businesses. That's what we have to focus on: Who are you going to take care of? Who is your customer? That meat, that's what turns the door. That's what gets people in here."

CHAPTER 17

SIX DEGREES OF DELICIOUS: A LANDSCAPE OF CHEFS IN MINNEAPOLIS

WRITER: EMILY SCHNOBRICH :: **ILLUSTRATOR:** SARAH BARGA POLLASCH

"Cooks coming and going to other restaurants. Hanging out. Helping out. Our relationships are developed in very personal, very stressful, very close situations. They are certainly built to withstand a lot of hardship. Bonds are developed and then people move on."
— **Adam Vickerman, head chef, Cafe Levain**

You hear it all the time. Some out-of-towner or new neighbor comments on the size of Minneapolis: "This place is like, *just* the right size. There's so much to do here but you can always count on seeing a familiar face. Wherever you go."

It's a charming quality, one that many residents count high on their list of reasons for sticking out the heavy winters and crabby summers. We love this place because we see ourselves in it. And when we look into our bowls, we see us too. Our food is where we come from.

27 TRAVAIL KITCHEN AND AMUSEMENTS
4154 WEST BROADWAY AVE, ROBBINSDALE

BAR LA GRASSA
800 NORTH WASHINGTON AVE **26**

THE BACHELOR FARMER
50 2ND AVE N

BOROUGH MINNEAPOLIS
730 NORTH WASHINGTON AVE **25**

24

HAUTE DISH **23**
119 WASHINGTON AVE N

Landon Schoenefeld

23 **22** **20** **19** **2** **3** **4** **5** **15** **11** **8** **6**

112 EATERY **22**
112 NORTH 3RD ST

BUTCHER & THE BOAR
1121 HENNEPIN AVE **21**

PORTER & FRYE
20 1115 2ND AVE S

CAFÉ & BAR LURCAT
1624 HARMON PL **19**

LA BELLE VIE **18**
510 GROVELAND AVE

BURCH STEAK AND PIZZA BAR **17**
1933 COLFAX AVE S

Isaac Becker

19 **22** **26**

Carrie McCabe-Johnston

3 **4** **16**

NIGHTINGALE **16**
2551 LYNDALE AVE S

BRYANT-LAKE BOWL
810 WEST LAKE ST

BARBETTE **15**
1600 WEST LAKE ST

14 **13** THE GRAY HOUSE
610 WEST LAKE ST

Tyler Shipton

20 **25** **27**

Kim Bartmann

1 **12** **14** **15**

12 PAT'S TAP
3510 NICOLLET AVE

10 TILIA
2726 WEST 43RD ST

9 PICCOLO
4300 BRYANT AVE S

TRATTORIA TOSCA **11**
3415 WEST 44TH ST

Steven Brown

10 **20**

Doug Flicker

9 **20**

Six Degrees of Delicious

A Landscape of Chefs in Minneapolis

1. **Red Stag Supperclub** 509 1st Ave NE
2. **The Bulldog Northeast** 401 East Hennepin Ave
3. **Brasa Premium Rotisserie** 600 East Hennepin Ave
4. **Restaurant Alma** 528 University Ave SE
5. **Sea Change** 806 South 2nd St
6. **Wienery** 414 Cedar Ave
7. **The Craftsman** 4300 East Lake St
8. **Cafe Levain** 4762 Chicago Ave S

Alex Roberts 3 4

Tim McKee 5 18

Krista Steinbach 24

Erik Anderson 5 20

Adam Vickerman 5 8 11 15

Peter Botcher 8 15 21

Remle Colestock 8 23

Brian Crouch 8 18

This is a journey across three dishes. From Alex Roberts's masa cake in northeast Minneapolis, to Landon Schoenefeld's deconstructed hotdish downtown, to Adam Vickerman's simple plate of mushrooms in the city's southside, the road between these dishes is cluttered with connections, sewn by the hands of chefs who have learned from one another, worked shoulder-to-shoulder, and helped to define fine dining in Minneapolis and the Upper Midwest. After all, stories about food don't begin with just a finished meal.

Stories about food are like trees. Great trees with root systems that sprawl beneath the soil, touching rocks and bones and living things. Or they are rivers, gathering water, carrying fishes, bits of glass and plants, rushing faster, growing stronger with every mile. They're even kind of like that pop culture riff on the theory of six degrees of separation, Six Degrees of Kevin Bacon. One cook isn't far from another. Together, they make up a tangled, edible landscape.

SPICY MASA CORN CAKE | CHEF ALEX ROBERTS
Brasa Rotisserie, Northeast Minneapolis

Start with Alex Roberts, whose Restaurant Alma has been a quiet soldier for innovative, seasonal food in Southeast Minneapolis since 1999. Roberts is rare among Minneapolis-based chefs because he spent his formative cooking years in New York. At first glance, he doesn't seem to have the hometown connections that other industry folks do. But with Alma, and its sibling restaurant Brasa, Roberts has created his own family in the industry.

"Alex really made me think twice. He always gave me that 'it's always gonna be a lifetime struggle' thing, but he never lost his cool. He's a smooth operator and he's good with people," says chef Landon Schoenefeld. Working for Roberts in both Alma and Brasa, Schoenefeld learned some of his most important lessons as not only a chef, but as a teacher in his own kitchen.

Roberts wants to give his people power over their own destinies. "I try to apply the Golden Rule," he says. "I think people are looking to be respected and empowered with knowledge, to be proving themselves and to learn new skills."

It's a simple but satisfying rule, much like the masa corn cake Roberts serves at Brasa. Like a Mexican gordita, this mini round of corn flour is fried until puffy. Then it's topped with spicy tomatillo sauce, crunchy pickled onions, melted cheese, and a bit of cilantro for spunk. Such a snack doesn't scream "Midwest," but it's what marks a man who's all about community. From encouraging young chefs to fundraise for the Youth Farm youth development organization to advising the Dayton brothers on their restaurant The Bachelor Farmer, Roberts permeates the land.

In Minneapolis, "I think that we do have a little more camaraderie and a little bit more 'your success is my success,'" says Roberts. "There's room for all of us to succeed and we can help each other in some way."

Cross the Mississippi River and Alex Roberts's seedlings spring up right away, branching off further. For example, near the rushing waters in the Warehouse District, you'll find Brasa alum Tony Tushar cooking Scandinavian food under Paul Berglund at The Bachelor Farmer. Next to them there's gentle Krista Steinbach, former queen of cupcakes at Sweets Bakeshop in south Minneapolis. Now she turns out Swedish pancakes as The Bachelor Farmer's head pastry chef.

TATER TOT HAUTEDISH | LANDON SCHOENEFELD
Haute Dish, Downtown Minneapolis

Just a skip away, a red, retro arrow points the way to Haute Dish. Landon Schoenefeld owns it. This guy is fiery in hair and demeanor, and committed to that editing spirit Roberts taught him. At Haute Dish, Schoenefeld brightens up Midwestern favorites, like iceberg lettuce salads and mac 'n' cheese, scrutinizing their parts and making them new again.

Like tater tot hotdish, the Midwest's claim to tragic culinary history. Schoenefeld's take on this retro pantry staple is a luscious deconstruction. Tender short ribs play a sweet high note next to giant, silky, house-made tater tots. A swipe of porcini béchamel gives the whole thing a heady, groan-worthy quality. Each bite sheds light on a different corner of the Campbell's-based staple that some Minneapolitans disown without thinking.

"I used to call myself the Kevin Bacon of cooks," Schoenefeld says. Sure, he sautéed and chopped at Roberts's restaurants, and his short ribs are good enough to rival Brasa's braised beef. But Schoenefeld's really run the spectrum, from slinging loaded hot dogs at the Wienery to learning perfect technique from Brian Crouch and Steven Brown at Restaurant (now Café) Levain.

"It was cool to go from place to place using the same ingredients," he says of working at Alma and Levain at the same time. Both kitchens saw the same duck from Wild Acres Farm and the same foraged mushrooms.

"It was the subtle differences, you know?" Schoenefeld collected them all and made them his own. Even Haute Dish's physical space is a place meticulously repurposed, down to the funky extra hand sink in one of the single-person bathrooms. Just a remnant of the previous tenant. A scar from the past.

A couple blocks from Haute Dish, Isaac Becker's 112 Eatery waits for the evening crowd, and his pasta place Bar La Grassa keeps it classy further down Washington Avenue. After Schoenefeld worked at 112 Eatery, Becker was the one who nudged him northeast to Alma.

Continue downtown to stately Porter & Frye, a kitchen filled with memories of Schoenefeld rubbing elbows with Tyler Shipton of Travail and Borough, just blocks from Bar La Grassa; Erik Anderson, who seared fish at the Guthrie Theater's Sea Change before moving to Tennessee; and Doug Flicker, whose dainty-plates spot Piccolo conducts exciting flavor experiments without being garish.

Just past the heart of downtown, Peter Botcher, who worked with Schoenefeld at Restaurant Levain, turns out excellent sausages at Butcher & the Boar. Then beyond the shimmering Walker Arts Center, there's Tim McKee's famous fine dining spot La Belle Vie, where Brian Crouch ended up, and Burch Steakhouse & Pizza Bar, Becker's latest creation. Another step, perhaps, on someone else's journey.

Just down Lyndale Avenue is a swanky restaurant called Nightingale. It's part owned by Carrie McCabe-Johnston, a calm cook who who spent some of her most important learning years at Brasa and Alma. Roberts himself gave her plenty of advice she opened her own place.

Further on in stylish Uptown, Barbette stands solid and gem-like as ever. The first of Kim Bartmann's restaurants (which include Red Stag Supperclub, Bryant-Lake Bowl, and Pat's Tap), the French bistro was a stop on Schoenefeld's journey to Haute Dish. Now, head chef Sarah Master infuses Barbette with the colors of her New Orleans education, after working at Porter & Frye, Spoonriver, and Restaurant Alma as well.

And east on Lake Street sits the quiet Gray House, owned by Ian Gray, who makes killer salads and fresh pastas. Gray hails from Becker's Café Lurcat and Trattoria Tosca, where Adam Vickerman first set the stage as head chef in 2009.

STEWED MUSHROOMS | ADAM VICKERMAN

Café Levain, South Minneapolis

Soon the path softens into residential south Minneapolis. This far from Alex Roberts's territory, shops are more colorful. Unruly yards and broken fences alternate with polished homesteads. West of Lake Harriet, Steven Brown's restaurant Tilia sees a line out the door. And in Café Levain's corner retreat on Chicago Avenue, Adam Vickerman cooks up simplicity. He makes sure to say that. But just one bite of his stewed mushrooms is proof times a million that the kid is golden.

These mushrooms are meaty enough to be a main course. The medley varies season to season but in summer, oysters, shiitakes, chicken-of-the-woods, and hen-of-the-woods all find their way into the pan. Vickerman caramelizes and glazes them with butter, cream, and sherry vinegar. His mushrooms make the sort of thoughtful meal that recalls Alex Roberts, even though he and Vickerman have never worked side by side. Still, the care is there, even in the most commonplace of dishes, absorbed by proxy through Schoenefeld and other chefs at work.

In 2003, at age 19, Vickerman began growing into his own character as an intern at Levain. He watched Schoenefeld work the line "like a machine, a perfectionist," traits he recognized later at Haute Dish when he and co-worker Remle Colestock helped open the restaurant. "Landon's cooking is very personal and very soulful," Vickerman says.

He also recalls Steven Brown and Peter Botcher as the leaders of "an incredibly talented group of passionate individuals [at Levain] who were very nurturing yet stern and focused." They molded him in ways beyond the kitchen. Although he left for Barbette with Botcher, later opened Trattoria Tosca, and spent time with Erik Anderson at Sea Change, Vickerman found his way back to the roost on Chicago Avenue. Unlike Schoenefeld, who turned his experiences into something brand new, Vickerman has focused and perfected his learning on the place where it all began.

"Steven Brown always told me I'd eventually forget about him and what he did for me at Levain," Vickerman says. "It ain't happening." Which is perhaps why Vickerman has such a deep understanding of his kitchen. With a crew as small as three, he says, "teaching at Levain is a basic trait," and personable training is key.

By learning from a few, Vickerman has felt the pulse of a multitude of other Minneapolis chefs. This path from corn cake to mushrooms is full of blurred lines and overlapping pages. But both Vickerman and Schoenefeld say that one of the best parts about cooking in Minneapolis is seeing the look on other industry workers' faces when they taste their food.

"Those are the flattering moments for me," says Schoenefeld. "When you're recognized within your industry."

Truly, that great tree — or river, or road — that stretches across the Mississippi depends on these moments of support and understanding. The landscape is fluid, and it takes many hands and years and steps to make one worthy dish. And one delicious city.

CHAPTER 18

OPEN ARMS, OPEN FARMS

WRITER: JASON WALKER **:: CARTOGRAPHER:** MATT DOOLEY [WITH FARM MAPS BY THE FARMERS]

As books like *The Omnivore's Dilemma,*"multiple academic studies and any sustainable farmer can tell you, there are myriad differences between practitioners of "big agriculture" — large corn and soybean farmers, livestock feedlots, Monsanto, Syngenta and their ilk — and small-scale, locally focused farms that practice sustainable farming methods.

One of the most glaring is that sustainable farmers tend to encourage all comers who wish to visit their farms, while "big agriculture" tends to discourage farm visits and has even pushed for so-called "ag-gag" bills that would criminalize hidden-camera video recording on factory farms, processing facilities and slaughterhouses.

Small farmers often sell their products directly from the farm, host events from educational demonstrations to all-out hootenannies, and even welcome volunteer labor from those wishing to get out of the house and get their hands dirty. Several, like Round River Farm in Finland, Minnesota, even practice bed-and-breakfast style "agritourism" and have a reservable cabin or other amenities where visitors can spend the night. Most are generally optimistic, happy places where the farmers' sense of connection to the land and overall satisfaction with their career choice overcomes hours of backbreaking labor, unpredictable income and often cruel government regulations.

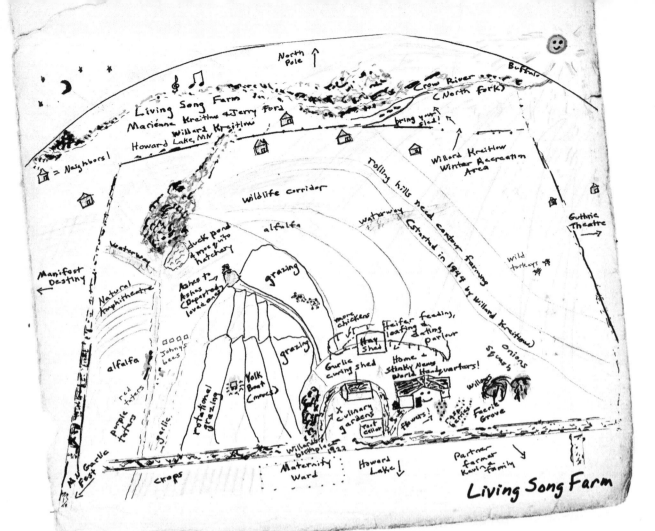

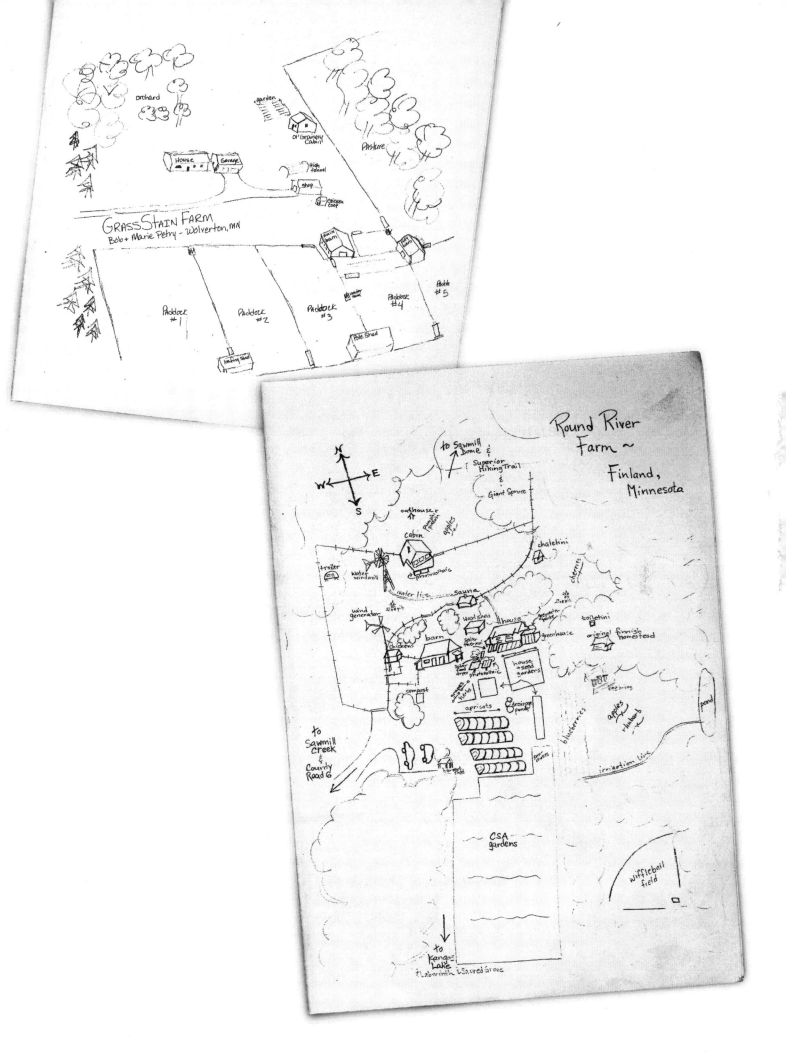

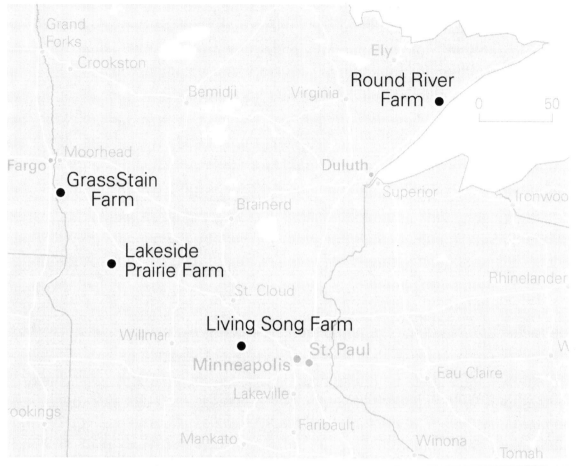

Luckily, the Upper Midwest is dotted with more sustainable, family-run farm operations than you might imagine, and despite a looming crisis involving future farmers (the average age of the American farmer is nearly 60), there are many diverse options for those wishing to visit a farm, find a zen-like connection to food and community and perhaps educate their kids or even themselves about where their food comes from and its impact on our land, water and economic system.

Here, then, are a few farms that not only practice sustainable farming methods but also welcome visitors. If you are looking to gather eggs, see the benefits of grass-fed livestock, learn more about heirloom vegetables, get tips on building high-quality soil or just want to connect with nature, these farms might fit the bill.

But first, a few rules:

- Don't show up unannounced; call first.
- Nearly all farms have dogs, many of them large, that will rush to greet you upon arrival. Most will be friendly.
- Farms with animals usually have electric fences. Don't go a-wandering into an unexpected jolt.
- Dress properly. Showing up in flip-flops and an expensive white shirt won't really work — wear boots and clothes that you won't mind getting dirty.

So go visit a local farm. You'll make new friends. You'll get fresh air and sunshine. And you'll walk away with a better appreciation for what goes into the production of your salad, BLT, steak, ice cream, tortilla chip or eggs Benedict.

And don't leave without some dirt under your fingernails.

LIVING SONG FARM | *7616 25th Street SW, Howard Lake, Minnesota | 763.244.6659 |*
livingsongfarm.com

A fourth-generation farm that has been using sustainable practices since the 1940s,
Living Song Farm raises dairy heifers, grass-finished beef, hay, garlic, onions, potatoes, and
squash — all under the steady hand of 91-year-old Willard Kreitlow, who still farms the land
with his daughter, Marienne Kreitlow, and son-in-law Jerry Ford.

Living Song's philosophy revolves around diversity: animals, vegetables, hay, and pastures
constantly moving around to more closely mimic the way nature would do it. According to
Ford, diversity gives his farm a resilience as well — if one thing fails, it doesn't break the
farm — but does require a broader knowledge and can be labor-intensive.

"We believe that a healthy farm is a beautiful farm, and we are so blessed with
lovely hills, woods, creeks, wetlands and a lake," Ford said. "Since we've been practicing
rotational grazing of the cattle and chickens, we have been delighted with the wildlife
that have reappeared: bobolinks, harrier hawks, kingbirds and a host of others that
find a home in our pastures and what we like to call 'esthetic spaces.'"

Living Song produces foods that are easy to store — it has a root cellar designed by a
family member to hold squash and potatoes, and its garlic and onions are cured for
storage. This not only gives the farmers a well-stocked larder, it gives them the ability to
sell produce well into the winter.

"People seem to come here and, even though their purpose was to pick up eggs or garlic,
or to learn about our sustainable practices, they start to relax and slow down," Ford said.
"We try not to hurry them, though if you're not careful, we'll put you to work.

"And we sometimes find them napping on the lawn. We consider that a compliment."

LAKESIDE PRAIRIE FARM | *20503 180th Avenue, Barrett, Minnesota 56311 | 320.492.2526 |*
lakesideprairiefarm.com

Situated between two lakes in the picturesque rolling hills of central Minnesota, Lakeside
Prairie Farm is a prime example of young farmers taking food production into their own hands.

Farm partners Bryan Simon and Ryan Heinen began farming in late 2012 and are working
to restore Lakeside Prairie's acreage into its natural state of oak savanna prairie. They're
raising pastured beef, oats and a couple acres of vegetables, all with the goal of creating a
symbiotic balance that benefits the land.

In their early 30s, Bryan and Ryan each have backgrounds in conservation and land
management, and that experience has now been boosted by a drive to produce food
without compromise.

"We are growing food that is healthy, flavorful, and nutrient dense," said Simon. "Food
that doesn't deplete our soil, doesn't pollute our water and air, or alter the climate. And we're
growing our food in a way supports a rich diversity of wildlife and a vibrant rural community.
We are not hoping to feed the world, we're seeking to feed our neighbors."

Lakeside Prairie's diversification and family focus makes it a great place to visit. From
Heinen's custom-built chicken wagon to its gorgeous lakefront views to the genuine warmth
of the two farm families, Lakeside Prairie is an encouraging preview of decades of ethical,
productive Upper Midwestern farming.

Seeing the farm's transformation from mismanaged land into native prairie is both
educational and moving. By grazing cattle, enriching the soil with diverse crop production,
encouraging native plant growth and using prescribed prairie burns, the farmers' mission is
to remake Lakeside Prairie Farm into how it looked 200 years ago – oak savanna prairie
currently makes up less than one percent of Minnesota land, and it used to encompass
one-third of the state.

"Tallgrass prairie is pretty much gone in the U.S.," Heinen said. "Plus, we want to raise
grass-fed beef and the prairie needs grazing and fire. We'll utilize that to hopefully make a
living, but also to help bring some diversity back to the land."

GRASSSTAIN FARM | *1762 160th St, Wolverton, Minnesota 56594 | 218.995.2002 | grassstainfarm.blogspot.com*

Located in the Red River Valley about 20 miles south of Fargo, Bob and Marie Petry have been "grass farming" for several years at their 20-acre GrassStain Farm, a picture-postcard farm of rolling grassy fields, red outbuildings, and woods.

But farming was in their blood long before they arrived at GrassStain; Bob and Marie both grew up on farms, and both have agriculture-related degrees from North Dakota State.

So, what is "grass farming," anyway? Well, the most visible proponent of the method is Joel Salatin, the Virginia farmer profiled in "The Omnivore's Dilemma" as well as the more recent documentary film, "American Meat." Farmers like Salatin and the Petrys see grass as the basis for their food production: Nature provides the grass through sun and rain, and their animals take turns grazing on that pasture, which provides food for humans as well as food for the soil in the form of manure. It's a cycle that produces richly flavored, healthier meat as well as weather-resistant, nutrient-rich soil that is perfect for prairie grass production.

The Petrys raise Jersey cows, pastured pork, chickens and eggs, and have both a small garden and an orchard.

"After moving around for several years, we were thrilled to find this 20-acre farm full of trees, grass, and buildings," Marie Petry said. "It's the perfect place for us to grow good food and share with friends. And nothing is more satisfying to Bob than sitting down to a delicious meal totally grown on this farm."

If you visit GrassStain Farm, try to do it when the Petrys' children, Elizabeth and Karl, are home — the family plays together as a bluegrass quartet.

"One time we entertained guests with turkeys 'singing' along with the fiddler, who was wearing a horse-head mask," Marie Petry said. "You had to see it to believe it! For us, farming is our work and our play; our food and our fun."

ROUND RIVER FARM | *5879 Nikolai Road, Finland, Minnesota 55603 | 218.353.7736 | round-river.com*

You've heard of and probably know people who want to get back to nature, start a farm and live peacefully off the land and off the grid, but rarely do their ambitious plans come to fruition.

Not so David and Lise Abazs. Their Round River Farm in Finland, Minn., is a solar-, wind- and human-powered homestead amid the Sawtooth Mountains that uses sustainable growing methods such as green manures, crop rotations and companion planting on their sandy loam soils. The farm sells CSA shares of vegetables and raises sheep for wool, chickens for eggs, and bees for pollination and honey.

The family, which includes sons Colby and Tremayne, harvests wild rice as well as balsam and other greens from their forested acres to weave holiday wreaths. The Abazses are also now experimenting with seed production for a new regional seed-saving initiative and cultivate an extensive array of rhubarb varieties.

When Lise and David bought the land in 1988, it was an abandoned Finnish homestead.

"We moved into the cabin on the property and began to re-clear the overgrown fields using pickaxes and pigs," David said. "Like the original Finnish homesteaders, we first built the sauna, then a stone barn, which at various times has housed goats, sheep, a milk cow and a draft horse. The chickens eventually got a stone coop also, as we had a seemingly endless supply of this building material. For our water source, we had a well drilled through 400 feet of bedrock, then put up a refurbished 1924 water windmill to pump it. When our family outgrew the cabin, we built a new house, all the while slowly opening up more space for gardens."

Guests can also rent the "Chaletini," an 8-foot-by-8-foot two-story playhouse-turned-cabin, for overnight stays. Lodgers may use the sauna, walk to the nearby Superior Hiking Trail and Kangas Lake, and sleep amid the livestock, vegetables and unique forest/farm melange of Round River Farm. Tranquility awaits, but as David said, "recognize that you are visiting a working farm and the best visitor is the one that weeds while they ask questions."

CHAPTER 19

HOW WE THINK ABOUT PIZZA TODAY: AN EXPLORATION OF CRUEL, UNFORGIVING SCIENCE VERSUS WHATEVER JUST FEELS RIGHT, MAN

WRITER AND ILLUSTRATOR: JEFF NELSON

Illustrator Jeff Nelson has strong feelings about pizza, and he poured his thoughts on the local scene into the map that accompanies this chapter. What follows are some choice excerpts from a wide-ranging and at times distressingly discursive essay by Nelson.

ON HOW TO IDENTIFY GREAT PIZZA:

The easy and sloppy route is to invoke Supreme Court justice Potter Stewart's infallible belief in his own 50-Shades of Grey-dar in regards to identifying pornography, "I know it when I see it," and apply it to pizza eating: "Good pizza? I know it when I eat it."

ON PIZZA CRUST:

A pizza's crust is like a band's bass player: absolutely necessary, not terribly interesting, and if you don't keep your eye on it it will take the opportunity to get so high that it will pop. That being established, once you find a good one, you never want to let it go, whether it's the chewy crust at Pizza Luce, which is this writer's Platonic ideal for "Minnesota-style" pizza,[1] or the Neapolitan crust of Punch (crispy on the outer rim with a not-so-crispy Dagobah center).

ON LIGHTLY APPLIED SAUCE:

I like my sauce as rich and thick as a room full of Koch brothers, but this is not the desired effect for many of the more recent SOFEO[2] establishments. Black Sheep Coal Fired Pizza makes a fennel sausage and green olive pizza with a sauce that flits about your mouth like a fairy trying to escape. It is so good that I can almost forgive them for single-handedly perpetuating the evils of Big Coal. Almost. Okay, fine: forgiven.

1. PIZZA LUCÉ
2. PSYCHO SUZI'S MOTOR LOUNGE
3. ELEMENT WOOD FIRE PIZZA
4. PIZZA NEA
5. STADIUM PIZZA & DINER
6. ANDREA PIZZA
7. GINELLI'S PIZZA
8. MESA PIZZA
9. CRESCENT MOON PIZZA
10. CAMPUS PIZZA
11. PARKWAY PIZZA
12. DI NOKO'S
13. FAT LORENZO'S
14. JAKEENO'S
15. SLICE of NEW YORK
16. LEANING TOWER of PIZZA
17. BURCH STEAK & PIZZA BAR
18. GALACTIC PIZZA
19. DULONO'S
20. PIZZERIA LOLA
21. MICHELANGELO'S MASTERPIZZAS
22. MOZZA MIA
23. HELLO PIZZA
24. PIG ATE MY PIZZA

ON SAUCE CON GUSTO:

On the other end of the flavor rainbow is Red's Savoy Pizza. The red sauce at Red's is so intense that you begin to have premonitions of the nightmares you will have before you have paid your bill. Your subconscious addresses you with the smooth, trained voice of a game show announcer informing you of what you have won: "First, you'll be torn apart by a pack of wild dingoes, but instead of teeth, they'll have cheaply-made Rose Art colored pencils, and instead of dingo faces they'll all look like Prince Charles, but with vertical snake pupils. The Eagles will be playing an acoustic version of "Witchy Woman" over and over in the background. You'll keep trying to yell for help, but Don Henley will just look at you and slowly mouth the words: 'You deserve this.'"

Here's the thing though: it's completely worth it. Plus, the St. Paul location has an aquarium.

ON DEEP OR FOLDABLE PIZZA:

The Twin Cities' king of deep dish pizza is DiNoko's. It marries toppings and cheese (and, if we may delve into pizza polygamy momentarily, it also marries crust and sauce[3]).

Cossetta is my favorite pizza to fold in half in order to eat.[4] The fresh onions and green peppers should not taste as uniquely wonderful as they do. They are juicy and crunchy — they taste just as green peppers and onions on pizza should taste. They are immovable ingredients from the pizza topping canon, a canon which is continually petitioned.

ON AMBIANCE AS PIZZA ENHANCER:

Is there anything more lovely than lounging on the riverside patio at Psycho Suzi's on one of summer's first lazy afternoons eating pizza and watching water sports enthusiasts wipe out on their wakeboards in front of a giant gravel farm? Maybe it's the liters of rum drunk from vessels shaped like shrunken heads — the effect of which is so deleterious that one is lulled into thinking that it would be a capital idea to take one of the tiki god glasses home, even though the bar has one's credit card information and has demanded a deposit and said vessel will cost one as much as an Arabian stallion by the time one has followed through.

Equally unique and enjoyable is Dulono's, possibly the only restaurant in all of the Twin Cities that could unpretentiously double as a set for a David Lynch movie. This undoubtedly works in Dulono's favor as pizza just tastes better when you're pretending to be Kyle MacLachlan. This is a fact. Try it.

ON THE RELIABILITY OF THE ACCOMPANYING MAP:

I regret that I have not yet been to every single place on my accompanying map. One such place is Pizzeria Lola. That isn't quite true. I drank a beer there, but I haven't eaten there yet. I'd like to. The same goes for Pig Ate My Pizza. Few places so demand to be visited, by both the merit of their name and sterling buzz.

---

[1] I totally stole that from my friend Jeff. See, Jeff is from Chicago and thereby genetically pre-disposed toward recognizing subtly different pizza styles (e.g. Saint Louis-style versus, say, East Saint Louis-style). Eating pizza with Jeff is the culinary equivalent of hunting butterflies with Nabokov.

[2] SOFEO or "See Our Fancy Exposed Oven?"

[3] Imagine the HBO polygamy series "Big Love," but with Bill Paxton as the crust, Jeanne Tripplehorn as sauce, Chloë Sevigny as toppings, and, typecast yet again, Ginnifer Goodwin as cheese. Actually, don't imagine any of that. Bad idea.

[4] Also my favorite establishment to refer to using the singular, as in "Cossetta" rather than "Cossetta's." Both are correct (at least according to the restaurant's multiple uses of both) but when given the choice, one should always use the form that *The Splendid Table*'s Lynne Rossetto Kasper would use.

CHAPTER 20
FREE SMELLS

WRITER: MAJA INGEMAN :: **ILLUSTRATOR:** JERRY INGEMAN

The day I knew I'd declare an economics major was the day I learned about externalities.

It was the first week of an introductory undergraduate course, and my professor was explaining how many transactions result in additional costs or benefits — spillover effects — to an otherwise uninvolved third party. Secondhand smoke? Negative externality. That rowdy college party down the block that's keeping you up at night? Negative externality (unless you fancy yourself a party-crasher and derive an inordinate amount of joy from drinking with college kids). Walking by Izzy's Ice Cream and getting a whiff of the fresh waffle cones still sizzling on the iron? POSITIVE EXTERNALITY.

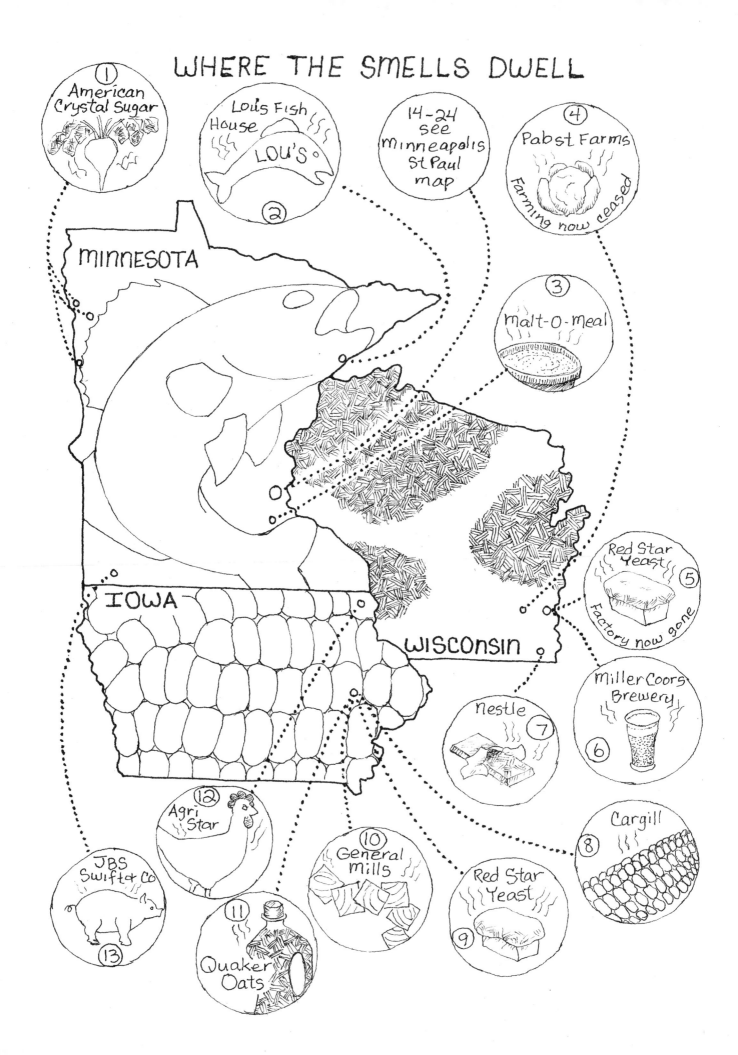

WHERE THE SMELLS DWELL

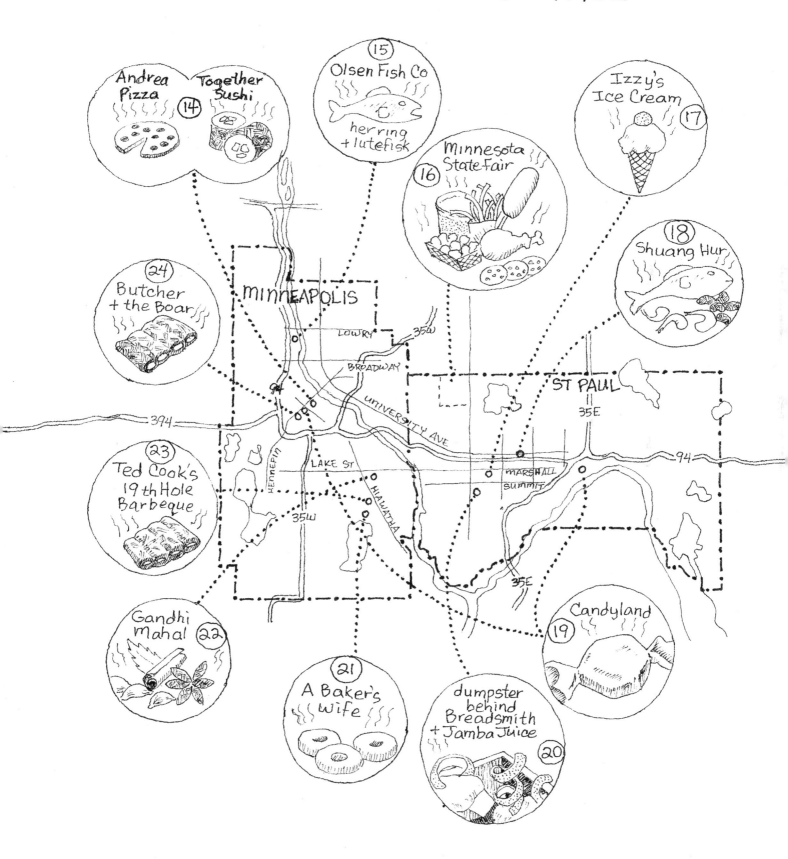

WHERE THE SMELLS DWELL
in MINNEAPOLIS and ST PAUL

National sandwich chain Jimmy John's has capitalized on this concept of externalities, advertising "Free Smells" in every storefront — and with good reason. Scent has a powerful ability to trigger emotion and memories, those that are inextricably linked to important landmarks and even seemingly insignificant interactions. Seattle bar/restaurant Canon has gone to great lengths to play on these emotions with their cocktail "Campfire in Georgia," infusing French oak with a rich cinnamon syrup, then lighting it on fire upon serving to envelop the drink — and your hands — with a lasting, cinnamon "smoke" scent that transports you back to memories of campfire songs, s'mores, and good company (all the best parts of a bonfire, sans the mosquitoes). Though Minneapolis hasn't ventured that far off the beaten path, a marked increase in bitters companies (among them craft bitters upstarts Bittercube, Dashfire, and Easy & Oskey) and use of aromatics shows that the Midwest is intrigued by the impact of aroma on food and drink.

Recent research suggests that scents, whether good or bad, may affect us in more ways than we realize. Beyond the normal means by which we process smell, a German scientist found that blood cells are attracted to other cells that possess a certain scent. So it's natural that growing up near strong scents would have an impact on our memories and perceptions of place — even the most putrid, sour smells can become tied to time spent in a particular place and remind us that we're home. So, without further ado: a few of the smells that have infiltrated our lives in the Upper Midwest.

CROOKSTON / MOORHEAD / EAST GRAND FORKS, MINNESOTA

Chances are, if you've baked *anything* sweet in the last few months, you may have used Crystal Sugar — but it doesn't smell as innocuously sweet throughout its entire production cycle as one might think. People who call northwestern Minnesota or North Dakota home are all-too-familiar with the diverse olfactory byproducts of sugar beet production: from the scent reminiscent of a freshly mown lawn when the leafy beet greens are first removed from the roots, to the faint blend of sweetness and dirt when the beets are plucked from the ground, to the smell of diesel engines running. According to Clare Carlson, a former sugar beet farmer, "farmers like the smell of diesel exhaust. I am guessing the rest of the world isn't quite as enamored." The clincher, though, comes into play each fall during the annual sugar production "campaign" when the harvested beets are sorted, cleaned, and boiled, extracting as much sugar as possible and converting the pulpy remains into animal feed.

All this boiling and cooking yields a scent that Clare's brother Craig describes as "molasses mixed with freshly turned, loamy soil... you get used to it for the most part." But the memorable scent — the one that Clare's brother Craig finds "harder to develop an appreciation for" — is that of decaying plant matter. When the supply of harvested beets exceeds the capacity the plant can process, they're stored outside and allowed to freeze. If the beets thaw early, or matter goes unused, the sour, sewage scent wafts through town. Think of that the next time you sprinkle some sugar on your cereal.

TWO HARBORS, MINNESOTA

Lou's Fish House has skyrocketed in popularity since it made its claim to fame in the July 2010 issue of *Martha Stewart Living*. But it's not fame that makes Lou's interesting — or the other famed fishhouses of northern Minnesota, Morey's Seafood and Dockside Fish Market among them. It's the heady smell of wood smoke and fish permeating the highway outside, and the sight of Lake Superior just across the street, that conjure memories of fishing, and campfires, and summer.

NORTHFIELD, MINNESOTA

Northfield is home to two colleges and 20,000 people, the vast majority of whom either adore or loathe the presence of the Malt-O-Meal factory (#3) down the street. From one Carleton alumna: "I can fully confirm that Northfield (yes, the whole town) does indeed smell like freshly baked brownies when Malt-o-Meal makes their cocoa puffs. The only downside is that the smell makes you constantly hungry for baked goods, and probably accounts for at least half of everyone's freshman 15." Another alum felt the opposite: "I hated [the smell], actually. [It] reminded me of classes and tests and papers."

OCONOMOWOC, WISCONSIN

Most of us know the Pabst family as the creators of a Midwest grunge-hipster brewing empire — but they were also avid conservationists with a 1,500-acre tract of farmland. Once used for horse breeding and dairy farming, in more recent years the land was used to grow beans, cabbage, peas, soybeans, and corn. All well and good, but locals described the farmland in the fall to smell less of freshly tilled land and soil, and more of the sour, effervescent scent of sauerkraut — the cabbage often stayed in the ground past its prime, where it was left to ferment. (If it were up to us, we'd have been sneaking a hefty dose of caraway and fennel onto the fields at night to try to spice things up a bit!) Alas, head there now, and you'll get a different scent entirely: the scent of construction, as a new development (replete with a Walmart, Sam's Club, and "upscale shopping center") is planned over the next decade.

MILWAUKEE, WISCONSIN

Ask a former Milwaukeean what scent was omnipresent in their hometown, and nine times out of ten they'll say "yeast." It's hardly a surprise: Milwaukee's the home of the Brewers, in terms of both baseball and macrobreweries, and the yeasty smell is produced by more than one manufacturer. Most sniffable: the (now-dismantled) Red Star Yeast factory (#5) on the north side of the Menomonee Valley. Cruise into town on I-94 prior to 2006, and you couldn't miss the smell: pungent, damp, organic in nature, and distinctly yeasty. "When it rained when I was a kid the smell of yeast would rise from the valley and hover over its perimeter. I never got used to it." Even since the factory was closed and operations were moved to Cedar Rapids, Milwaukee residents are still graced with a similarly yeasty smell — the Miller-Coors factory (#6) is just to the northwest and emits a warm, earthy scent that only grows stronger in the evening.

BURLINGTON, WISCONSIN

Just south of Milwaukee: a teeny town named Burlington, that's brave enough to dub itself "Chocolate City, USA" (thereby one-upping Hershey's "Chocolatetown" moniker — the town beat out Hershey in a chocolatey legal battle that made the *Wall Street Journal* in the late 1980s). Much of the town's livelihood stems from the Nestle chocolate plant (#7) established there in 1966 — so much that they've held a chocolate festival for the past thirty years to draw tourists to town, raise money for local charities, and celebrate the chocolate that makes the town "famous." On windier days, the smell of the chocolate — rich, sweet, almost more enticing than it tastes — washes over the town. Sweet, indeed.

CEDAR RAPIDS, IOWA

Lined with manufacturers producing syrup, cereal, and frosting, the corridor along I-380 in Cedar Rapids isn't for the delicate-nosed. Dubbed by some the "city of five smells" — an adulteration of the chamber of commerce's campaign for the "city of five seasons" and nod to the town's stinky 2008 reopening of "Mount Trashmore" to accommodate flood debris — a heavy dose of treacly sweetness pervades the air for miles.

According to Leslie Burke, an HR coordinator at Quaker Oats (#11), "people complain all the time about the smell, but it's not us! Whenever we make apple-cinnamon oatmeal it smells just like apple pie." It's easy enough to believe. While its 12 floors of Cap'n Crunch, Aunt Jemima's syrup, and flavored oatmeal production coalesce to emit a syrupy-sweet melange of scents, Quaker's not the only culprit — and it's only a stone's throw away from a number of other strong-smelling food producers.

The real killer? Corn syrup. The scent hangs in the air with the same cloying viscosity as its finished product, slowly evolving from a one-note corn-influenced sweetness to a heavily caramelized to burnt smell as you move down the river — much the way it smells when you burn sugar on a stove. "You can't miss it — the Cargill plant (#8) is on the north edge of town, but you can smell it from the freeway," says Conrad Lichty, a born-and-bred native of Cedar Rapids.

Further down the road: more overwhelming sweetness, this time from the General Mills plant (#10) (from whence all Betty Crocker frosting originates). At least it's a bit better contained. And the infamous Red Star Yeast plant (#9), relocated to the shared delight (and, perhaps, nostalgic dismay) of so many Milwaukeeans? Here, it's barely recognizable, drowned out by the smoke and diesel fuel of tens of tankers carting freshly processed ethanol from the Archer Daniels Midland plant a block away.

POSTVILLE, IOWA

Postville's name went on the map when an Orthodox Jewish family from Brooklyn converted a shuttered meatpacking plant into the largest kosher meat processing plant in the country — and it imploded when a 2008 ICE raid removed 389 employees and revealed abusive working conditions, precipitating the temporary closure of the plant. Since the plant was reopened as "Agri Star" (#12) under new management, the tiny town has continued to absorb (and lose) wave after wave of short-term migrant workers from all over the world, following in the footsteps of the Hasidic community that moved to Postville to work at the plant for good. Since the town is so teeny (there's not even a stoplight in sight), the smells of the town are more concentrated than most: aromas of spice and garlic from the Mexican restaurant (a remnant of one of the immigrant communities) mingle with hints of diesel fuel, dead meat, and fecal matter, which seem to amplify on your way out of town as they blend with the scents of surrounding livestock farms. Though the plant's odor isn't all sunshine and rainbows, the plant has proven itself to be the town's lifeblood: and for that, any smell would stand.

WORTHINGTON, MINNESOTA

In case you haven't gotten your fill of animal waste, this one's even more pungent: while passing the pork rendering plant on your way into Worthington, the town quote "you'll come to love us" takes on a new meaning. Though the town is known for its "Turkey Days" festival, its largest (and smelliest) employer is JBS Swift & Company (#13), the meatpacking plant that has boosted Worthington's population even though most rural areas are on a decline. Like Postville, it's not the most pleasant scent — according to Worthington native Jenny Mammen, "it smells like baked fecal matter... in the late summer it's the worst." It's true: mid-August's densely humid air seems to absorb the putrid odor without letting go, and on windier days it spreads into town (after all, there are less than two miles between the plant and the town center). "After you've lived there for awhile it becomes second nature," Jenny says — but the smell of porcine waste continues to be a nose-pincher for out-of-towners.

TWIN CITIES, MINNESOTA
...For the worker bees

9-to-5ers in downtown Minneapolis are all-too-familiar with the weird conglomerate of odors in the skyway — at times appetizing, others nauseating. A perfect convergence of the two? The point at the corner of 8th Avenue and LaSalle, where grease and garlic from Andrea Pizza (#14) coalesce with the slightly off, fishy scent of Together Sushi. If you decide to stop for a bite, stick with a pepperoni-pineapple-jalapeno slice from Andrea — it's slathered in a serviceable tomato sauce bursting with garlic and dried herbs, and the pineapple and jalapeno help to brighten an otherwise salt-and-grease bomb. Head to Together Sushi, and it's the decisive equivalent of drunkenly scarfing grocery store sushi at 3 a.m. — except you're probably not drunk, and it's made fresh, so it's harder to excuse the gooey glob of fishy salmon, flavorless rice, and too-bright pickled ginger. Another benefit of this double-trouble skyway stop? Your clothes will reek of garlic. All. Day. Long. Take *that*, business casual.

More likely to impress your co-workers: a stop at the ultra-sweet Candyland (#19) around the corner (or the original, old-school location in downtown St. Paul), with row upon row of taffy, obscure and old-fashioned candies, and the famous "Chicago Mix®" of cheese popcorn, plain popcorn, and caramel corn. The tiny store pumps out caramel corn and straight-up sugar sweetness extending at least half a block down the street outside and permeating some of the neighboring businesses, giving passersby the near-feeling of being "a kid in a candy shop."

...For the fish fanatics and spice fiends

Among all the Asian grocers in town, somehow Shuang Hur's (#18) St. Paul outpost — just off the edge of "Little Mekong" — has us hooked. Perhaps it's the fact that the 30-foot fish counter faces the entrance, giving your nose an instant onslaught of fish and squid on ice — not unlike a summer afternoon of gutting walleye off the dock. Yet unlike any seafood vendors in town (Coastal), the dried goods aisle adds a hefty dose of depth — from the briny tingle of dried shrimp, to the pungent tang of fermented, salty black beans, to the warm spice of coriander, anise, and galangal.

A different twist on fish — where fish is supposed to smell strong (kind of): Olsen Fish Company (#15), the global leader in lutefisk production. Tour the factory, and the odor is actually more benevolent on your schnozz than cooking it in your kitchen — because Olsen produces about two million pounds of herring per year, the spices (coriander, peppercorns, onions) and sweet-sour tang of the high volume of pickled fish overpower the lutefisk's scent. The herring scent is actually kind of pleasant, familiar, one with which so many Scandinavian-American families grew up serving with crispbread and cheese. If you're one of the rare few nostalgic for the phlegm-like scent and gelatinous taste of lutefisk (or masochistic enough to seek out olfactory revulsion), consider heading to Madison, Minnesota for the Norsefest lutefisk-eating contest or pick your poison (your local church/ VFW's lutefisk dinner, that is).[1]

And another twist on some of these same spices — particularly the coriander — plays out in Gandhi Mahal's (#22) fragrant Indian cuisine. Spice is king here, from the brilliant heat of the vindaloo you can smell from the sidewalk outside, to the betel-fennel mixture offered gratis as a digestif on your way out.

...For the sweet tooth

Macalester College alumni may be smart, socially responsible, and ready to take on the world by the time they graduate, but the first couple weeks away from their parents, they're looking for a cheap, sustainable meal. What better way to harmlessly kill two birds with one stone than a dumpster dive? While dumpster diving — the "art" of salvaging "treasure" (or food) from another man's trash was a popular pastime for many Mac first-years at the beginning of the year, the allure wore off quickly for all but the most dedicated freegans after the first outing. The most prized dumpster diving destination among first-timers: the shared repository behind Jamba Juice and Breadsmith at the corner of Grand and Snelling Avenues (#20). Breadsmith's day-old bread — the "treasure" to be gained — was often double-bagged, protecting it from picking up any funky odors — which was *almost* a shame, because the entire dumpster — and often the surrounding alley — shone with the bright citrus of tens of pounds of freshly discarded orange peels.

Head down the street and hang a right on Cleveland to reach Izzy's (#17), the ice cream shop know for its tiny melon-baller "Izzy scoop." The ice cream is sweet, creamy, and bursting with flavour (we're particular fans of the strawberry crème fraîche ice cream and kalamansi sorbet), but the waffle cones are where it's at. These ain't your childhood Styrofoam sugar cone — they're ever-so-lightly sweet, crunchy enough to hold their own against rapidly melting ice cream, and smell like a vanilla-scented dream — one that you begin to crave from the moment you reach the street corner and catch the first whiff of fresh cones, hot off the presses.

Cross the river and you'll find an unassuming old-school bakery that you'd swear fumigates the entire block with a cloud of almond extract and powdered sugar. An aromatic blend of yeasty, baking dough and simple frosting, the aroma at A Baker's Wife (#21) instantly recalls an afternoon baking in grandma's kitchen — and many of the pastries fall right in line. From well-executed, down-home cookies to bars, breads to our personal favourite, the almond paste-filled pastry, these are desserts that make you feel at home.

...For an endless summer

While only the die-hards fire up their Webers year-round, Ted Cook's 19th Hole (#23) is the place to go for that same charcoal-kissed, smoky flavor in the dead of winter. The smell of tender, blackened meat at this South Minneapolis barbecue joint is almost stronger outside than in — in part due to several high-velocity fans and a squeaky ceiling fan spinning at full blast to both cool the room and help dissipate the scent. Forego the sides and ketchup-sweet sauce here, and stick to the unadulterated ribs for the full effect.

Your better bet for sauce (thick as molasses, with the flavor rounding out its sweet-spicy profile to boot) comes from Ted Cook's flashier sit-down restaurant cousin, Butcher and the Boar (#24). It's several times the tiny takeout restaurant's size — and with the larger real estate comes a barbecue scent that carries even further. Contributing most notably: a hefty fire pit near the outdoor beer garden that belches a consistent stream of deeply porky smoke that wafts along the wind, enticing (or repelling) hungry carnivores from a few blocks away.

And — for the experience you only really need once a year (or three, or four times — but two weeks is enough) — the Great Minnesota Get-Together serves up an epic cloud of grease and sweat that at once allures and sickens. After all, how many other destinations do you visit with the fully-executed intent to eat yourself sick? From the deep-fried salt bomb cheese curds shipped in fresh from Ellsworth, Wisconsin each day to the oily, sweet batter scent of funnel cakes, the myriad loud, overblown scent variants on grease, sugar, and salt commingle in a way that's only acceptable at the fair.

[1]For a more or less complete listing of lutefisk dinners across the upper Midwest — and the country — visit lutfiskloverslifeline.com

1. American Crystal Sugar
   · Highway 75 South, Crookston, Minnesota 56716
   · Business Highway 2, East Grand Forks, Minnesota 56721
   · 2500 North 11th Street, Moorhead, Minnesota 56560
2. Lou's Fish House, 1319 Minnesota 61, Two Harbors, Minnesota 55616
3. Malt-O-Meal, 319 Water Street S, Northfield, Minnesota 55057
4. Pabst Farms, 1370 Pabst Farms Circle, Oconomowoc, Wisconsin 53066
5. Red Star Yeast, Milwaukee, Wisconsin (CLOSED)
6. Miller / Coor Brewery, 4000 West State Street, Milwaukee, Wisconsin 53208
7. Nestle, 637 S Pine Street, Burlington, Wisconsin 53105
8. Cargill Corn Milling, 1710 16th Street SE, Cedar Rapids, Iowa 52401
9. Red Star Yeast, 3350 10th Street SW, Cedar Rapids, Iowa 52404
10. General Mills, 4800 Edgewood Rd SW, Cedar Rapids, Iowa 52404
11. Quaker Oats, 418 2nd Street NE, Cedar Rapids, Iowa 52401
12. Agri Star, 220 North West Street, Postville, Iowa 52162
13. JBS Swift & Co., 1700 Minnesota 60, Worthington, Minnesota 56187
14. Andrea's Pizza / Together Sushi; 811 Lasalle Avenue, Minneapolis, Minnesota 55402
15. Olsen Fish Co., 2115 N 2nd Street, Minneapolis, Minnesota 55411
16. Minnesota State Fair, 1265 Snelling Avenue N, Saint Paul, Minnesota 55108
17. Izzy's Ice Cream, 2034 Marshall Avenue, Saint Paul, Minnesota 55104
18. Shuang Hur, 654 University Avenue W, Saint Paul, Minnesota 55145
19. Candyland
    · 27 S 7th Street #6, Minneapolis, Minnesota 55402
    · 811 Lasalle Avenue #104, Minneapolis, Minnesota 55402
    · 435 Wabasha Street N, Saint Paul, Minnesota 55102
    · 212 Main Street N, Stillwater, Minnesota 55082
20. Breadsmith / Jamba Juice, 1577 Grand Avenue, Saint Paul, Minnesota 55105
21. A Baker's Wisconsinfe, 4200 28th Avenue S, Minneapolis, Minnesota 55406
22. Gandhi Mahal, 3009 27th Avenue S, Minneapolis, Minnesota 55406
23. Ted Cook's 19th Hole Barbeque, 2814 E 38th Street, Minneapolis, Minnesota 55406
24. Butcher and the Boar, 1121 Hennepin Avenue, Minneapolis, Minnesota 55403

CHAPTER 21

INTO THE PINES AND OVER THE FIRE: EPIC WILDERNESS MEALS IN THE BOUNDARY WATERS CANOE AREA AND BEYOND

WRITER: ALYSSA VANCE :: **CARTOGRAPHER:** MATT DOOLEY

Way up in the northeastern corner of Minnesota, nestled next to the Canadian border and tucked within the Superior National Forest, sits more than one million acres of pristine wilderness. The Boundary Waters Canoe Area (BWCA) is guarded by the U.S. National Forest Service and is one of the most coveted hiking, camping, and canoeing regions in the country. It is dense with thousands of lakes and waterways that were formed millennia ago when the glaciers that originally covered the region began to retreat, leaving behind a region sprinkled with pine, water, and bedrock. There are more than 2,000 campsites in the BWCA alone — and that doesn't take into account the popular surrounding camping destinations like Grand Marais, Ely, and the Lake Superior shoreline.

CANADA

Saganaga
Lake

Sea Gull
Lake

Neglige Lake

Boundary Waters
Canoe Area Wilderness

B.W.C.A.

Brule Lake

Judge CR
Magney
State Park

Malberg
Lake

Superior
N.F.

Kawishiwi
Lake

Superior Hiking Trail

Cascade River
State Park

Superior National

Forest

Temperance
River
State Park

George H.
Crosby
Maniton
State Park

Superior Hiking Trail

N

0   10   20 Miles

G. H. Manitou
State Park

Land Cover

Tettegouche
State Park

open
water

wetland

deciduous
forest

evergreen
forest

agriculture,
grassland

Bean and
Bear Lake

Silver Bay

Lake Superior

Split Rock
Lighthouse
State Park

Gooseberry Falls
State Park

Apostle Islands

National Lakeshore

Spending any time in wilderness demands work. And in this region the work is earned by portaging canoes, strapping on backpacks, and traveling by foot or water for long — and often strenuous — stretches, over land and water. However with this work comes reward. And don't the best rewards come in the form of food?

Below is a collective narrative of memorable wilderness meals in northern Minnesota. It begins by the rock-laden Lake Superior shore, travels north and west through the still waterways and thick pines of the BWCA, and trails off at International Falls along the Canadian border.

Highway 61 is a road adjacent to the Superior Hiking Trail — a 296 mile stretch that follows the Lake Superior shorelines and connects Duluth to the Canadian border. Silver Bay is a small town on that highway, roughly 50 miles north of Duluth. If you turn inland when you reach it, you'll have access to a hilly three-mile hike that leads you away from the sprawling Lake Superior shoreline, into a walkable roller coaster of rocky hills, and arrives at two bodies of water: Bean and Bear Lake.

"We hiked the trail in early July. The air was thick with heat and humidity, and most of the trail was spent under a blanket of trees. You're constantly take long steps to hike up or gingerly walking on a downward slope. As a novice hiker, it was challenging. But all worth it when we reached the peak that juts out over Bean Lake — a crisp, quiet, bright blue lake in the middle of all these trees. We camped at Bear Lake, just beyond it. We used our tiny camping stove to heat a hearty curry soup with coconut milk, sliced chorizo sausage, carrots, and lentils. Dessert was a sweet, crunchy muesli square. Eating both while staring out at this peaceful lake was one of the most satisfying moments of that summer." — **Alyssa Vance, Minneapolis resident**

George H. Crosby Manitou State Park sits 20 miles northeast of Bean and Bear Lake. The land was donated by its namesake, the mining magnate George H. Crosby. It boasts more than 3,000 acres of backpack-only camping grounds — an effort to preserve as much untouched nature as possible. The Manitou River cuts through the park and eventually spills into the chilly Lake Superior water.

"The day after we arrived, we took a seven-hour hike down the river and back up the Cedar Ridge Trail, coming back to camp via the Humpback Trail. One of the best hikes of my life thanks to the constantly changing scenery and the beautiful cascades on the river, but probably among the more exhausting. Coming back to camp, we realized that we are all several steps beyond starving. So we devised an improvised dinner plan based on what we had: Wisconsin-made summer sausage, a lot of Fraboni's bacon grease in our skillet, a couple large bags of add-water-and-heat potato soup. First thing we did was cube the summer sausage and fry it over the campfire in
bacon grease. Then we got an enormous pot of soup going, which we fortified with the slightly crispy, bacon-boosted summer sausage. I don't think there's any way this kind of cooking could carry over into the everyday modern world, but after burning piles of calories on the trail, and in the cool of night by the fire, it was one of the richest, creamiest, most satisfying things I've ever eaten." — **James Norton, Minneapolis resident**

Kawishiwi Lake is a three-mile shot straight north of George H. Crosby Manitou State Park. Because it sits on the southeastern edge of BWCA border it's considered an accessible entry point for a portage. It's also an irregularly shaped lake — so there is a surprisingly long shoreline and plenty of small bays. The head of the Kawishiwi River sits on the north side of that lake. If you head towards it and hike north for seven-plus miles you'll eventually meet with Malberg Lake — a 400-ace body of water accessible only via canoe.

"The best food I've ever had in the BWCA was a delicious meal of breaded northern pike and smallmouth bass, lightly fried with chicken-of-the-woods mushrooms and ostrich fern fiddleheads that we foraged. We didn't have breading, so we slowly toasted some rye bread we had until it was crumbly, and coated the fish prior to frying in some grape seed oil someone had. It really tasted of the North Woods." — Matthew Kumka, Minneapolis Resident

Saganaga Lake is 20 miles northeast of Malberg Lake, and is cut in half by the Canadian border. At more than 13,000 acres, it's the largest body of water within the BWCA. Sea Gull Lake is just south of Saganaga Lake. The nearly 5,000 acres of water are dotted with more than a hundred small islands and surrounded with pine and granite cliffs.

"The first time I visited the BWCA was with my dad when I was five-years-old. I started to go annually after that, through high school, and eventually worked at a canoe outfitter during my college summers. I made a lot of "hobo dinners" — a bunch of potatoes, meat, butter, and veggies in foil and tossed directly over the fire. We also made a version of apple pie. We pressed pre-made apple filling between two slices of bread and put it in a press over the fire. We picked berries, too. There was a lot of burnt forest area up there and it was blueberry heaven. There are a lot of beauties that come after a fire, and one of those is berries." — Sarah Kaiser-Schatzlein, Minneapolis Resident

Neglige Lake is a relatively small and narrow body of water about 15 miles south of Sea Gull Lake. It's considered one of the more remote lakes, since it's difficult to access and has just one campsite. Because it is an operating fishery, the water is flush with two species of trout: brook and rainbow.

"It was our first time in the BWCA. We took turns carrying the canoe. I was on duty during the last portage to Neglige Lake. We bulldozed through about a mile of underbrush. It was hot out, and pretty challenging. When we finally got to the lake it was early evening and there were fish jumping out of it. We caught about 10 to 12 brook trout, then gathered these big, flat stones, and heated them over a fire for about an hour.* We put the fish — whole — in foil with butter and spices. It tasted like a more tender piece of salmon. Oily, flavorful meat. The meat pulled right off the bone." — Chris O'Brien, Minneapolis Resident
*Editor's note: Heating stones directly over a fire can occasionally result in high-velocity stone shrapnel.

Angleworm Lake is roughly 30 miles east of Neglige Lake. It's a long, thin body of water. Much like the shape of... a worm. To get to it, campers hike along the Echo Trail — 14 miles long and filled with red and white pine and scenic overlooks.

"Four of us portaged two miles from Echo Trail to Angleworm Lake. We were carrying a 23 foot, 4-person canoe! We had stopped at Fitger's Brewhouse on our way up and filled up a few Nalgene growlers of beer. Our first campsite dinner was pizza: chicken, walnut, caramelized onion, garlic, pesto. We grilled the chicken and caramelized the onions before we left, carried the dough in a gallon-size plastic bag, and just added water and yeast before we cooked them on the cast-iron skillet." — Jeremy Nelson, Minneapolis Resident

The town of Ely is 13 miles south of Angleworm Lake. It's considered one of the gateway cities to the BWCA. Like many towns along the Iron Range, the first economies were influenced heavily by logging and mining. International Falls is over 100 miles northwest of Ely — right at the Canadian border.

"We took a 68-day-long canoe trip from Ely to Canada for our honeymoon. Along the trail, there was this amazing series of lakes with narrow waterways that had been cleared. We romanticized that they had been maintained for centuries. One lake was crystal clear blue, and we could dive down 20 feet and see one another. I spent about a month or two dehydrating food to prepare for the trip. I had never had fish tacos, and I wanted to make them. We fished almost every day and caught northern, walleyes, and the obligatory brook trout. I made my own tortillas on the trail and used dehydrated tomatoes, cheese, and dried beans. Life was so simple: paddle, eat, sleep." — **Andrea Strom, Ely Resident**

CHAPTER 22

REMEMBER WHERE YOU CAME FROM

WRITER: SOLEIL HO :: **ILLUSTRATOR:** ALLEGRA LOCKSTADT

Over the past few years, it's become evident that Minneapolis is resolutely entering the age of the New Immigrant Chef. These are the children of Leeann Chin's generation, brought up in the United States but raised by parents who were still very connected to their countries of origin. Popularly known as 1.5 or 2nd generation immigrants, the former includes people who immigrated before or during their early teens, whereas the latter refers to the native-born children of immigrant parents.

These young chefs have injected the city with a fresh perspective and initiated diners into the unique, border-busting mindsets that they grew up with. Finding their own ways through a trail blazed by the four horsemen of the this-ain't-fusion apocalypse — David Chang, Roy Choi, Danny Bowien, and Eddie Huang — this new crop of chefs cook with a sense of compromise, rather than collision. The chefs at Gai Gai Thai, Pizzeria Lola, Saffron, and The Left Handed Cook have been wowing the city's diners with their adventurous-yet-faithful cooking, so I really wanted to ask them just who or what they were being faithful *to*.

SAMEH WADI

WORLD STREET KITCHEN

SAFFRON

LYNDALE

ANN KIM

HELLO PIZZA

PIZZERIA LOLA

FRANCE

XERXES

LAKE

THOMAS KIM

KAT MELGAARD

THE LEFTHANDED COOK
THE RABBIT HOLE

KRIS PETCHARAWISES

GAI GAI THAI

NICOLLET

They represent the vanguard of the new in Minneapolis, part of the core set of tastemakers that have lit the local restaurant scene on fire. What follows is a sampling of their perspectives on their heritages, American food, and the culinary magic that happens when those two halves of their selves intersect.

KRIS PETCHARAWISES | *Gai Gai Thai*

The ingredients of the Thai street food and breakfast bowls that you'll find at this humble mobile kitchen constantly rotate according to what's in season, which makes their farmer's market locations the perfect setting for them. Petchawarises has made his name crafting dishes that are both unmistakably Thai and full-on Minnesotan.

COMING TO AMERICA

I was born in Bangkok, Thailand, and six months later my family decided to move out to the States because my mom was trying to go to nursing school in Georgia. The reason we chose Georgia was because my dad's sister's husband was going to grad school down at Georgia Tech. It seems kind of random to people, why a Thai family would go down to Georgia, for sure. My dad was also going for his Masters in engineering, so it was natural to go to the States, just because the options were a little bit better. So I was raised by my grandparents until I was about 3. It's your typical immigrant story: an Asian family brings their kids, they work and have to leave the kids with the grandparents.

HOME ECONOMICS

I have a lot of memories of having meals with family, with my parents and aunts and uncles eating together. It's very social in Thai culture — it wasn't a meal unless the family was getting together. It's a good way for people to bond.

With Thais, pretty much everyone likes to go out to eat a lot. It wasn't just home cooking, but I grew up eating a lot of stuff outside, street food. The definition of street food in the States is really different from what it is in Thailand. Thai street food isn't about cooking in a heavy truck or box where you can't really interact with people or show them how things are made; it's about just being out there, just enjoying the company, smelling everything and seeing the process. I prefer more of the Thai style. It's fun to see regulars, it's fun to interact with people. It's one of the nice things about being at Kingfield [Farmers Market].

THE CROSSOVER HIT

The red cabbage slaw on our menu has the flavors of the Thai papaya salad, but with a mix of local ingredients. Obviously papayas aren't native to Minnesota, so red cabbage is our way of making it Midwest-style, using what's here. We also like to support our fellow market vendors, buying their strawberries, corn, kale, all of that good stuff. In that regard, we've been really successful in taking what the market has and giving it really nice Thai flavors.

HOW I MAKE IT WORK

The Thai flavor profile is all about sweet, sour, and salty. The red cabbage slaw still adheres to the spicy and the sour and the sweetness — all of those flavor profiles. The red cabbage in addition adds a bit of sweetness to it that you also have in papaya. So while it's not exactly the same, we're not throwing out all the different flavors out there just for the sake of authenticity. In a way, we're using the old template but with respect to what's available locally.

You gotta respect the flavor profile. You can't just put peanuts in something and call it Thai. A lot of the big food conglomerates like to do that. It's like, you can't just put ketchup on something and call it American, you know? I think growing up and being around the food and cooking it, messing around as a kid, gives you a real advantage in knowing the flavor profile. At the same time, I think when someone from the outside respects the craft and the trade, that's a good thing for the culture. If you appreciate the flavors, do the food justice and respect, that's fine.

ANN KIM | *Pizzeria Lola, Hello Pizza*

The exquisite pizzas that you'll find at Kim's two locations in southwest Minneapolis are among the best you'll find in the metro. Rather than copying any given region's pizza, she created her own style, featuring lovely, chewy crusts that support dreamy toppings like Iowan guanciale, piquillo peppers, and Korean BBQ short ribs. She and her team have shouldered the lion's share of responsibility for putting Minneapolis's pizza scene into the national spotlight.

COMING TO AMERICA

My family immigrated here from Korea in 1977. All I remember is that I was 4 years old, and that it was July. We immigrated to Minnesota and came here because that's where we actually had a relative, my mother's younger sister. Our first home was in Apple Valley. Not the most likely place to immigrate to, but that's where we ended up. My maternal grandmother also came with us because both of my parents were working multiple jobs and they needed someone to take care of my sister and I.

HOME ECONOMICS

When I was younger my grandmother did the majority of the cooking. There weren't any places where we could find any of the Asian ingredients and produce that my mother and grandmother were used to. You can imagine back in the '70s, there weren't a lot of markets here and the Korean community wasn't very large. My grandmother grew a lot of produce that was native to Korea. She grew perilla leaves and she would ferment and pickle those and we'd have them all year to eat. Things like garlic chives, different types of zucchini that we'd get from Korea that they wouldn't have here. My grandma would preserve, pickle, or saute them so we'd have those side dishes: *panchan*, as they call them in Korean.

Also, every November, there was a farm — there was a small Korean community, not a big one, but there was a farm that people went to that had a lot of Napa cabbage in the fall. We would buy a ton of it and ferment it at home. I remember we would sit in the laundry room to wash and salt hundreds of pounds of cabbage. And then we'd use our kiddie pool to basically salt and brine the Napa. I remember helping my mom and grandmother stuff the chilli peppers into the cabbage and stuff them into jars and we'd have it all winter long. There was a lot of home cooking going on.

THE CROSSOVER HIT

When I opened Pizzeria Lola, Korean-style pizza toppings definitely weren't a thing that I was intending on doing. But at one point, I just thought, I wonder what it would taste like to have kimchi on a pizza? I thought, you know, it's similar to sauerkraut and we can experiment with it. I had no intention of putting it on the regular menu because I really didn't think it would sell. So I ran the Lady ZaZa, a pizza with kimichi and Korean sausage on it, as a special for about a week, and then people loved it. I had to put it on the permanent menu. People have also been ordering kimchi on the side with their pizzas; we might be the only pizzeria in town that also carries chopsticks! I just think it's so strange and funny that a lot of our customers' first experience with kimchi is on a pizza. It's really cool to see. It makes me really proud and happy to be able to bring the elements that I grew up with, things that I love and that I didn't really have a true appreciation for until I got older, to people in a new way.

HOW I MAKE IT WORK

For me, I have to go by my gut and intuition with things that I grew up with and my palate and I just try to create things that I think taste good and that other people would like to eat as well. I keep it really simple. I think I try to take things that are rustic and simple and elevate it and surprise people. Like with pizza. People just tend to think of it as junk food. You don't think about it, none of the meats are house-made, the cheeses are just this shredded cheese. But the way we do it, everything from the crust to the cheese to the meat are house-made. So for me it's about taking these simple things and really putting thought into it and elevating it to make it special. That's what I think I do well and if I stick to that formula I hope the restaurant will be here for 50 years.

SAMEH WADI | *Saffron, World Street Kitchen*

With multiple nods from the James Beard Foundation, an *Iron Chef America* appearance, and two completely different and successful restaurants to his name, this young chef has earned himself a secure seat among the best chefs in the region. At Saffron and World Street Kitchen, he flexes both his love of home cooking and his extensive knowledge of global street food, respectively.

COMING TO AMERICA

Around the time of the Gulf War in Kuwait, a lot of my family started to come over to America from our homes in the Middle East. In 1997, I moved to Minnesota. I was 13, and it was my freshman year of high school. Moving into the suburbs was kind of a shock to me. The kids I went to school with didn't even know how to find the Middle East on a map. I did Middle Eastern calligraphy in art classes at school, and I was extremely proud of being able to show people that piece of my culture and where I came from. I took that very seriously. But I also came here really openminded toward change, to having a future here.

HOME ECONOMICS

My father taught my mom how to cook when they first got married. They both have really good palates. My father was very internationally inspired, and would bring different ingredients home from his travels to experiment with. Like when we were living in Kuwait and had never heard of soy sauce or fish sauce, he brought it back from Southeast Asia for us to try. My mom is more traditional, and cooks for the basic Middle Eastern diet. She's my biggest influence as a cook, and really made me appreciate the classics that have been handed down from generation to generation. My family takes food extremely seriously, so cooking with them was really like a rite of passage.

THE CROSSOVER HIT

A while back, I was looking in my brother's basement and found a stash of recipes that my mom and dad had collected for the cookbook they were trying to write. I spent two weeks reading the recipes, which were in Arabic, and I stumbled upon a recipe for slow-cooked green beans written by my grandmother. It took me instantly to my childhood, when my mother would make them for us. It's a peasant dish, but I felt then that I had to put it on my menu. The problem was that Saffron's menu at the time was too refined for it. So I shut down the restaurant for a week to rework everything just so I could put this dish on the menu. I didn't want it to hide behind some puree, a foam, or microgreens. Just green beans and a lemon wedge. I'm still confident that this dish can be appreciated by Joe Public. It's still on the menu.

HOW I MAKE IT WORK

When I first came to America, my brother sat me down and told me, "Here you can be whatever you want. But whatever you do represents our family, our culture. You are an ambassador of the Palestinian people. Represent well." I really took that to heart. Saffron is a reflection of that journey, and of who I was when I opened the restaurant. The idea for Saffron has been in my head since culinary school. It's influenced by Middle Eastern, North African, and Mediterranean cuisines. At the time I opened it in 2007, no other chefs in town were doing this kind of food. I really wanted to showcase the food that I grew up with.

On the other hand, World Street Kitchen is more of a reflection of me as a person. It's loud, bright, and everything's out in the open. The idea behind the menu is that it's the kind of food that I want to eat. Because you know, sometimes I just want some fucking tongue tacos! I want to be able to eat whatever I want, wherever I want. And I love that about international street food. It's the same at World Street Kitchen, and there's no wall between the cooks and the public. You can talk to the cooks, have a relationship.

Saffron is me then, and WSK is me now. The restaurants represent two sides of me. I'm Arab American and proud of it. But I have to wonder, why wasn't I involved in something more useful than being a chef? Still, if I had to do it all again, I wouldn't change a thing.

THOMAS KIM AND KAT MELGAARD | *The Left Handed Cook*

Since their little restaurant in Midtown Global Market busted onto the scene in summer 2012, partners Melgaard and Kim have charmed diners with a bold mixture of Asian, Latin, and Midwestern flavors and a hefty dose of punk rock aesthetics. That delicate balancing act shows in dishes like their kimchi- and curry-inflected poutine, as well as the novel-yet-homey Bop Bowls on their menu.

HOME ECONOMICS

Thomas: [I have] first-generation Korean parents and then we had our extended family living with us as well: my mom's two sisters and their kids. It was the full-on Korean experience. No American food at all. My mom still to this day will not cook a single American dish. Not because she refuses to, but she just doesn't know how.

Kat: I didn't have any experience with Korean food growing up, actually. It was literally meat and potatoes every day growing up. It was a lot of roast beef, mashed potatoes, scalloped potatoes, pot roast, any kind of slow cooking, steak, hamburgers, potato salad. Any kind of meat and potato combination. I definitely grew up in that very Middle American food landscape. It wasn't until I moved to New York that I had Korean food or any kind of Asian food besides your typical Chinese. It was weird at first, as somebody that was adopted. At the time I was growing up, for adoptees, it wasn't like your parents would teach you about your culture, your ethnic culture. It was more like, you're my kid and that's all there is to it.

Thomas: The funny thing is, I think Kat and I, regardless of what our family was, came to the same result. The kind of reactionary thing where we went against our childhood and now we have that camaraderie. The end result is kind of similar: We both have tattoos, are really into art, and we have that big city culture.

I would also rebel against my parents, like, if dinner was always rice and kimchi, I would insist on steak and potatoes. Something that my mom just didn't know how to make or wouldn't make. It turned into a situation where she was, like: "Just make it yourself." That's what kickstarted me into making food for myself. It made me pretty self-reliant, and made me more comfortable in the kitchen. It was a good and bad thing. My mom probably would have been happier if I ended up as some crazy Korean food chef. Unfortunately not.

THE CROSSOVER HIT

Thomas: We have a dish that's called the Notorious P.I.G. That one's like the kimchi scallion pancake, and we treat it like a tortilla. We incorporate chimichurri into it to give it a nice South American herbal flavor, then we top it with carnitas which are very Latin American, but we dress it with roasted scallion sauce and hoisin, which brings it back to being a little bit more Asian. We top it with Cheddar cheese, which is our homage to American culture. That base of it is Korean, but then it delves into the Latin aspect of it, which I have been heavy into, living in L.A. You can't help but be immersed in that style of cuisine.

I'm taking that Korean flavor profile, then interpreting it in my own way, then presenting it to a different palate. When we emulate the flavor profile, it turns into this weird, secondhand cuisine. But it works, I think.

HOW WE MAKE IT WORK

Thomas: We look at ourselves less as Asian and we look at ourselves more as American, but we tap into our upbringing which happens to be Asian. But it could have been anything.

I try not to have any sense of guilt over things being inauthentic. From my personal lens, this is my background and I'm trying to look at this cuisine through that particular lens. Someone else might see it differently, and that's good because it brings all of these interesting facets to this cuisine. I think whatever you grew up with thinking were essential ingredients, that's the formation of the cuisine you continue to push forward. Thankfully, I wasn't narrow-minded enough to just put myself into one cuisine. I went first Italian, then American, then Japanese. It really broadened my approach to things.

CHAPTER 23

SMALL TOWNS, GOOD EATS

INTRODUCING A NEW CULINARY STATISTIC: THE CHATTERBOX SCORE

WRITER: CHUCK TERHARK :: **CARTOGRAPHER:** NAT CASE

When judging a meal, context matters. Sometimes it's everything.

I learned this lesson one Memorial Day weekend in the Boundary Waters, after a day of paddling and portaging away from civilization and a night of eating little more than gorp and gummi bears. The next morning I woke at dawn, grabbed my fishing pole, and swore a solemn vow to the grumble in my stomach that it would have walleye for breakfast. An hour later I filleted four fish while my camping partner made a fire. He cooked them in a little oil while I paddled across the lake to dispose of the fish guts; on my way back, a bald eagle swooped down where I'd disposed of the guts and carried them off. I could smell breakfast from the middle of the lake. After eating it, I laid down on a sunny rock and entertained myself with the thought that somewhere nearby an eagle was digesting the same meal as me. That walleye breakfast was, and will probably always be, the greatest meal I have eaten.

Was it the best walleye I'd ever eaten? Certainly not. There are many restaurants in the Twin Cities that can cook a walleye better than we did. But context matters.

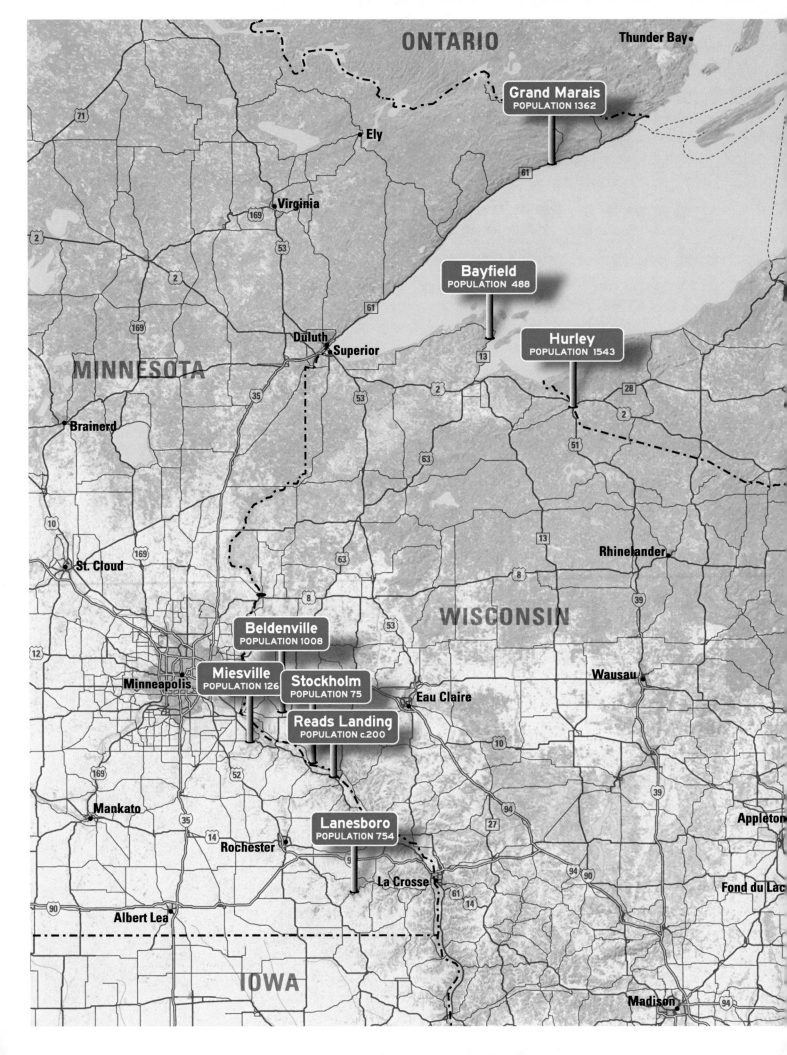

I think about this often when I'm at a restaurant in a small Midwestern town. You know the type: a diner, or a supper club, the last place in town holding out against the constant encroachment of McManifest Destiny. The kind of place where you just want to sit and take in the atmosphere and charm. As for the food, well, you take what you can get. Sometimes, though, you get more than you expect.

Some of my most fondly remembered meals have been in places like this. Good meals, some of them great meals, all bolstered not so much by the food as by its distance from the crush of the urban world.

There's value in these places. Not just cultural or nostalgic value, but real culinary value. A good small-town cafe may not stack up head-to-head with the best that a big city has to offer, but it offers something else, a chance to enjoy good food where you may not have expected such a chance. Sometimes that value is so great that it tips the scales, leading to such exaggerated claims as, "Such-and-such roadhouse makes the best burgers the state has ever seen," or, "No barley soup will ever be as good as the one I used to eat in the cafe in the farm town where I grew up." (And sometimes you find a true gem, an honest-to-goodness incredible restaurant in the middle of nowhere.) This is how Americana propagates itself, through stories that, true or not, are believed, rendering the difference meaningless. You could call it "Chatterbox Syndrome," after the fictional Lake Wobegon cafe — because such experiences turn us all into Garrison Keillors, blubbering and sentimental, pining for simpler, tastier times.

Context matters. But how much does it matter? Is it possible to capture the ineffable quality of these small-town eateries? To grade them on a curve that accounts for their locales, their intangible charms, their *je ne sais what-have-you?*

Probably not. But that doesn't mean we can't try.

And so I offer, more as a thought experiment than anything else, a new metric by which to judge the outstate dining experience: the Chatterbox Score.

CALCULATING THE CHATTERBOX (CB) SCORE: CB = (Q X A X O X S) / P

Q = Quality of food

A = Atmosphere

O = Originality/Creativity

S = Service

P = Population of nearest town

The values Q, A, O, and S fall on a 1-10 scale and are assigned subjectively by the author. These values are all multiplied, and then divided by the population of the restaurant's nearest town. A "perfect" score is, theoretically, 10,000*: Tens across the board in a town inhabited by one lonely world-class chef. This is, of course, unlikely. Far more typical would be fives across the board in a town of 625, which would net a CB score of exactly 1. So let's call 1 an "average" score, and develop some rough guidelines from there:

1-2: Average ("This is about what I'd expect.")

2-3: Good ("Hey, this is... good.")

3-4: Very Good ("Wait, what's this place doing out here?")

4+: Incredible ("Holy.... I would drive hours to eat this!")

*My walleye breakfast, having been prepared and consumed on the shores of an uninhabited lake, would have to be divided by zero. In other words: Incalculably awesome.

Some things to emphasize as we proceed: A restaurant's CB score does not directly reflect its overall quality as a restaurant. It is simply intended to quantify that value of a place that makes it feel oddly and excitingly out of place in its surroundings, the way a quarter looks when it's lying on a sidewalk. The "what's *this* doing *here?*"-ness of a place. Many of the greatest restaurants in the world would have extremely low CB scores, simply because many high-quality restaurants are located in heavily populated areas. Those would be diamonds in, say, jewelry boxes: Beautiful things deserving of celebration, but which also happen to be located exactly where you'd expect them to be. We're looking in the rough here.

Without further ado:

THE TOP TEN RESTAURANTS BY CHATTERBOX SCORE IN RURAL MINNESOTA/WESTERN WISCONSIN

WILD RICE

Bayfield, Wisconsin
Population: 488

CB Score:
Q: 8
A: 9
O: 7
S: 8
/ 488
= 8.26

Let's begin with the crown jewel of rural Wisconsin dining. A world-class kitchen churning out trend-forward dishes with a focus on local and seasonal ingredients, all in a modernist, nouveau-Scandinavian gem of a building (designed by Duluth architect David Salmela) within few hundred feet of the Lake Superior shoreline — this restaurant just shouldn't be out here, serving foie gras ravioli and pumpkin seed sweetbreads. Thank the old spirits of the North Woods for Mary Rice, the Andersen Windows heiress who has chosen to use her fortune for culinary good in Minnesota and Wisconsin (and for civic good, too: one percent of your final bill at Wild Rice goes to the Bayfield Rec Center). She has built a gastronomic empire in Bayfield and revels in the unexpected, which explains Wild Rice popping up like a morel in the middle of these woods. Would it survive without her angel investment? Who cares. Sometimes a sugar mama is a sweet thing indeed.

A TO Z PRODUCE AND BAKERY

Stockholm, Wisconsin
Population: 75

CB Score:
Q: 5
A: 8
O: 5
S: 2
/ 75
= 5.33

A to Z—colloquially known as "the Pizza Farm"—regularly draws huge crowds despite being a 90-minute drive southeast of the Twin Cities. One reason is that drive itself, a gorgeous wend through bluff country regularly punctuated by incredible river views and delightful river towns. The other is the destination: An organic farm that, once per week on Tuesdays for six months out of the year, harvests all the ingredients necessary to make woodfired pizza and bakes them right there on the farm for anyone who makes the drive. And many do, waiting in long lines and passing the time sipping boxed wine and lounging on blankets within earshot of the cow pasture. The pizza itself is fine, but out here it's all about the atmosphere. The utter tininess of Stockholm helps, too.

KINGS PLACE

Miesville, Minnesota
Population: 125

CB Score:
Q: 6
A: 4
O: 6
S: 4
/125
= 4.6

Towns as tiny as Miesville are lucky to have even one claim to fame, but, spoiled as they are, Miesvilleans have two: The Mudhens, the town's championship baseball team; and King's, home to some of the state's most sought-after burgers. They serve 30-odd variations, each with a baseball-themed name and toppings out of (appropriately) left field. (Fried eggs, baked beans, sauerkraut and peanut butter regularly crop up. Although not on the same burger—at least not yet.) The service and atmosphere are about what you expect, but the burgers outclass nearly every big-city beef patty you'll find.

HARBOR VIEW CAFE

Pepin, Wisconsin
Population: 814

CB Score:
Q: 7
A: 8
O: 7
S: 7
/ 814
= 3.37

You know any town that prides itself on its connection to *Little House on the Prairie* (Laura Ingalls Wilder was born nearby) is going to play up its charm factor, but there's nothing put-on about Harbor View Cafe. It's just a great little checkered-tablecloth bistro serving French-inspired comfort cuisine on the shores of Lake Pepin, a welcome stop amid the stream of bakeries and antique malls on Great River Road. Don't miss the house specialty: sauteed Alaskan halibut in a black butter caper sauce.

SHADY GROVE

Beldenville, Wisconsin
Pop: 1,008

CB Score:
Q: 8
A: 8
O: 7
S: 7
/1,008
= 3.11

I like supper clubs. I've been to many of them. But when a person says, "I like supper clubs," they really do mean all supper clubs, because they are all the same. They are all dark, they all serve steak or fish with mashed potatoes and some canned vegetable or other, and they all endeavor to achieve a level of sophistication surpassed by most decent restaurants decades ago. (A favorite supper club story: While dining at a very nice one in a very small Minnesota town, a friend ordered a "whiskey, neat." It arrived in a green bejeweled goblet—the "neatest glass the bartender could find.") All of this makes me hesitate to call Shady Grove a supper club, as it is a legitimately wonderful restaurant, serving a chef-driven seasonal menu with fresh ingredients grown right there in the property's vegetable garden. And yet it has all the feel of a supper club, with a full bar (at a table near us sat a 103-year-old woman who attributed her longevity to, among other things, the restaurant's gin martinis) and plenty of steak and seafood on the menu. The service was so-so, but was more than rectified by the friendliness and attentiveness of Steve and Heather Snook, the restaurant's kindly husband-and-wife owners.

MAGGIE'S

Bayfield, Wisconsin
Population: 488

CB Score:
Q: 7
A: 4
O: 7
S: 6
/ 488
= 2.4

The other Mary Rice restaurant on this list, Maggie's, is Wild Rice's wackier, more approachable little sister, decked out in pink (the flamingo is evidently Rice's spirit animal) but imbued with the same guiding principles as its handsomer spinoff in the woods. Don't miss the fried whitefish livers — a house specialty for decades, and now imitated all over Great Lakes country.

ANGRY TROUT CAFE

Grand Marais, Minnesota
Population: 1,362

CB Score:
Q: 8
A: 7
O: 7
S: 8
/ 1,543
= 2.0

Tucked into one of Minnesota's most picturesque scenes, the Angry Trout Cafe in Grand Marais pulls off the neat trick of making the North Shore somehow even more visitable. The owners are localphiles to a fault, even sourcing the menu's caviar from Lake Superior herring. (The Scandinavian delicacy is so sought-after that Sweden imports the fish's roe from Grand Marais fisheries — though local demand is lagging.) Visitors love the scratch ingredients, and the fish is as fresh as it gets.

READS LANDING BREWING

Reads Landing, Minnesota
Population: 200

CB Score:
Q: 5
A: 5
O: 3
S: 5
/ 200
= 1.86

Another spot whose score is helped out by the tininess of its hometown, Reads Landing Brewing is, as the name implies, all about the beer. The brewery's house varieties are all quite good, but the real surprise is the rest of the beer list, which boast craft and microbrews from all over the country, with a nice bias for the local stuff too. Someone in Reads Landing in a proud craft beer snob. (I'm guessing this is the smallest town in Minnesota that sells Surly Darkness.)

OLD VILLAGE HALL

Lanesboro, Minnesota
Population: 754

CB Score:
Q: 5
A: 7
O: 5
S: 7
/ 754
= 1.62

The self-proclaimed "Bed and Breakfast Capital of Minnesota," Lanesboro also offers plenty for day-trippers who don't feel like staying the night. For foodies, chief among these attractions is the Old Village Hall, a historic downtown building topped with a bell tower and bragging rights as the town's best restaurant. It does meat and potatoes right, with plenty of surprise to balance the comfort, and you can't beat the cozy atmosphere.

LIBERTY BELL CHALET

Hurley, Wisconsin
Population: 1,543

CB Score:
Q: 6
A: 7
O: 6
S: 8
/ 1,543
= 1.3

"The Bell" has been serving authentic Italian cuisine in Hurley for nearly 100 years, first to the hungry miners and lumberjacks of northeastern Wisconsin and the Upper Peninsula, and now to the downhill ski crowd (hence the "chalet" sobriquet). Family owned for generations and fiercely adored by locals, the Liberty Bell specializes in the staples of old-style Italian-American: pizza and lasagna, as well as a family-secret Caesar salad.

CHAPTER 24
THE SONGS OF THE SOUTH MINNEAPOLIS ICE CREAM TRUCK: A FIELD GUIDE

THE SONGS OF THE SOUTH MINNEAPOLIS ICE CREAM TRUCK: A FIELD GUIDE

WRITER/ILLUSTRATOR: ANDY STURDEVANT

1. "TURKEY IN THE STRAW" (Author unknown, circa 1820s)

In most parts of South Minneapolis, the dominance of "Turkey in the Straw" as the song of choice of most ice cream truck operators between late April and very early September is unchallenged. "Turkey in the Straw" is the heavyweight champion of ice cream truck songs. To hear "Turkey in the Straw" echoing through the stucco cottage-lined streets of the southside is to become mentally primed for the taste of Bomb Pops and Batman-shaped frozen novelties with gumball eyes.

It's a weird choice for entrusting with the public face of children's ice cream. "Turkey in the Straw," like the entire repertoire of ice cream truck songs, predates the Twenty-first Century. In fact, it predates the twentieth. It's a traditional folk song from the 1820s or so, initially made popular by blackface minstrels, and adapted and re-adapted hundreds of times over the past two hundred years for all sorts of purposes: children's tune, drinking song, Civil War marching anthem, campfire sing-along, racist novelty number, rural hoedown favorite, and even a vulgarity-laden goof ("do your balls hang low?" asks one well-known variation). By the time Walt Disney immortalized it in "Steamboat Willie," it was already a hundred years old.

How did this ancient song, and many others that are equally ancient, become the public face of children's ice cream in South Minneapolis and elsewhere in the United States? In fact, we don't even have to leave South Minneapolis to learn a key part of the story.

Virtually any song you hear emanating from an ice cream truck is originating from a small black box, mounted near the dashboard, with two knobs (one controlling volume, one controlling song choice) and an on/off switch. Under the right-hand knob are emblazoned the words "MINNEAPOLIS, MN." This box is the Digital II, manufactured by the Nichols Electronics Company. It contains, on a solid-state chip inside, the eight all-time most popular ice cream truck songs, including "Turkey in the Straw."

The Digital II is a product of the greater southside, manufactured by Nichols Electronics

C H E V Y   S T E P   V A N

NICHOLS ELECTRONICS
DIGITAL II

12 VOLT TRIP GONG
(MOUNTED TO HOOD OF ECONOLINE)

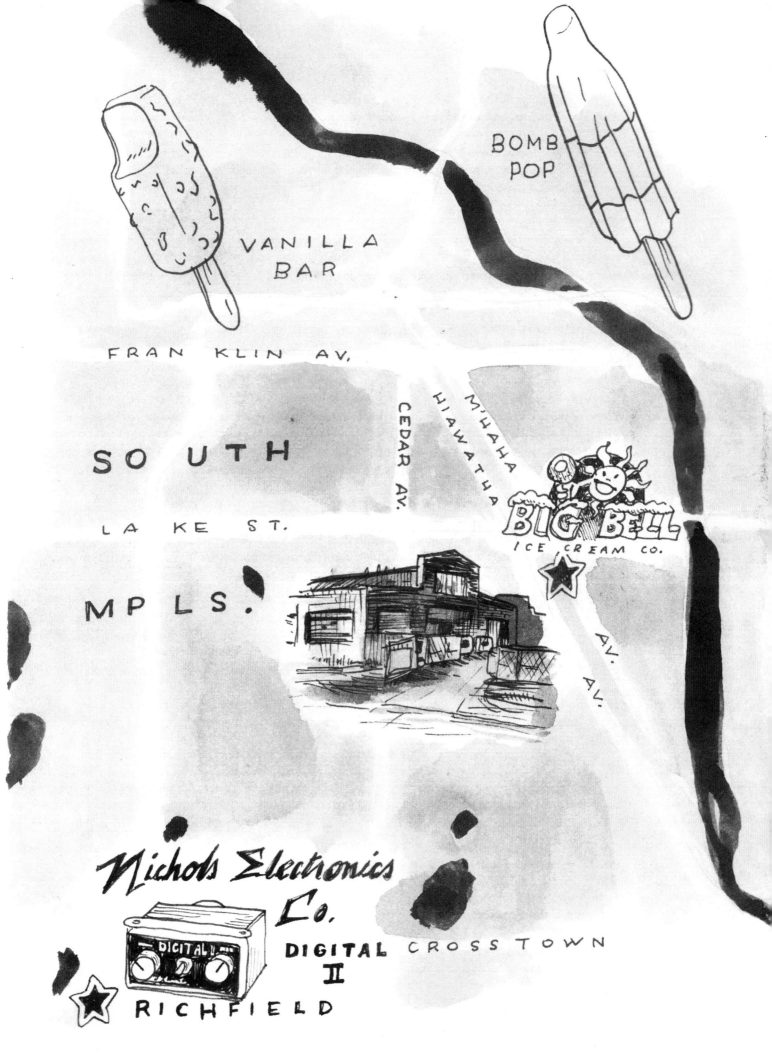

about ten blocks over the city's southern border in the first-ring suburb of Richfield. It uses digital technology to evoke the tinkling, automated music of the pre-modern era. It's a long chain of nostalgia going way, way back.

Ice cream trucks were associated with chiming, jingling bells for most of the Twentieth Century. According to musicologist Daniel Tannehill Neely (who outlines this hidden history beautifully in a 2005 article in Esopus magazine), ice cream parlors of the Nineteenth Century often contained music boxes, where patrons could hear tinkling versions of classical and operatic favorites while enjoying their ice cream. When mobile ice cream carts became part of the urban landscape, early proprietors used bells and music boxes to nostalgically link their wares to the parlors of old. At the end of World War II, a Los Angeles-based truck driver rigged a crude, battery-draining system to amplify this chime music over speakers. He was, like any ice cream truck vendor, selling nostalgia, so he stuck with Nineteenth Century standards like "Sidewalks of New York."

The Nichols Electronics Company, founded in 1957 by a Minneapolis engineer named Bob Nichols, was the first to create transistorized amplification systems for this chime music, which operated much like guitar pickups. (Ironically, one of the disputed authors of "Turkey in the Straw" was a performer in the 1820s named George Nichols — no relation to Bob.) In 1985, Nichols improved on this model with the Digital, a box that completely eliminated moving parts, making its operation even simpler. The Nichols Electronic Company is still located in Richfield, and is still the world's leading producer of electronic music boxes. The technology has changed greatly, but repertoire has not. "Turkey in the Straw," chiming in a strangely disembodied bell-like timbre and reaching back well beyond living memory, draws a direct line back to America's oldest associations with ice cream.

But the last word on this particular song should go to perhaps the most famous mobile food vendor in all of literature, Ignatius J. Reilly in John Kennedy Toole's novel A Confederacy of Dunces: "I suspect that you imagine 'Turkey in the Straw' to be a valuable bit of Americana. Well, it is not. It is a discordant abomination. Veneration of such things as 'Turkey in the Straw' is at the very root of our current dilemma."

2. "THE ENTERTAINER" (Scott Joplin, 1902)

"The Entertainer" is one of the most modern of the Digital II's eight songs, have been composed just on this side of the Twentieth Century in 1902 by Scott Joplin. It's still best known today for its role in the 1973 Robert Redford-Paul Newman film The Sting. It was massively popular throughout the 1970s, both through its association with the film and its role as a surprise smash hit for the classical record label Nonesuch, which issued an anthology of ragtime music in 1970 with "The Entertainer" front-and-center, resulting in million-plus sales and several Grammys.

Most of the ice cream truck trade in South Minneapolis comes from the Big Bell Ice Cream Company. Located in an industrial corridor along Minnehaha Avenue in the Longfellow neighborhood, the Big Bell compound is wedged between a passenger light rail line, a commercial rail line, and a few streets that cut diagonally through the grid system. Despite its pleasant nearby bungalows and its mix of older residents and younger families, it's one of the parts of town that could still reasonably be called "sooty." It's a corridor that has slowly resisted the de-industrialization of the rest of the city for the past fifty years. Big Bell's neighbors aren't boutiques and bistros — yet — but instead the likes of the Acme Foundry, Leder Brothers Metal Co., Industrial Plastics of Mpls Inc., and the Crosstown Sweeping Corporation.

Make no mistake, the Big Bell headquarters is a compound. It's located in an old warehouse, surrounded by automated twelve-foot high gates and barbed wire fences. Trucks are parked inside, and some on the streets outside. On a busy day at the height of summer, it's quite a scene when the gates are open — drivers walking around, getting in and out of trucks, repairmen in grease-stained coveralls consulting with one another. The majority of Big Bell's fleet are Ford Econolines and E-350s, or Chevy Step-Vans and GMC Value Vans. Occasionally, you'll see a modified mail truck such as the Grumman LLV. But for the most part, it's step vans. "Step van" is one of those genericized trademarks like Vaseline, Jell-O or Xerox that originally referred only to Chevy's particular model, but is now used interchangeably for any medium-duty delivery van of this type. These are sturdy, reliable automobiles are intended to make it easy for drivers to access the cargo in back, shifting from driving duties to vending duties with ease.

The drivers are personable people. Most of them work very long shifts, eight hours a day, seven days a week during the summer. It's a seasonal business.

"The Entertainer" is, like any of these songs, a quaint, old-timey number that evokes received feelings of nostalgia for an era that ended well out of living memory. But it also has a strong claim on modernity and urbanity, not only as an artifact of the not-so-distant 1970s, but also a pure product of America's cities. "The Entertainer" was modestly popular in Joplin's time, a ragtime composition that formalized the urban dance music of the early Twentieth Century red-light districts and working-class neighborhoods. It is music of cities and for cities.

Ice cream trucks, too, are a product of cities. Tonier suburbs like Bloomington, Edina, and Wayzata have noise ordinances that prevent ice cream trucks from playing their Digital IIs while they roll through the streets. Besides, the suburbs don't support the kind of density needed to insure worthwhile sales. "Sometimes I'll get calls from a mom who says there are 10 kids in the neighborhood who want ice cream," Big Bell driver Kahsay Gebreamlak told the Star Tribune in 2007. "But we oftentimes don't go there because that could only mean $10 to $15 in sales." Most neighborhoods on the southside, on the other hand, boast populations where a full quarter of the residents are under 18, and they're all packed into a small, dense area that is easily driven through. The cacophonous jingle of "The Entertainer" and "Turkey in the Straw" fit right into the bustle of these boisterous, kid-inundated summer streets in the city's residential pockets.

3. "LITTLE BROWN JUG" (Joseph Winner, 1869)

Another odd choice for selling children's frozen novelties, "Little Brown Jug" was historically a bleary-eyed testament to the joys of functional alcoholism in a cozy, domestic setting: "Me and my wife live all alone / In a little log hut we call our own / She loves gin and I love rum / And don't we have a lot of fun! / Ha, ha, ha, you and me / Little brown jug, don't I love thee!" Of course, there is not a kid alive today that knows these words. Like most hard-edged Nineteenth Century folk songs, this one was neutered over time as it was passed down from generation to generation, making its way from frontier saloon to big band arrangement to kindergarten music class over the course of seven or eight generations.

While Blue Bell provides much of the ice cream to the southside, it doesn't provide all of it. In the years before the food truck revival in Minneapolis, ice cream vendors constituted the vast majority of licensed food trucks in the city. It's not difficult to get a license, and if you can provide the initial investment (the truck itself) and get it past inspections, you too can be an ice cream truck vendor. There are a number of independent vendors, most identifying themselves with DIY vinyl lettering on the sides and front bearing the owner's name ("Tarik's Ice Cream" is a popular one in my neighborhood).

These trucks are more likely to be Econolines. A used step van in average condition can go for well over $25,000. An Econoline is more practical for daily use, and you can get a good used one for a few thousand. All you need is the ice cream and a license, and you're set.

Well, actually, you need the chimes, too.

The retail price of the Digital II is around $200, which makes it fairly affordable, but not necessarily in everyone's price range. A few trucks have iPods or stereos wired to amplifiers, but these are quite rare. The most common cost-effective, though, is mounting a low-voltage alarm bell to the hood of the truck, wired into the van's electrical system. One manufacturer of these models notes that the alarm has "two gongs to overcome ambient noise levels" — exactly the criteria an ice cream jingle must meet.

A few of the independent vendors around South Minneapolis will have these setups, driving around and making their arrivals known with what sounds disconcertingly like a fire alarm, fired off in short blasts. The Digital II is designed with a volume control to adhere to local noise ordinances. The alarm bell-equipped vans have to take their chances. These alarms distill the ice cream jingle to its essence: stripped of the melody and nostalgic cultural associations of an ancient but still faintly recognizable song like "Little Brown Jug," you're left with just the chiming of a bell.

4. "LA CUCARACHA" (Author unknown, before 1800)

Telling the story of a cockroach that loses a leg and must limp along with only the five it has remaining, "La Cucaracha" began as a corrido (Mexican ballad) reputed to have been brought over by a Spanish naval captain, and adopted during the Mexican Revolution as a national song. Depending on who's singing it, where, and which of the thousands of additional verses that have been written since are being utilized, the song can take on complex political, satirical and cultural implications. Columnist Cecil Adams once called it the "equivalent of 'Yankee Doodle' — a traditional satirical tune periodically fitted out with new lyrics to meet the needs of the moment."

I don't know when this came into heavy rotation. But it seems to be used in South Minneapolis, at least, as a bid for the attention of the area's Hispanic population. In 2000, the Powderhorn Park neighborhood, in the heart of South Minneapolis, was 22 percent Hispanic. In 2010, that number was 32 percent. Many are Mexican, and this song is undoubtedly known not only by American schoolchildren — we learned it in music classes in the late 1980s — but also by generations of Mexican families.

5. "SAILING, SAILING" (James Frederick Swift, 1880)

Another jaunty, seemingly indestructible song from the British Isles that will outlive you and me and our children's children.

Not only are the musical offerings remarkably consistent, but the treats offered from the ice cream truck are equally consistent with my own youthful memories. You can choose from the equally indestructible frozen visages of Batman (created in 1939), Bugs Bunny (1940), Tweety Bird (1942), the Pink Panther (1964), and the Teenage Mutant Ninja Turtles (1984) — almost the exact same options I had back on the streets of my hometown suburb back in the late 1980s. The non-branded goodies, like snow cones, Bomb Pops, vanilla bars, vanilla sandwiches, and turtle bars, have remained unchanged for decades, as well. The ice cream truck delivers continuity, if nothing else.

6. "CAMPTOWN RACES" (Stephen Foster, 1850)

Another song with a wild, disreputable, and racially troubling past that, over time, has become an American classic, beloved by children, the elderly, and wholesome, church-going people all over the country. Perhaps Foster's most famous song, he drew upon the wild, vernacular minstrelsy music of the early Nineteenth Century to imbue the lyrics and careening, reckless melody with a sense for the utter joy of gambling.

Ice cream trucks have not been without their controversies in Minneapolis. There were a surprising number of robbings and shootings involving ice cream trucks and their drivers throughout the so-called "Murderapolis" era, when violent crime in the city was at an all-time peak. In May 1995, Minneapolis City Council Member Dennis Schulstad of the 12th Ward proposed an ordinance that would put an end to ice cream trucks on residential streets. The 12th Ward is a largely residential section of Minneapolis, located in the city's sleepy southeast corner, not far from Big Bell's Snelling Avenue compound. In previous years, two children had been killed, on unrelated occasions, when they were struck by cars after purchasing ice cream from trucks.

"When an ice cream truck is out in the street ringing its bell, you are encouraging children to run out into the street," Schulstad warned. "This is an attractive nuisance we're putting out on the streets."

"I'm not saying [ice cream trucks] are the devil, and I'm not accusing them of not doing things right," he said. "I'm just saying we should talk about it."

The motion was passed on to the Council from the Public Safety Committee with no recommendation, and was defeated handily.

Schulstad served as alderman from 1976 to 1997. He was, at the time, the only Republican on the council, and the last one to serve since.

7. "RED WING" *(Kerry Mills and Thurland Chattaway, 1907)*

Made famous by Nebraska Ho-Chunk tribe member, actress and singer Lillian St. Cyr in the early Twentieth Century, this song's titular character was named for the Dakota chief Hupahuduta, also known as Red Wing. She also took the name "Red Wing" herself professionally. Occasionally, the song has been associated with the Minnesota town of the same name, most famous for its ceramics and leather boots. It was wildly popular at the time it was published, as most of these songs were.

Despite being the most recent of the songs here, however, "Red Wing" is the one with the smallest presence in the collective cultural memory today. To the extent that it's recognizable at all, it's only as an ice cream truck jingle. "Camptown Races" or "The Entertainer" still turn up in classrooms and ringtones and occasions when someone sits down at a piano to show off. Not so with "Red Wing." It's preserved, like an ice-bound vanilla sandwich wedged into the bottom of a freezer, only as a very small aspect of the frozen novelty industry. Kerry Mills and Thurland Chattaway, who adapted it from a Nineteenth Century German children's song about a farmer, couldn't have imagined that the only place that "Red Wing" would be heard in a hundred years was in a ghostly electronic rendition emanating from diesel-powered trucks selling ice cream to kids.

8. "BRAHMS'S LULLABY" *(Johannes Brahms, 1868)*

The Digital II can handle other songs besides these eight, of course. Regionally well-known in the Northeast is the equally loved and despised "Mister Softee" jingle, composed by a Philadelphia jingle writer in the early 1960s and one of the only songs in use requiring a license. Only Mister Softee trucks are permitted to play the Mister Softee jingle. All others risk a fine.

There's another popular jingle, often heard around the southside and elsewhere, that begins with a vaguely irritated-sounding woman saying, "Hello?" and then launching into an insistent little melody that makes musical allusions to both "It's a Small World After All" and "Turkey in the Straw" without fully committing to either. No one seems to know what's actually called.

Of course other popular pieces of early and classical music make their way into the repertoire: "Greensleeves," the Sixteenth Century English folk song, is one you might hear occasionally. Or sometimes you'll hear a familiar melody from Mozart or Beethoven. I once encountered a driver in Powderhorn Park using a pre-1985 Nichols box. The older boxes had several moving parts, and broke down easily. This box was crackling its way through a severely degraded version of Beethoven's Bagatelle No. 25 in A minor, popularly known to piano recital attendees as "Für Elise." It was so spare and sad I thought it might be an original composition of some kind.

Johannes Brahms's "Wiegenlied: Guten Abend, gute Nacht" ("Good evening, good night"), Op. 49, No. 4 is another popular choice from the classical world. That's the one popularly known as "Brahms's Lullaby." It's the one that starts, "lullaby, and good night."

I never thought the Brahms lullaby was a great choice for a jingle; while it ties into the earliest classical and romantic music selections of the first ice cream parlors, the lullaby seems too closely associated with bedtime, not play time. But it's been consistently popular since 1957, and will probably continue to be.

Despite the limitless options one has in terms of customizable song choices in the early 21st Century, there's been a remarkably consistent and limited self-selection in the ice cream truck songs of both South Minneapolis and the rest of the United States. There's very little regional variation. There's very little stylistic variation. All the songs are old — in fact, incredibly old by contemporary cultural standards. Where else do you regularly hear songs from the 19th Century in your daily life? They're carefully selected to evoke a daisy chain of unbroken nostalgia: to you, a 21st Century adult in an American city, the tinkling, lo-fi chimes squawked out by a digital box remind you of your childhood, a pre-contemporary soundscape of blooping Ataris, MTV synthesizers, and Apple IIEs. And when your parents heard those same songs, they called back an even earlier era, of chiming early American folk standards pealing over the sounds of postwar city streets. And to their parents, those songs called back to the ice cream parlors of their parents' days, when eating ice cream meant the accompaniment of a music box...

And so on and so forth. Chiming music is a form of self-fulfilling nostalgia, a sound forever associated with ice cream because chiming music has always been forever associated with ice cream.

ACKNOWLEDGEMENTS

The team behind "The Secret Atlas of North Coast Food" is grateful to Chef Don Saunders of The Kenwood for cooking for our most committed backers with style and grace; to the wonderful and always-supportive team at Peace Coffee for hosting an exclusive signing and cupping event; to Becca Dilley for her invaluable role as a sounding board, brainstormer, and barrier between James Norton and insanity; to Jay Peterson for tolerating all of our pestering questions about books and answering helpfully and promptly; to Jamie Millard for the invaluable recommendation of our printer, BookMobile; to David Enyeart at Common Good books for his immediate enthusiasm about this project; to Aaron Landry for everything he's done for the site in general and for this book specifically; to Heather Porter Engwall and the team at the Wisconsin Milk Marketing Board for their support of our All-Star Cheesemakers chapter; to John Hines at WCCO for his longstanding support; to Natasha Georgia at Kitchen Window for giving us a Minneapolis home for our book; to our friends at the Current and Minnesota Public Radio for connecting us with one of the most literate and inquisitive audiences in Minnesota; to our copyediting team (Becca Dilley, John Garland, Tim Gihring, Peter Hajinian, Maja Ingeman, Elizabeth Mead Cavert Scheibel, Andy Sturdevant, and Chuck Terhark) for valiantly dispatching with this manuscript in one go, assisted by tapas, sangria, and autumn brews; to the Heavy Table team of writers, photographers, editors, information architects and more, for giving us a sturdy base upon which to build; to our contributors; and least but far from least, our Kickstarter backers (see below) who made this book possible.

THANK YOU TO OUR KICKSTARTER BACKERS, WITHOUT WHOM THIS BOOK WOULD BE YET ANOTHER INTRIGUING, UNREALIZED IDEA

Dale Yasunaga
Dan & Lisa
Katherine Nagel & David Schoppik
Deb Diepholz
Diana McKeown
Faysal
Jim Shultis
Jonathan Kaplan
Joseph & John
Kevin Diepholz
Lorenzo Lucid
Marcus McCrory & Heather Wilkie
Mark B. Abbott
Mary Safar
Rick & Ann Garland
Steinhaeuser Family
Susan Lacek

Anne George
Becca Dilley
Colin McFadden
David Duckler
Eric Schneider
Evan Pedersen
Fiona Carter
Frances Wilkinson
Izzy L Daye
Jessica Forbess
John Hines WCCO Radio
Julianna Simon
Julie Ingebretsen
Julie Pearson
Kelly Browne
Kelly Ingstad

Kevin Platte II
Kevin Winge
Marjorie Kelly
Michael Gordon
Mikael McLaren
Nathan Matter
Patricia Schnobrich
Sam Carlsen
Scott Kuhlman
Stephanie Kuenn
Thomas Ruhland
Tim Gihring & Lucy Lyon
Tim Ikeman
Varsha Seetharam
Vellee Deli

Aaron Day
Aaron Zierdt
Alyson Newquist
Alyssa Vance
Ashley Shelby
Bill Hibbard
Blake Nicholson
Charles & Nancy Rader
Charles & Rebecca Lyon
Chris & Kerry Lehr
Christian Krautkramer & Allison Grady

Claudia Holt
Deanna Kossett
Deborah Zanish
Donna & Tom Danielson
Douglas McPeek
Emily Schnobrich
Eric Halverson & Jessie Siiter
Eric Wittmershaus
Gabrielle Zuckerman
George Robbins
Ingrid Lind-Jahn
Jennifer Moe

Jill Lewis
Kara Merrill
Karen Dilley & Dick Thomas
Karen Nelson
Kelly McManus & Mike Olson
Lauren Ross
Lindsay Pohlad
Lisa Dircks

Maja Ingeman
Marcus Trapp
Margot M. Barry
Matt Dooley & Kaylee Spencer
Mike Lougee
Mom & Dad
Patricia Zurlo
Paul Kellett

Rebekah Tempest
Robert Ackerman
Ruth Baker
Sharyn Morrow
Susannah Brooks
Sweet Science Ice Cream
Teresa Mogensen
Tricia Cornell & Bruce Manning

Aaron Landry
Aaron Street
Abbey Nova
Adam Bezdicek
Adam Voreis
Adrian Cumming
Aidan Sullivan
Aleah Vinick
Alex James & Jade Johnson
Alexander Larson
Alexandra Aulisi
Alissa Rowinsky Wright
Allison & Michael Isenberg
Allison Hantschel
Amanda Aileen Fisher
Amazing Barstow & Meghan Sloan
Ameripride Linen
Amy Jensen
Andrea & Brian Strom
Andrew Watt
Andy Sturdevant
Ann Harste
Anna & Land Wilson
Anne Baker
Anne Kosseff
Anne Rucker
Anne T. Cook
Avneet K. Singh
Barb Paul
Ben Gurstelle
Ben Ross
Ben Sattler
Benjamin, Ashley &
    Penelope Pernitz
Bessie Cherry
Beth & Dan Salzl
Beth Dilley & Craig Kesselheim
Beth Sorensen
BG
Bill Kinney
Boese-Buck-Coland-Tschetter-
    Ward Clan
Brad Hayle
Brandon Boat
Brandon Warner
Brenda Johnson
Brent Hickman
Brett Myers
Brian Moen
Brian Scholin
Britta Shroyer
Cari Tan
Carol Walker
Carrie Rank
Catherine J. Reagan
Catherine Sallas
Chloe Copenhaver
Chris Drosner
Chris Giacomazzo
Chris Gwinn
Christopher Bannister
Chuck Terhark
Claire Carlson
Codi Cathleen Crooks
Conner
Cristina J. Spurr
Cynthia A Matson
Dan Haugen & Amy Softich
Dan Nelson — Loyal listener of
    WCCO radio.
Daniel & Jennifer Schaefer
Darby Ballis
Darla Kashian
Dave & Audrey Royer
Dave M.
Dave Stadley
David Friedman
David Goodwin
David Rapp
David W. Lee
Debbie Thompson
Denise Bielick

Diane Richard
Doug Zaun
Duluth Grill
Dustin C. Cook
DWITT
Elisa Poquette
Elise
Elizabeth K. Daniel
Elizabeth Koenig
Elizabeth Polter
Elizabeth Wefel
Ellen Guettler & Ben Pofahl
Emily
Emily Koppes
Emily Newhall
Emily Tritabaugh
Eric Hananoki
Eric Vogt
Erica Edwardson
Erica Mauter
Erik & Molly Olson
Erik Anderson
Evangeline "Lily" Neve
Eve Benesh
Flory Leow (Furochan)
Fresh Bar
Garrett Peterson
Geoffrey Kleinman
Gerhard's Brats
Gnocchi.Me
Graham J. Lampa
Grant & Julie Boelter
Grant Rykken
Hannah Rogal
Heather R. McLaughlin
Heidi Parker Tucker
Heidi Schallberg
Holly
Holly J. Perrotti
Ike & Maggie Whiting
J.D. Dresner
J.D. Gardner
James Priebnow
Jan Muchnikoff
Jane Stephenson
Janie Wise
Janine Anderson
Jason Alexander
Jay Dean
Jeanne Foels
Jeff & Angie Hawkins
Jeff Rosenquist
Jeffrey Benson
Jeffrey Johnson
Jennifer Schnobrich
Jenny Lu
Jenny Pfafflin
Jesse Lickel
Jessi Reddin
Jessica A. Johnson
Jessica Chapel
Jessica Matelski
Jessica Ward-Denison
Jilly Eldring
Jim Cosmano
Jim Lenfestey
Joe Radosevich
Jofish
John C. Champe
John Garland
John Kovalic
John Malone
John P. Haurykiewicz
John Quast
John Yasunaga
Jon & Bryn Orum
Jon Austin
Jonathan Gross
Joseph & Leah
Joseph & Shannon Pettini
Joshua Page
Karen Kersting

Karmen Gusa
Kate An
Kate Biederwolf
Kate O'Reilly
Kate Smith
Katherine M. Dahl
Katherine Niebur
Kathleen Cobb
Katie Eukel
Katie Pimlott
Katie Roth
Katie Swanson
Kent & Dave Linder
Kevin J. Lee
Kiah Smith
Kiel Hockett
Kirstin Hibbard
Kris Thayer
Kristen Schweiloch
Kyle Matteson
Kyle Nabilcy
Laura & Matt Tanner
Laura Arneson
Laura Bigger
Laura Seelau
Laurie Jesch-Kulseth (Relishing It)
Lee Egbert
Lee Zukor
Liana Krissoff
Linda Flory
Lindsay Bennett
Lindsay Christians
Lindsay Seebinger
Lindsey Hamilton
Lindsey Westman
Lisa & Jason Troutman
Lisa Nelson & Anthony Manfredi
Liz Hager
Liz Scheibel
Lizzie Breyer
Louis Cooke
Louise
Mark & Peggy Schultz
Mark MacLennan
Marshall & Ellie Behrens
Martha Grant
Mary Kay Cameron
Mary Lynch
matt gassman
Matthew J. Galligan
Matthew Lewinski
Max Broman. STP
Meg
Meg Finn
Megan & Tom Hill
Megan Culhane Galbraith
Micah Vono
Michael Amos
Michelle & Bill Jarvey
Michelle Loeffler
Mike Linzbach
Mike Rollin
Mike Skoglund
Mila
Molly Bloom & Andy DuCett
Molly Wright Steenson
Mr. Sheng & Tabatha
Naomi Nakamoto
Naomi Rask Golden
Naomi Scheman
Natalie Champa Jennings
Natalie Loots
Nate Moen
Nate Morris
Nathan Kelly Rice
Nathan Magel
Nicholas Coleman
Nichole Fromm
Nick Fauchald
Nicole Halabi
Nicole Soderholm
Nikki Aden

Noel & Timothy McCormick
Nori Heikkinen
Pat & Cara Callahan
Pat Hagen
Patricia Norton
Patrick Maun
Paul Isakson
Paul Maggitti
Paul Nordland
Paula Forbes
Peter Fleck
Peter Hajinian
Peter Norman
popwilleatme
Quinlan Faris
R Krishnan
Rachael Thomatz
Rachel Welch
Rich & Veronica Andrew
Richard Manser
Rick Borland III
Robert Bauer
Robert Winberg
Roberta Rosenberg
Robin Marohn
Roee Dori
Ron Charles
Ross Pfund
Roxanne Webber
Roy Zemlicka
Rueben Nilsson
Ryan & Alyssa
Ryan Fedder
Ryan Prins
S & N Phillips
S. Batz
Sarah Hunt
Sarah J. Morrison
Sarah Master
Scott Tappa
Sean Hess
Sean Silver
Sean Sullivan
Seth Steinbach
Sheena Schar
Shira Yechopetz
Steffanie Musich
Steffi Yasunaga
Stephanie Curtis
Steve & Julie Young-Burns
Steve Carey
Steve Davidson
Steve Himes
Steve Sundberg & Helen Delaney
Stuart Cox Jr.
Stuart Klipper
Susan Pagani
Suzanne LaPalm
Terri Peña
The Buttered Tin
The Perennial Plate
The Sommers Family
Thomas Gunn Jr.
Thomas J Collins
Thorsten Claus
Tim Gruber/Jenn Ackerman
Tod Foley
Tom Elko
Tom Ferguson
Tony Drollinger
Toony Iran
Tracy Armstrong
Trent
Trevor Owens
Tyler Farber
Tyssa Erickson
Ursula Murray Husted
Valencia R Grice
Valerie Plummer
viclum!
William Bottinick
Yann Novak